RescueLogic Software: The Complete Guide

By Dan Horon, Cadgraphics founder and president

Cadgraphics Incorporated
Makers of RescueLogic Software for Fire and Security Systems
PO Box 11737
St. Paul, MN 55111-0737

www.rescuelogic.com
(612) 722-3233

"Safety Made Simple"

RescueLogic Software: The Complete Guide

Copyright Information

ISBN

ISBN 978-0692228241

Patent Information

This guide contains proprietary information. Cadgraphics and RescueLogic techniques and technology are protected by United States Patents 6,229,429 and 6,369,695.

Trademark Information

Disclaimer

Table of Contents

How to Use this Guide

This guide shows you how to use RescueLogic software, step by step, with complete instructions and illustrations. If you're setting up your RescueLogic system for the first time, work your way through the pages of this book in order. Once your system is up and running, you can use this guide as a handy reference manual. Simply refer to the comprehensive table of contents or the index to find answers to your questions.

Specialized Type

"Quotes"	Items you select from a number of options, such as a pull-down menu, are set off by "quotation marks."
Bold Text	Words or characters you type are indicated in **bold**. For example, if the guide says to type **Control Panel**, you should type the words **Control Panel**.
Italics	Specialized terms are written in *italics*.
Small Caps	Keyboard keys, such as CONTROL and ENTER, are shown in SMALL CAPITAL LETTERS.

Basic Terms

Point	Position the mouse pointer until the tip of the on-screen arrow rests on the item you want to point to.
Click	Press and immediately release the button on the left side of the mouse.
Double-Click	Click the left button twice in a row.
Right-Click	Click the button on the right side of the mouse.
Drag	Hold the left button down as you move the mouse.
Drop	When you are done dragging an item into position, drop it into place by releasing the mouse button.
Highlight	Point and drag the cursor over the text you want to highlight.

Helpful Hints

Helpful Hint: Throughout this guide, watch for "Helpful Hint" boxes like this one, where you'll find tips, hints, and suggestions for making the most of your RescueLogic system.

Illustrations

This guide is illustrated with actual RescueLogic screen images, which were captured on a computer that runs Windows 7. If your computer uses a different Windows operating system, your RescueLogic windows might look different, but you will follow the same step-by-step procedures.

Introduction

On behalf of Cadgraphics Incorporated, I am pleased to offer you this complete guide to RescueLogic software.

Since I first created Cadgraphics in1988, the software has come a long way. Today's version still features the same graphics capability that made it a hit when it was introduced — along with an array of new features that customers have suggested and requested along the way, such as color-coded lists, customizable emergency instructions, and drag-and-drop device placement. Today's RescueLogic even works with networks and wireless systems, so you can access your alarm and system information from any PC on your site or on the web.

RescueLogic has been tried and tested in just about every conceivable type of facility, and it is guaranteed to work for you. We have designed it to be remarkably simple, and we have written this guide to show you how you can get your RescueLogic system up and running in practically no time. Every step is illustrated and explained in plain English, so you can sit down and get right to work. If you have a specific question, simply refer to the comprehensive table of contents or the index to find answers.

This book should answer most of your questions about RescueLogic. It is based on my own work with the software since 1988, as well as countless training sessions and project setups with customers just like you.

Our website at *rescuelogic.com* is another good resource for RescueLogic information and publications. If you have any questions or comments about RescueLogic, please do not hesitate to contact me. My e-mail address is *dan@rescuelogic.com.*

I am confident that you will discover RescueLogic is a remarkable way to ensure that your buildings are secure, your people and your property are safe, and that you can take the mystery out of your fire and security systems.

Sincerely,

Dan Horon
Cadgraphics Founder and President

Ways to Use RescueLogic

RescueLogic software was originally designed to show fire and security alarms on a floor plan. Since it was first introduced in 1988, our customers have discovered that it's also an innovative way to keep tabs on building safety and management. The next few pages will show you how you can make the most of your RescueLogic system.

Give First Responders Information on Demand

Rescuers can access RescueLogic for maps, floor plans, and emergency information.

Integrate Your Fire and Security Systems

Monitor all of your systems from a laptop or personal computer.

Connect Panels from Multiple Manufacturers

RescueLogic can get data from any panel or smart device.

Monitor HVAC and Building Controls

You can include information from any device that has an RS-232 port.

Check Your Site from Anywhere in the World

You can log into RescueLogic wherever you are.

Get Text and Email Alerts

Get automatic updates when devices go into trouble or alarm.

Link to Closed-Circuit Video

Show video from cameras with TCP/IP addresses.

Protect People and Property

Safeguard vulnerable people and populations.

Set Up Wayfinder Posts

Create information stations with maps, schedules, and local news.

Prepare Mass Notification Alerts

Be ready to provide emergency information to the public via text, email, and point-specific audible announcements.

Check "As-Built" Facts against Blueprints

Walk RescueLogic through your facility to make sure that your floor plans are accurate.

Demonstrate Code Compliance

Automatically generate printable reports and records.

Standardize Your Emergency Operations Plan

Use RescueLogic to document your site's emergency procedures.

Keep Facility Records

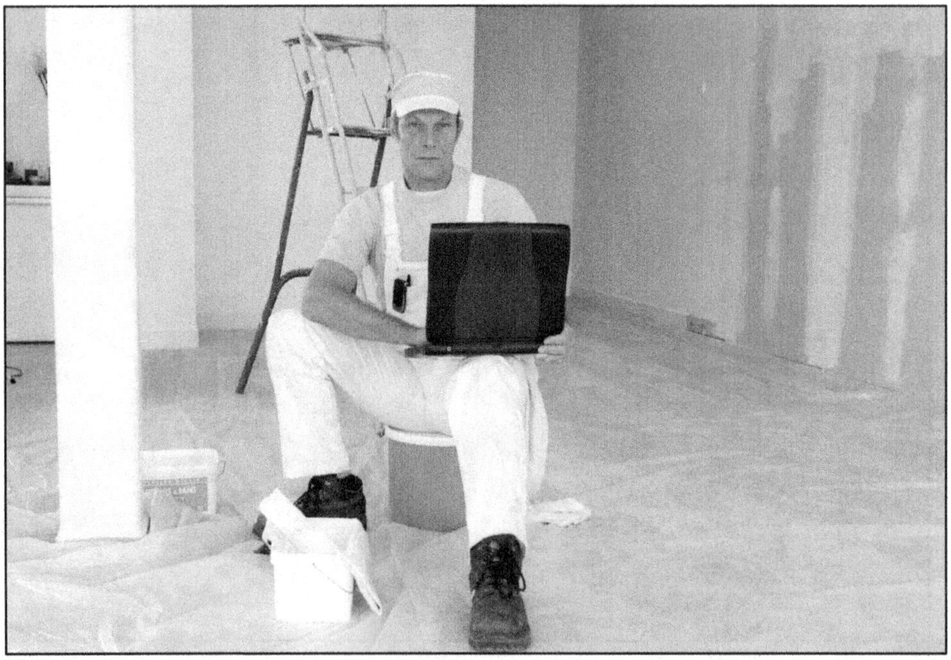

Some people even use RescueLogic to keep a record of ongoing maintenance needs, like touch-up paint colors and replacement bulbs for exit signs.

Chapter 1: Installing RescueLogic

RescueLogic is remarkably easy to set up and use. In every sense, RescueLogic really is "Safety Made Simple." In this chapter, we'll show you how to install RescueLogic on the laptop or computer of your choice.

Basic System Requirements

RescueLogic is easy to install and run on most readily available PCs, laptop, flat-panel, and touchscreen computers.

If you would like to know if RescueLogic will work with a computer you already own, use this checklist of basic system requirements:

- Any Windows-based PC
- RS232 or RS485 connections — one for each control panel or network interface port
- Sound card with speakers (optional)
- 17-inch monitor (19-inch recommended; larger monitors are better)
- Microsoft Windows XP Professional or later
- Mouse or touchscreen
- Portable USB thumb drive to transfer and store files

For best results, include:

- Internet access
- Email server information
- A serial server to connect the RS232 port to Ethernet

Compatible Options

You can add a wide range of readily available peripherals to your RescueLogic system, such as networking components, printers, and other devices.

Helpful Hint: If you want to use RescueLogic to control your fire alarm system — in addition to monitoring alarms — you should follow UL 864 requirements. You can call us for details, or contact the manufacturer of your fire alarm system for specific requirements and model numbers of the specific hardware that is UL listed with their equipment.

Please note that you are *not* required to use UL listed equipment if you simply want to monitor your site with RescueLogic.

Download the Software

To download RescueLogic software, go to **ftp://rescuelogic.com/RescueLogic.msi**. The file you'll want to download is called *RescueLogic.msi*.

You will be asked for the following login and password: **Login:** cgfolder1 **Password:** CGabc123

Download the file, and install it from your hard drive or a thumb drive.

You can also use the following links to download three add-on programs:

- Activity Reports: **ftp://rescuelogic.com/ActivityReports.msi** (74.0 MB) This is an add-on that makes it possible to compile reports of system activity.
- Mail Dispatcher: **ftp://rescuelogic.com/MailDispatcher.msi** (19.9 MB) This is an add-on that makes it possible to send automatic email alerts of system activity.
- System Watch: **ftp://rescuelogic.com/SystemWatch.msi** (22.5 MB) This is a stand-alone program to monitor your system from another computer.

Helpful Hint: Your internet browser might not allow downloads from FTP sites. If you can't access the files from the links, use an FTP program like this one: **http://filezilla-project.org/download.php**.

Budgeting and Planning

RescueLogic is priced by the number of points you plan to monitor. Typically, those points include field devices like smoke detectors, as well as control panels with monitored points like batteries and power supplies. Your fire alarm installer can tell you how many points you have in your system.

A standard RescueLogic system is designed for one central monitoring station. You can add more monitoring posts for a reduced fee.

Install RescueLogic on Your Computer

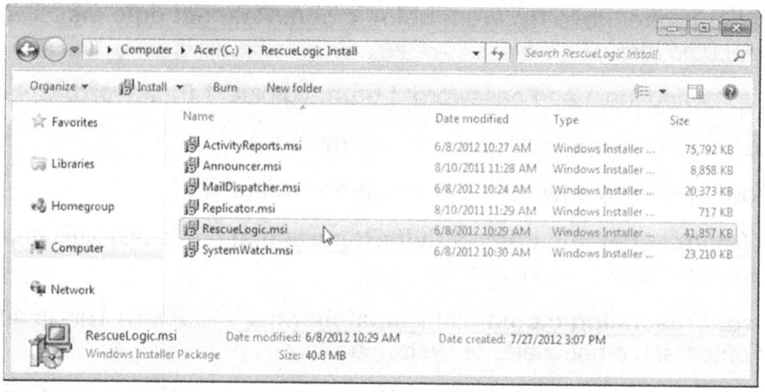

Browse to the download file. If you can't find it, search for "RescueLogic.msi" in likely folder locations.

Click to open the RescueLogic.msi file.

> **Helpful Hint:** One way to open a folder on your hard drive or on another computer is to type the folder name as a command. Click the "Start" button, and then click Run. Now type the program name.

The Setup Wizard will open. Click "Next" to continue.

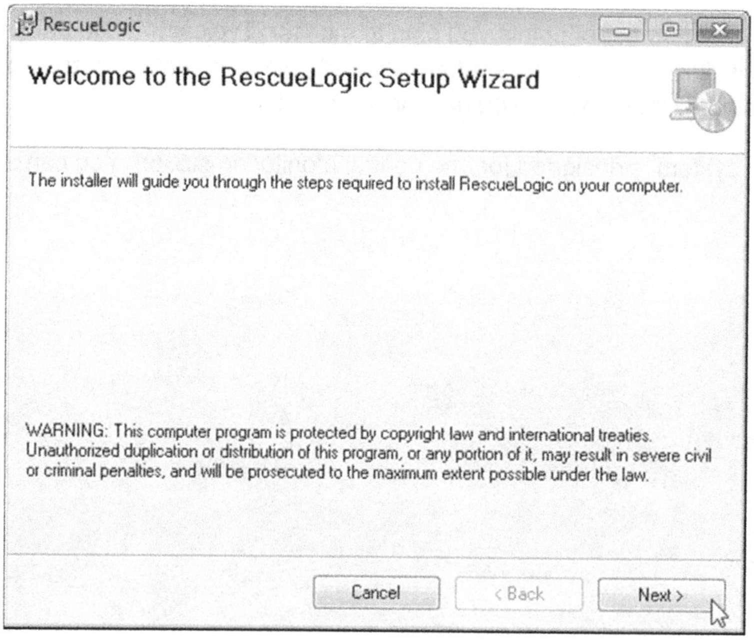

Read and accept the license agreement, and click "Next."

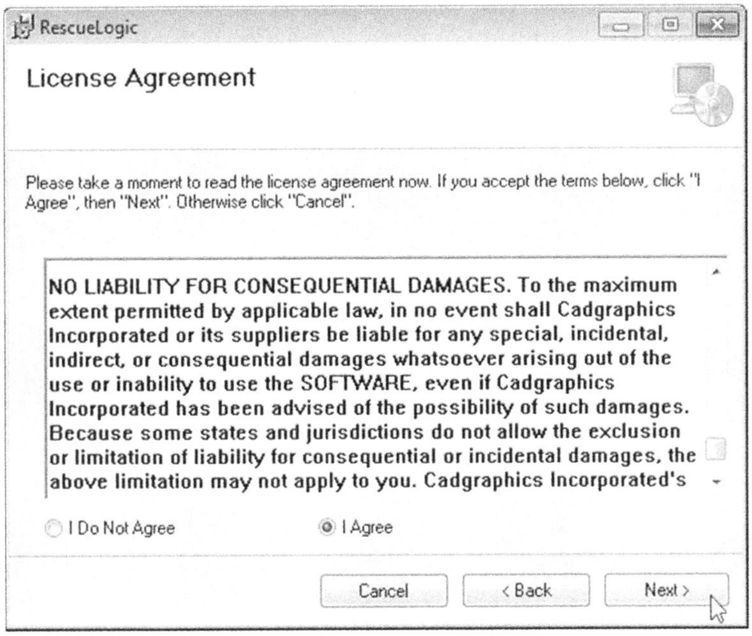

Select an installation folder. Most users go with the default that pops up automatically.

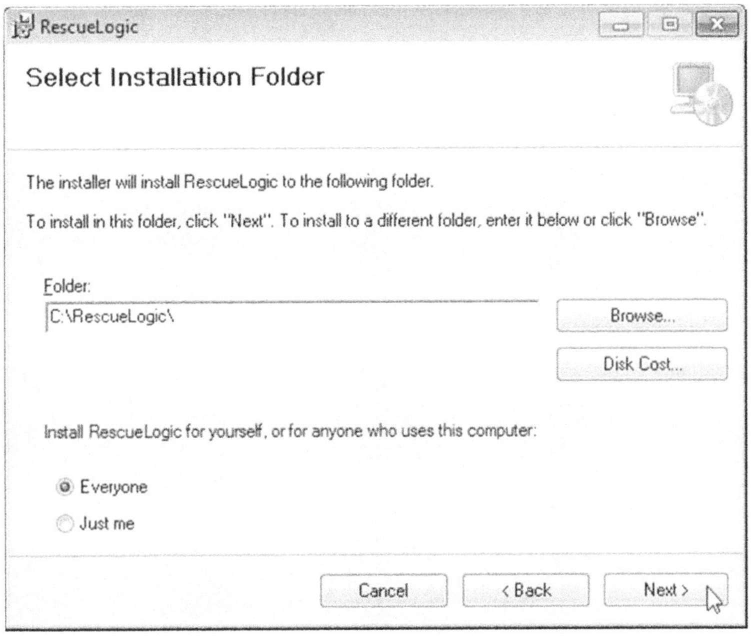

Click "Next," and the InstallShield Wizard will copy the RescueLogic program files onto your hard drive.

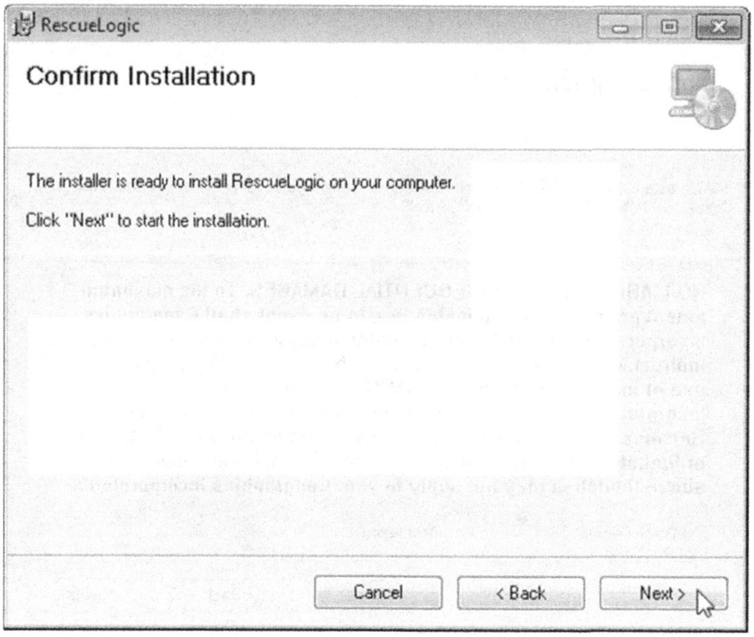

You'll see the progress bar move as the software is installed.

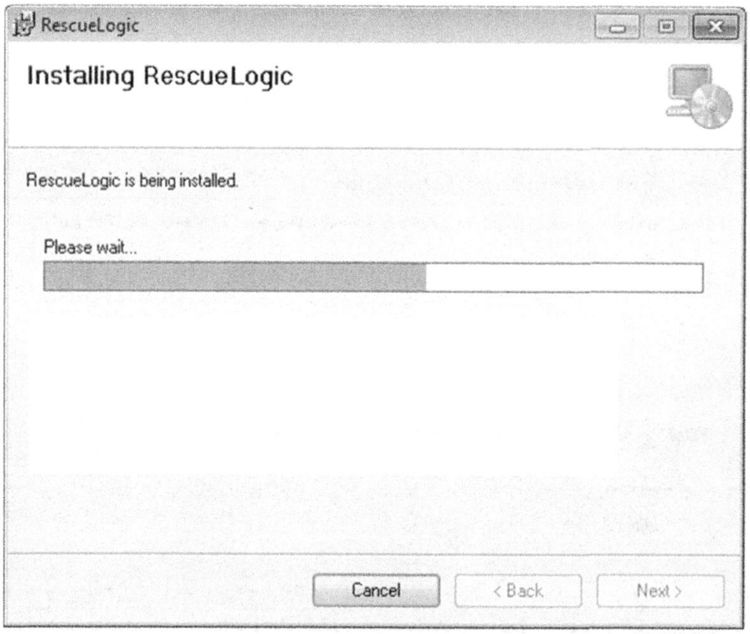

When RescueLogic has been successfully installed, click "Close."

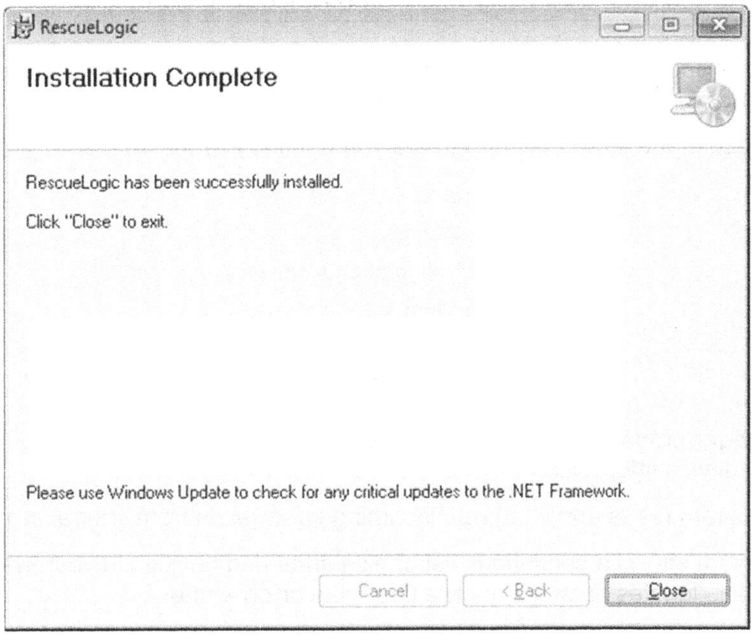

Helpful Hint: Whenever you finish installing new software, restart your computer.

What Gets Installed: RescueLogic Files

When you have completed the full installation process, the "RescueLogic" folder on your hard drive should contain the following files:

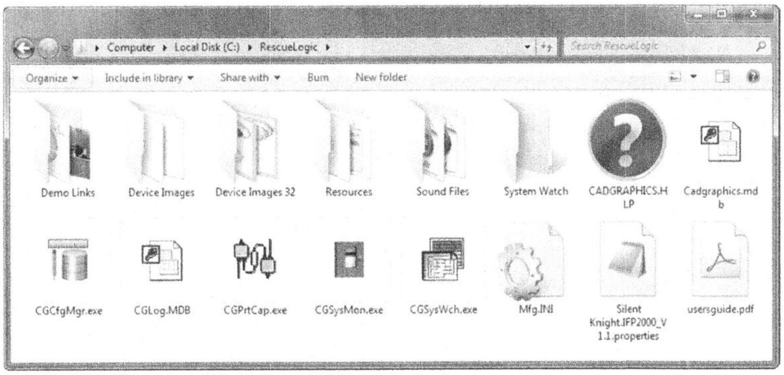

Other files (such as dll types) are also copied to the Windows System folder.

Helpful Hint: Secondary remote computers may be installed and connect to the main RescueLogic computer. If you install RescueLogic on a network, you can establish separate display settings for each station to suit each user's personal preferences. That's because a separate copy of system files and registry entries will be saved on each computer. Those remote stations will not have database files or the program files other than System Watch (CGSysWch.exe.)

The Software within the Software

The complete RescueLogic software package is actually several programs in one. You may use three or more of the programs to set up and use your RescueLogic system.

Here is an overview of each of the three main programs you will find in your RescueLogic folder:

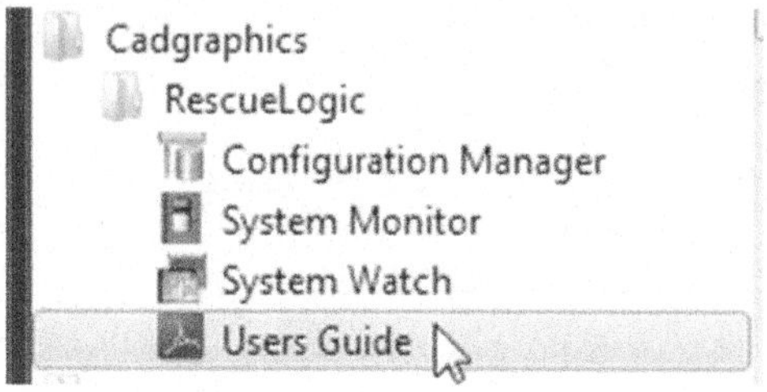

The **Configuration Manager** program customizes your system and enables RescueLogic to recognize your alarm panels and modify device information.

The **System Monitor** program reads and interprets incoming information from your alarm system.

The **System Watch** program shows a continuous list of all alarms and devices in your system, displays emergency instructions, and locates each alarm on a floor plan or on a map.

The **Users Guide** menu selection links to this file on your hard drive and opens it with your PDF Reader.

An optional **Activity Reports** program will make it possible for you to perform an extensive review of all events in your system. It includes files that are compatible with Crystal Reports, which you can use to create your own headers and report criteria. You could even format your periodic service and inspection reports to meet the needs of your local building codes.

Program Modification, Repair, and Removal

You can use the RescueLogic installation program to modify, repair, or remove RescueLogic from your hard drive. Click on the "Start" menu in the lower-left corner of your desktop. From the pop-up menu, choose "Control Panel."

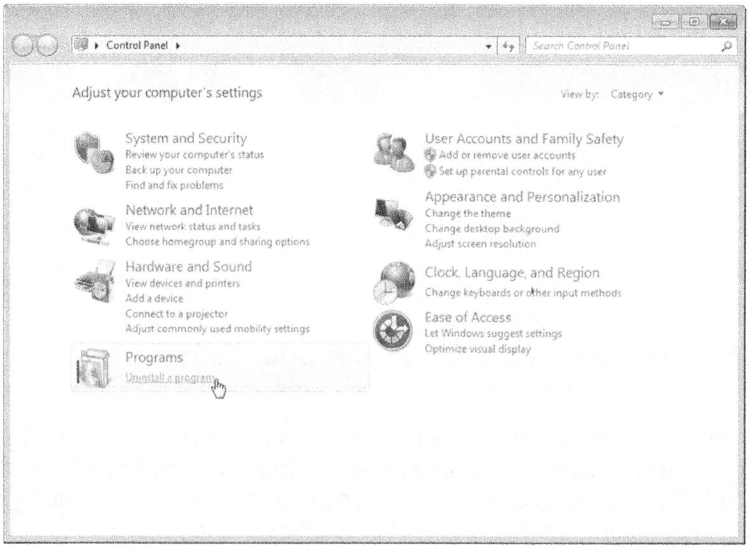

The "Control Panel" window will open. Double-click the "Add/Remove Programs" icon.

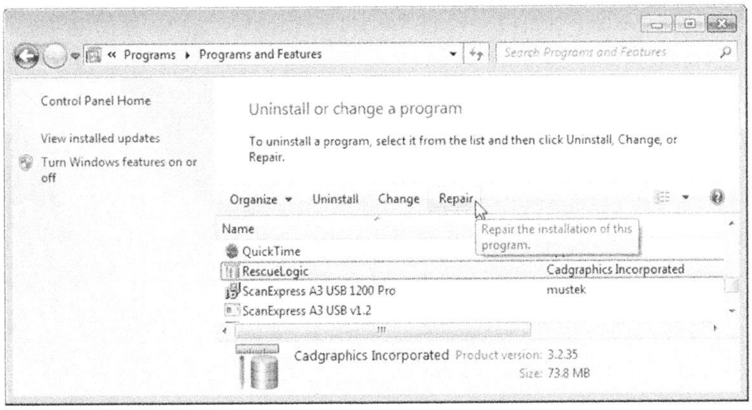

You can choose to modify, repair, or remove the program. Simply follow the on-screen prompts.

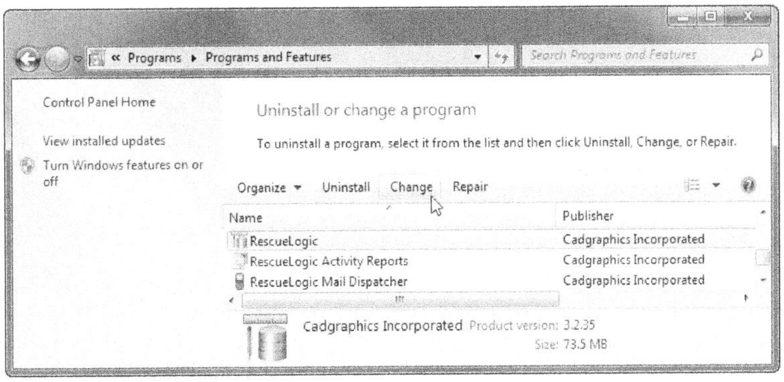

Chapter 2: Networking RescueLogic

RescueLogic users commonly install several RescueLogic stations throughout a facility. When you set up a remote RescueLogic station, other users will be able monitor your alarm system. They will see what you see — alarms, troubles, maps, and floor plans — and have access to your sound files and closed-circuit video, too. They can even zoom in and out of trouble spots, make notes for other operators, and set System Watch preferences to suit their needs. This chapter will show you how to network your RescueLogic system, quickly and easily, with readily available networking components.

Step 1: License Your Software

To install a remote copy of RescueLogic, you must have a multi-user license for the software. A single RescueLogic license will work with one computer. A multiple license lets additional computers gain access to that main computer. You can install RescueLogic on several machines, but it will only run simultaneously on the number of computers for which you have a license. For network license information, see Appendix A in the back of this guide.

Step 2: Configure Your Computer for File Sharing

If you would like remote computers to access your RescueLogic system, you should configure your main RescueLogic computer to allow file sharing.

The following steps demonstrate one way to allow access — but most business networks are highly specialized, so you may need authorization and assistance from your network administrator.

To begin, go to the "Start" menu on your main RescueLogic computer and open the Control Panel. Open the Network and Internet link.

On the next screen, open the Network and Sharing Center.

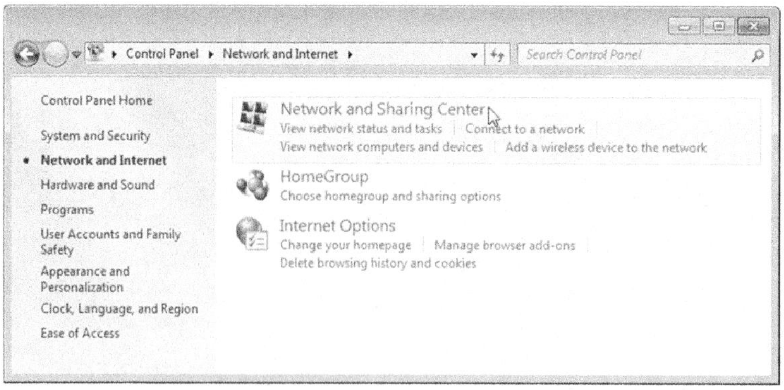

Choose homegroup and sharing options.

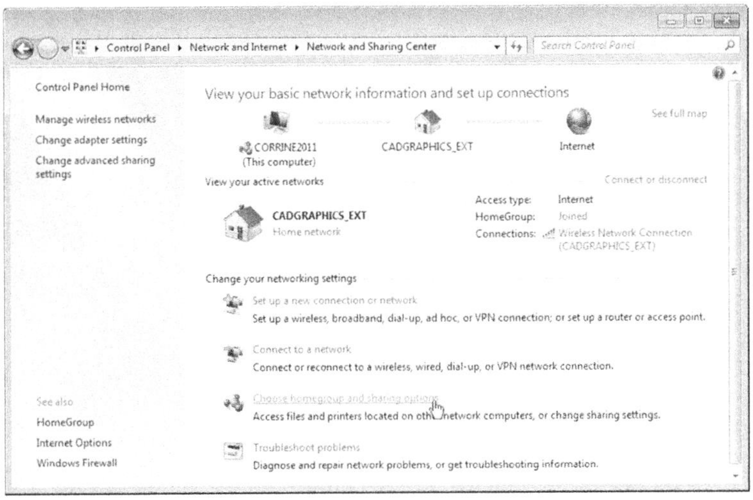

Change the advanced sharing settings.

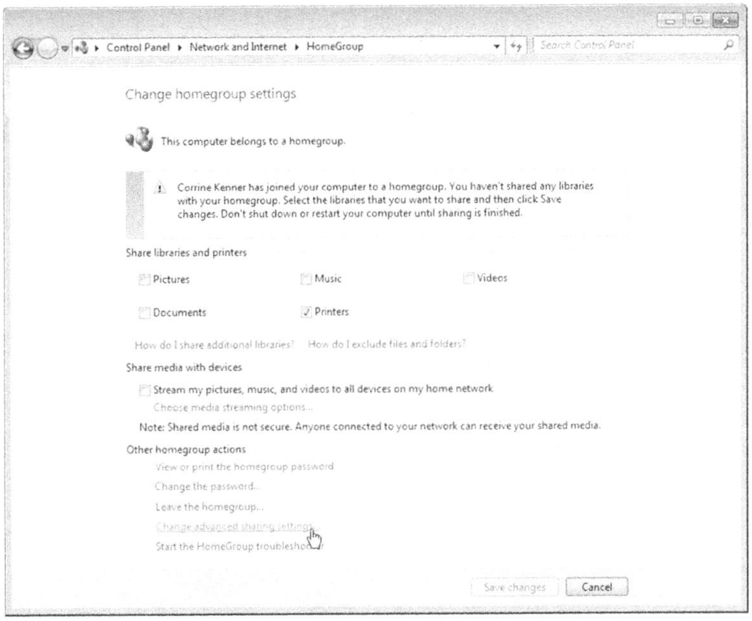

Turn on network discovery, and turn on public folder sharing.

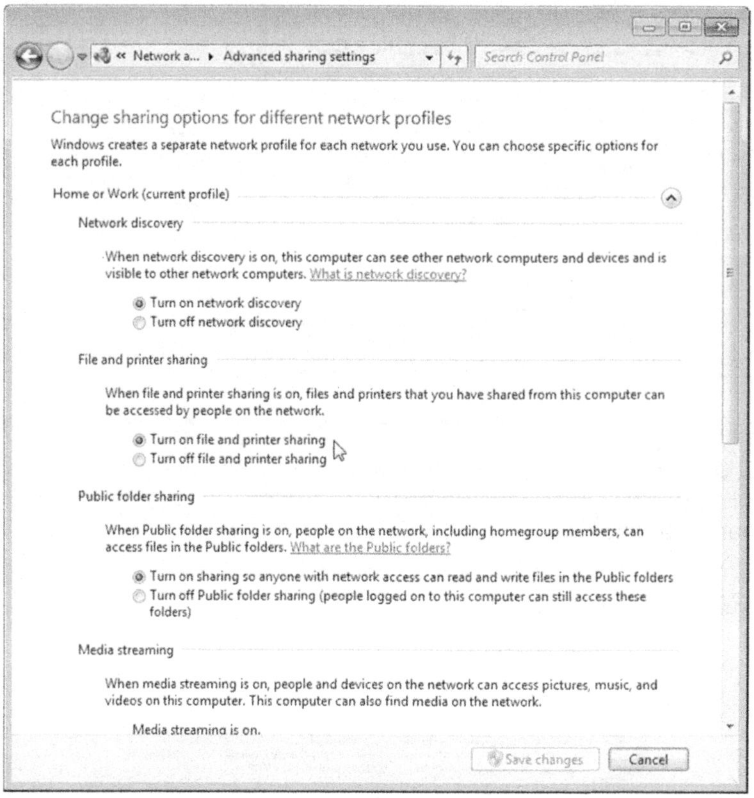

Scroll down to turn off password protected sharing and allow Windows to manage your homegroup connections. Then save your changes.

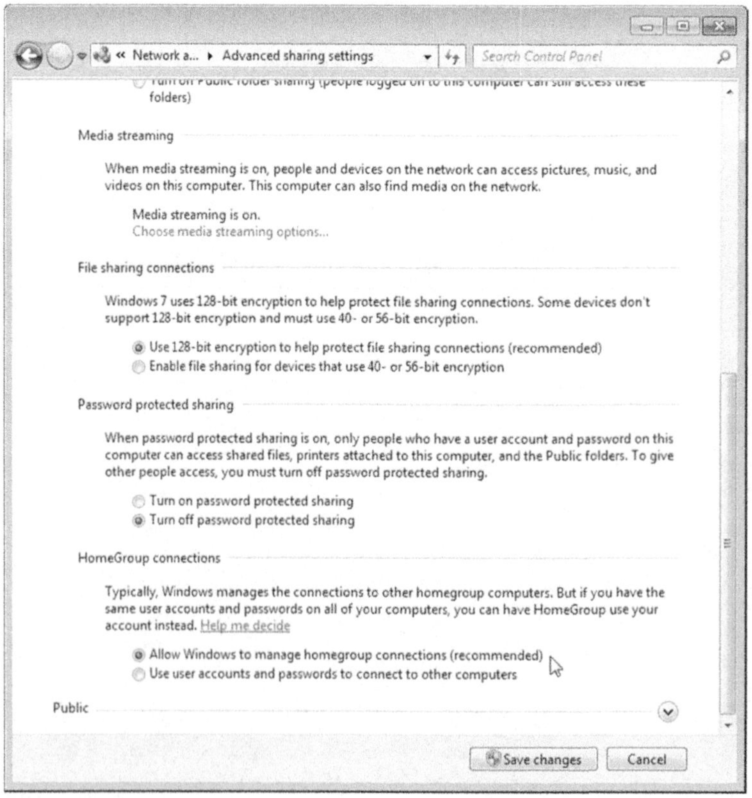

Step 3: Install System Watch on a Remote Computer

You'll use the System Watch add-on program to use RescueLogic on a remote computer. Since you've already installed RescueLogic on your main computer, you'll probably recognize the steps. They're almost identical.

If you already downloaded the add-on on your main computer, simply copy the file to a thumb drive and install it on your remote computer.

To download System Watch straight to your remote computer, go to **ftp://rescuelogic.com/SystemWatch.msi**. You will be asked for the same login and password you used before: **Login:** cgfolder1 **Password:** CGabc123

To begin, click on the SystemWatch.msi file.

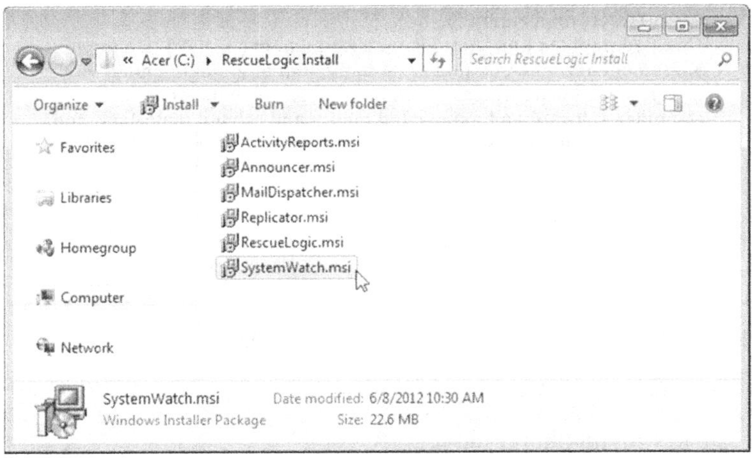

The installation wizard will open. Follow the on-screen prompts.

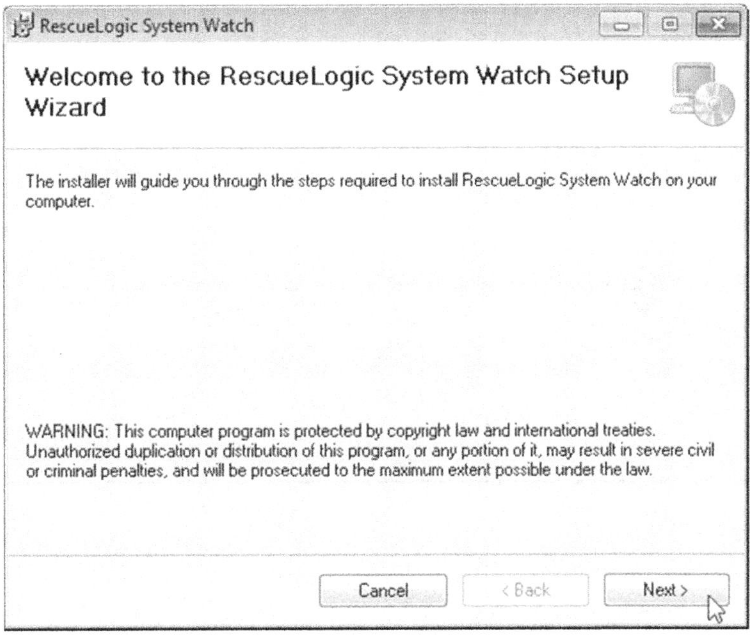

Accept the license agreement.

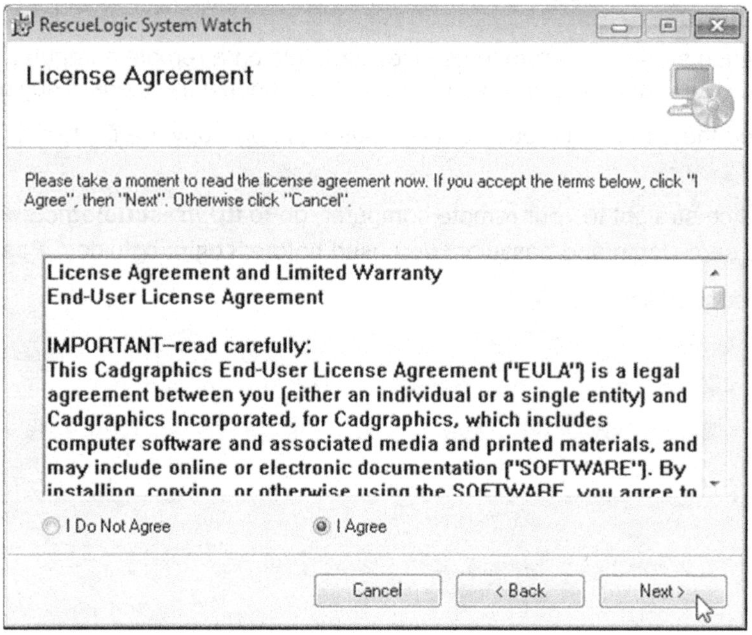

Select an installation folder. Most people go with the default suggestion.

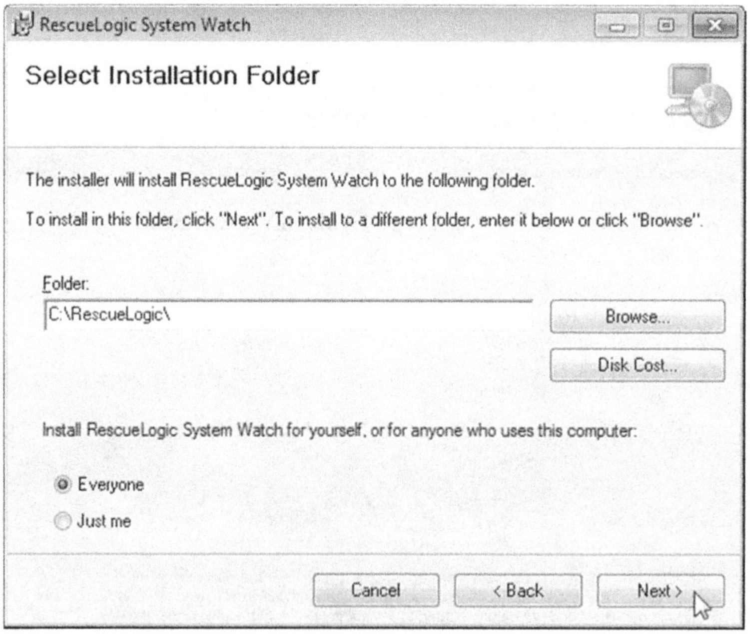

Click "Next" to start the installation.

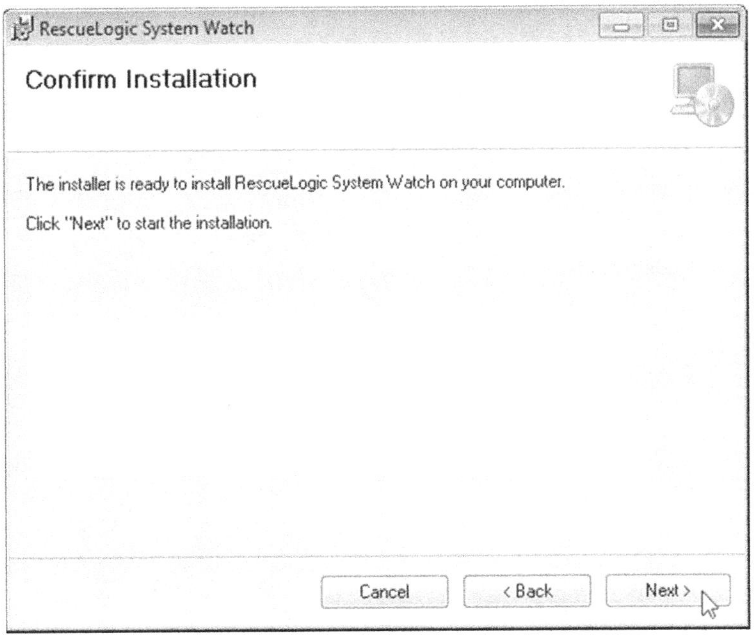

The installation program will install background files and drivers needed to access the main RescueLogic system over a network.

Helpful Hint: Generally speaking, remote users only need to access the System Watch program. However, remote users can access Activity Reports and Configuration Manager, too. Simply point a shortcut on the remote to the corresponding program on the main RescueLogic computer. Configuration Manager will allow one user at a time to change the system.

Step 4: Locate the Database

Go to the start menu and open the Cadgraphics folder.

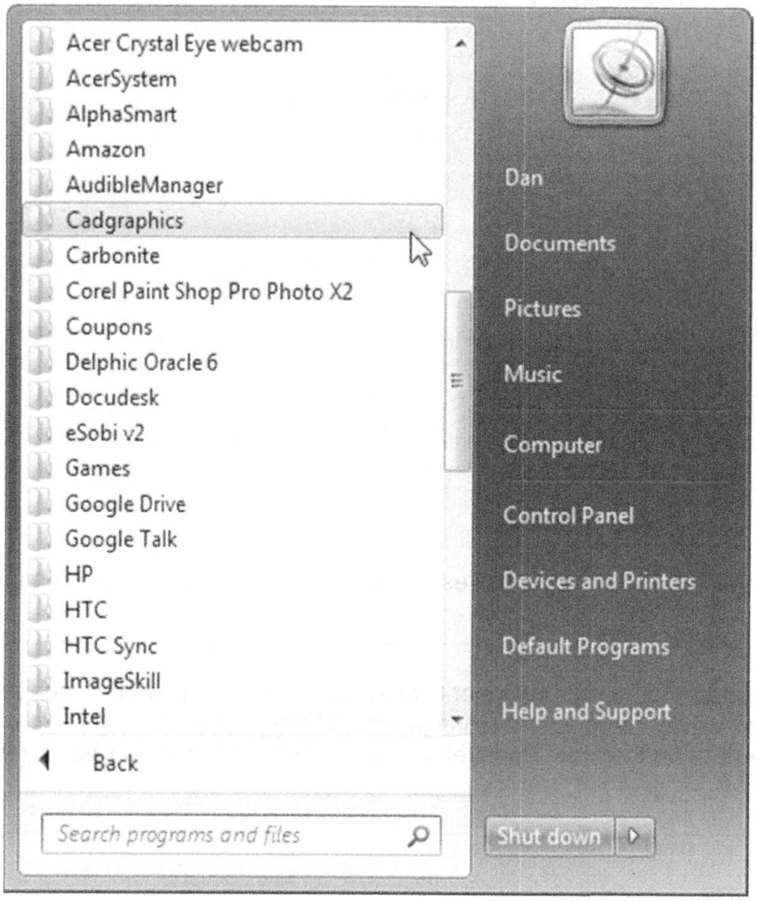

Click System Watch.

The System Watch install program did not copy a database file into the RescueLogic folder of this PC because the data is actually located on another PC or server. You will see a screen that says the database cannot be found. Click OK.

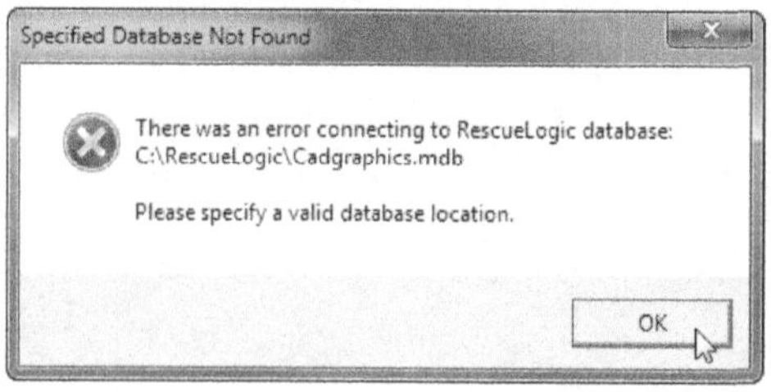

You'll be asked to locate the database. It's in the shared folder on the main computer. Type the complete path to the database file, or click the button on the right to browse the network and find the database.

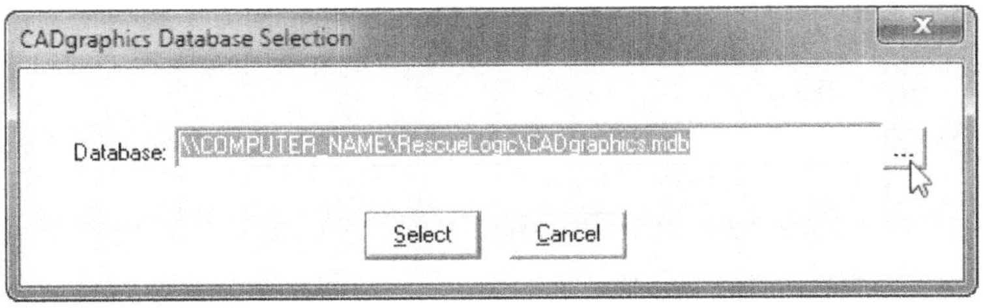

The System Watch screen will open.

Changing the database location

After the initial system is running, your network administrator might change the server name or the name of the shared folder. In that case System Watch Setup allows you to change the location.

Click the "Setup" button in the bottom-left corner of the window.

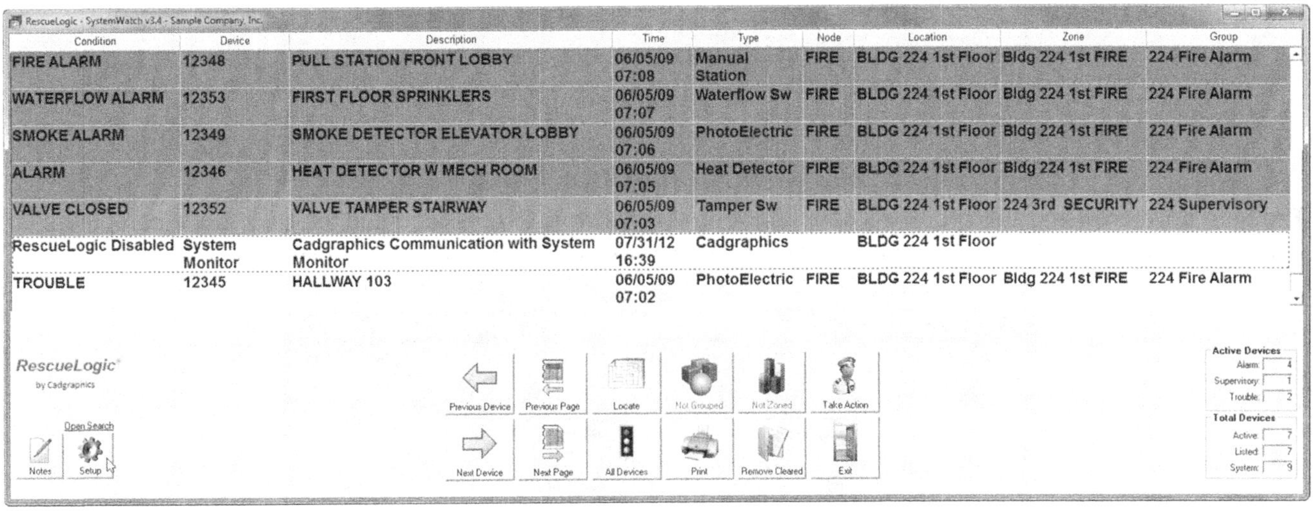

You'll be prompted to enter a password. The default password is the number "3."

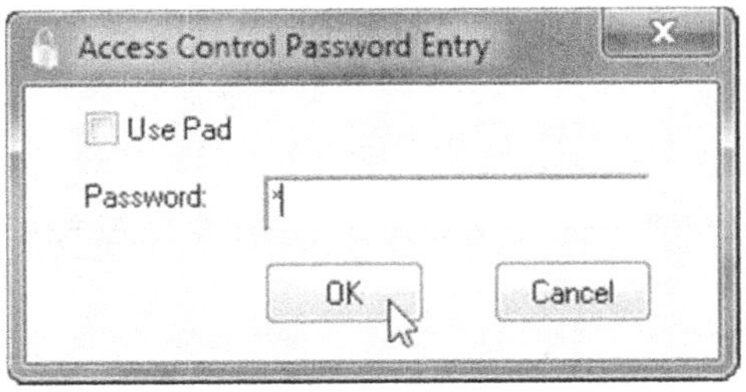

The System Watch Setup screen will appear. On the “Settings” tab, you will see the currently set location of System Monitor, which is where your database is located. Click the “Browse” button to find the new location.

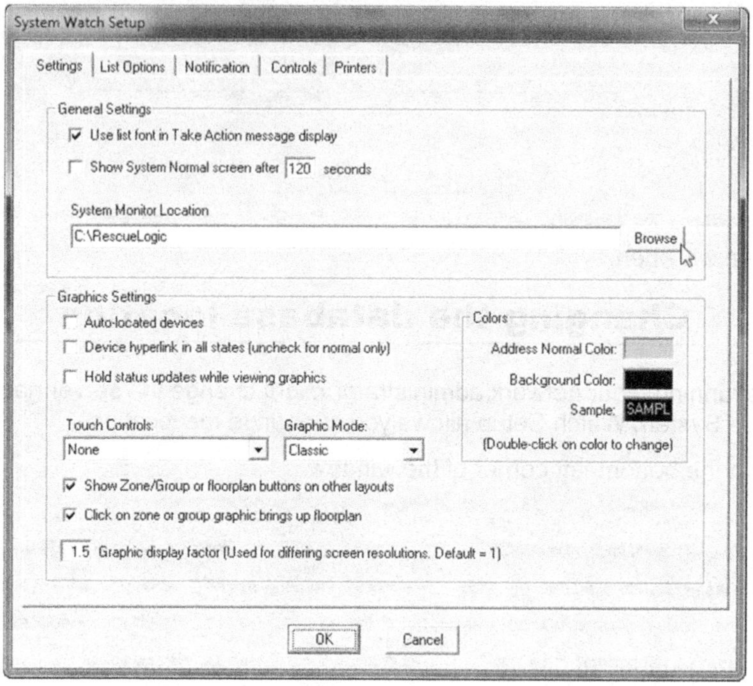

The hard drive browsing dialog box will open. Click on “My Network Places” and find the links to the computers in your workgroup on the network. You will need to find the RescueLogic folder on the main computer.

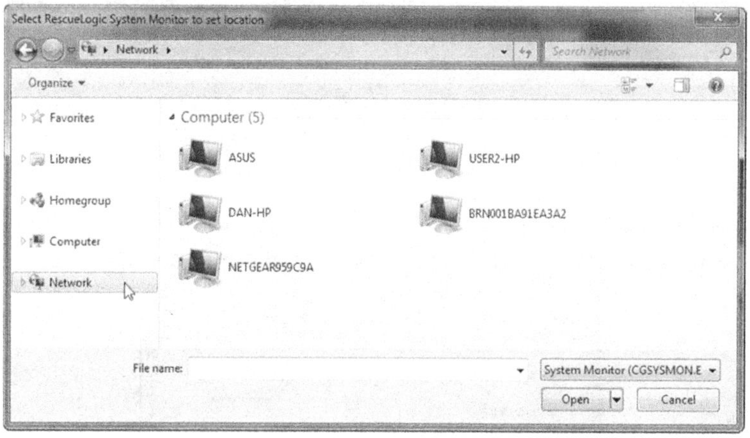

In this example, we know that the original RescueLogic program is housed on the DAN-HP computer.

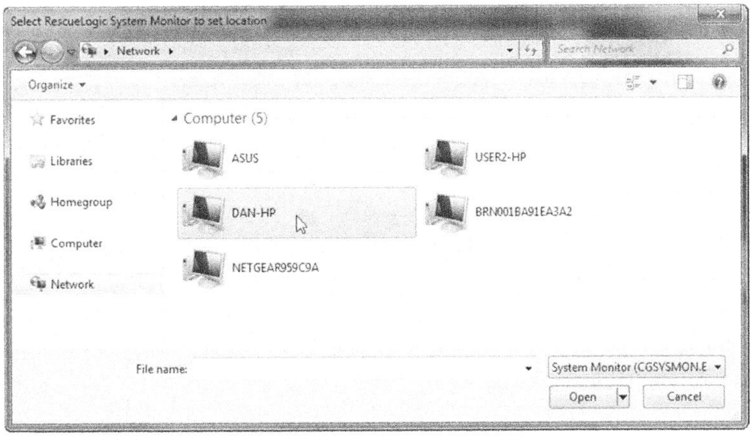

Among the shared resources on the main RescueLogic computer, you will see the RescueLogic program folder. Double-click on it.

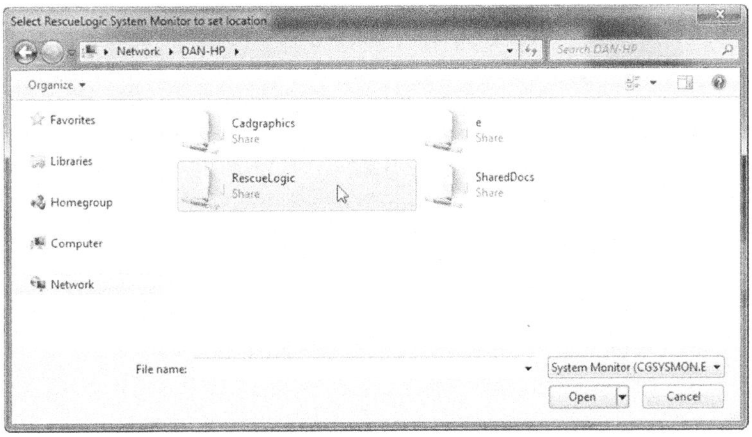

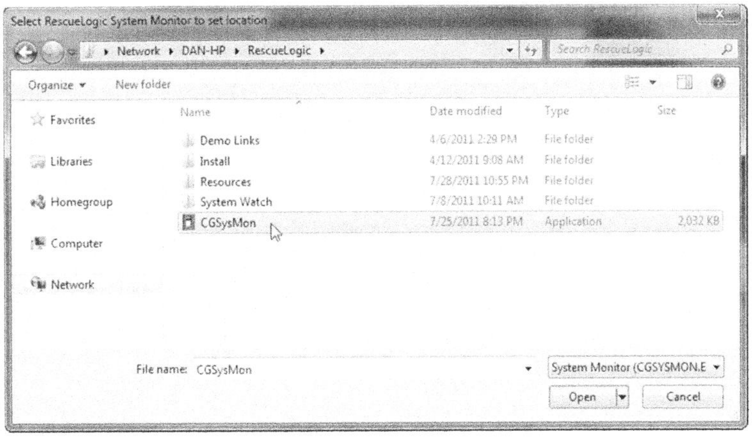

If you get an error message first, just follow the on-screen prompts.

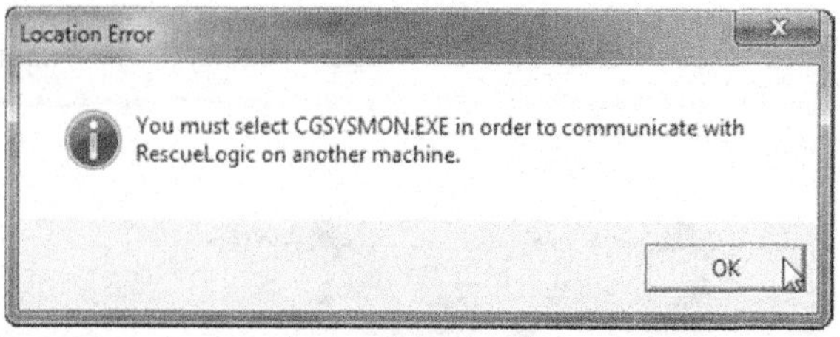

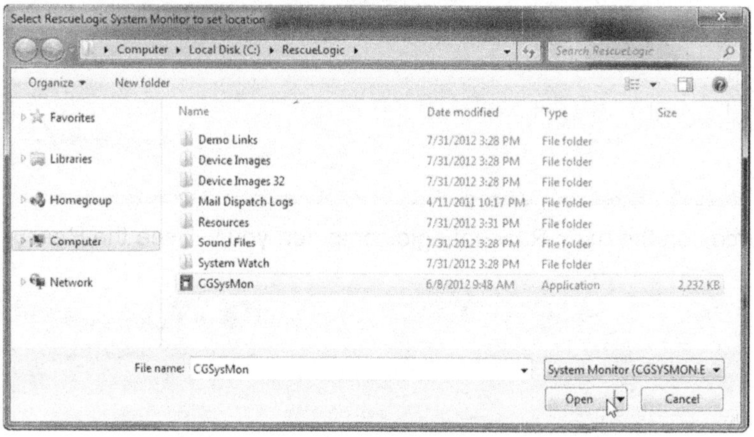

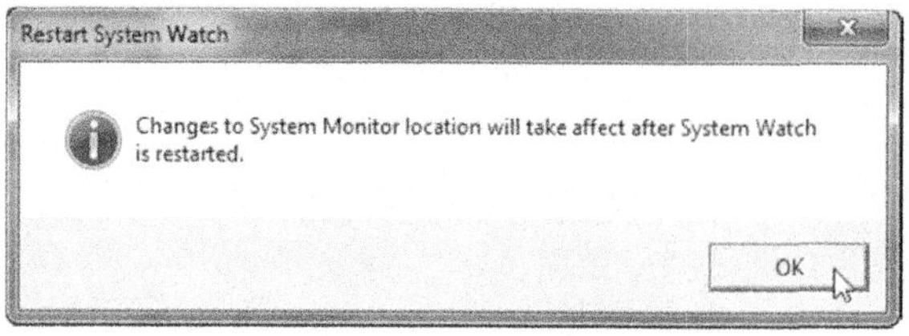

Step 5: Network Your RescueLogic Computers

You can network your RescueLogic system using an existing network, like the network you might already have in place for general office use to share printers or to share files and programs with co-workers. However, if the existing network has extremely heavy traffic or is otherwise unsuitable, you can also set up a dedicated RescueLogic network.

The networking components you will need are inexpensive and readily available. You will have several options:

If your RescueLogic monitoring stations are close together, you might simply run a crossover cable between two computers. CAT5/6 cable can run as far as 300 feet between two computers. You can extend that reach by using network switches at 300-foot intervals.

If you need to go farther than 300 feet, you might want to install high-speed fiber optic cable. You can use media converters to convert CAT5/6 cable to fiber optic, and then switch back to CAT5/6 cable at the other end of your network. Fiber optic cables can extend your reach up to a mile.

Talk to your network administrator or your Internet service provider about setting up a virtual private network (VPN). Tell them you need to set up file sharing between the two locations. You will probably find yourself talking with them about Internet access, cable modems, routers, security firewalls, and network switches at each location.

You could also install a wireless network. You can find readily available, inexpensive components almost anywhere.

The NFPA's 2013 fire alarm code designates a number of networking options. See NFPA, Chapter 12, and look for "Shared Pathways."

A Typical RescueLogic Network

Here is a sample diagram that shows a typical network setup: one main RescueLogic computer connected to an existing local area network, with a second computer that has a remote copy of RescueLogic software. Both computers share files across the local area network, and both share the same access to the Internet and a printer. This diagram also depicts a third RescueLogic monitoring station — a wireless laptop with a remote copy of RescueLogic and a wireless connection to the network, so it too can access RescueLogic files, the printer, and the Internet.

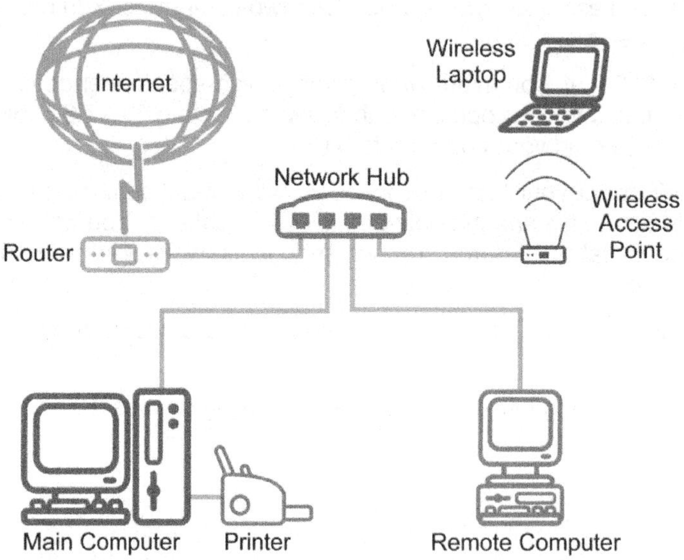

Helpful Hint: At Cadgraphics, we are happy to share what we know about networking hardware and peripherals. It tends to be rather generalized, because RescueLogic software is our primary focus. Advanced networking assistance is not part of our standard technical support program. However, we can direct you to several good resources for networking information, as well as current networking products. Please email *info@RescueLogic.com* for details.

Recommended Hardware, Software, and Peripherals

RescueLogic was designed to work with your existing alarm system, and to be compatible with a wide range of related software and peripherals. You can integrate RescueLogic with practically any components you like.

Here are some ideas of the types of devices you might like to add to your RescueLogic system.

CAD software	To create and edit CAD maps and floor plans for your site.
Drawing or painting software	Standard drawing or painting software packages can convert digital photos and CAD files into RescueLogic images.
Crystal Reports	Crystal Reports software will allow you to customize your RescueLogic reports and records capabilities.
Wireless network access point	With a wireless network access point, you can connect RescueLogic to your existing local area network.
Ethernet adaptor	Most computers come with a network adaptor.
RS232 Adaptor cables	If you need to add one or two COM ports to your computer, you can plug an adaptor cable into any available USB port.
Serial server	You can use your TCP/IP network to get information from alarm panels across your site by connecting a device server to your panels' RS232 port.
Fiber media converter	With a fiber media converter, you can switch to fiber optic communication and extend your network cable beyond 300 feet.
Crossover cable	Connect two computers together and create a mini network.
Portable data storage	Technicians and installers who work with databases should have a portable data storage device. Look for one that will fit into your pocket, plug into a USB port, and retain data for years.

Chapter 3: A RescueLogic Tour

Once your software is installed, take a few moments to explore RescueLogic's features and user-friendly interface, and get a feel for just how easy it is to set up and use RescueLogic software. This chapter will give you a guided tour of some of RescueLogic's most popular features.

A RescueLogic Test Run

After RescueLogic has been successfully installed on your computer, you will find it listed along with all of your other programs. You will find Configuration Manager under your Windows "Start" menu.

Just click on the "Start" button in the lower left-hand corner of your screen. You will see a new program group called "RescueLogic," along with icons for RescueLogic programs —Configuration Manager, System Monitor, and System Watch. (If your programs list is not alphabetized, RescueLogic may be the last folder in the list.)

To try a test run of RescueLogic based on a set of default images and files, open the "RescueLogic" program and click on "Configuration Manager."

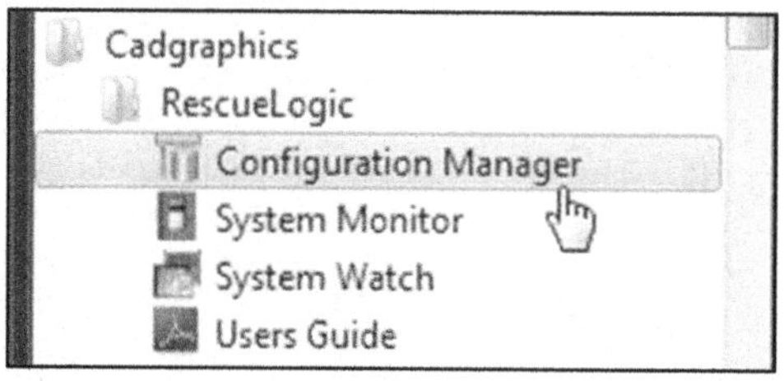

You may see a message window reminding you that your copy of RescueLogic is running in demonstration mode. Click "OK."

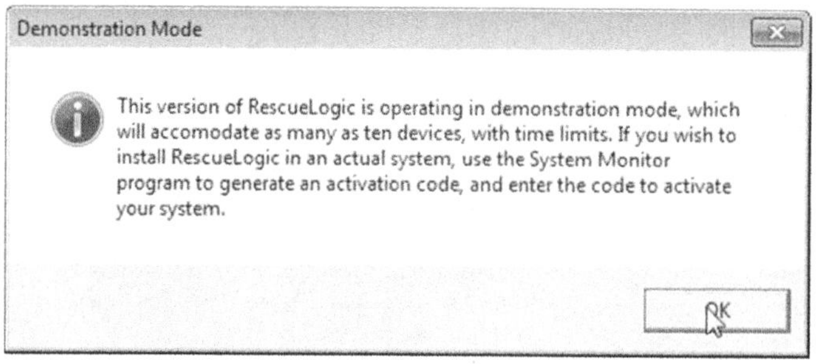

You will be asked for a password. Because you have not customized your system yet, the password is still the default, **password**. Enter the password and click "OK."

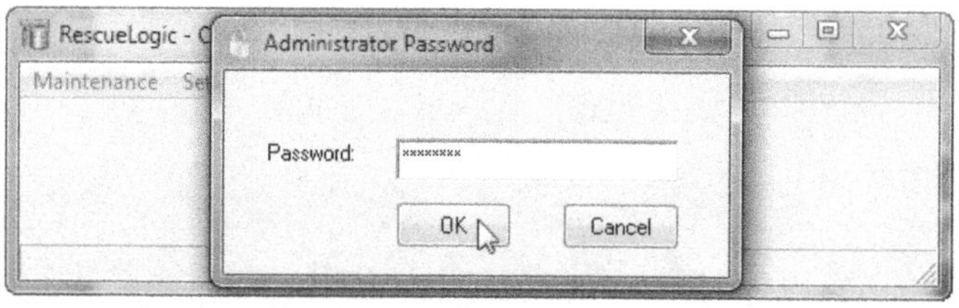

Go to the "Test" drop-down menu and click on "System Watch."

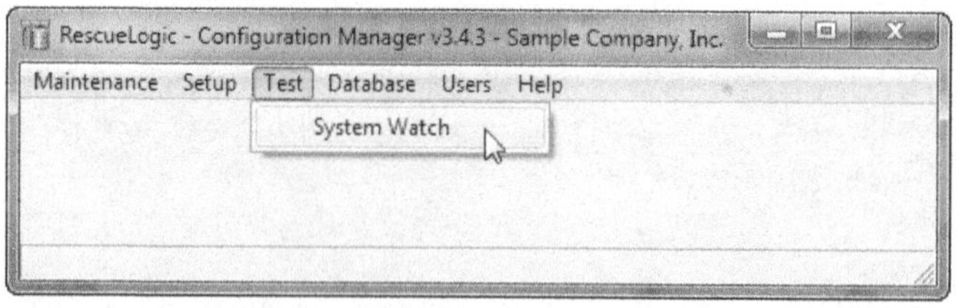

Helpful Hint: System Watch will run for ten minutes in "Test" mode, which is usually enough time to preview your work as you are setting up your system. The time limit is designed to ensure that the "Test" program does not mistakenly take the place of the real System Watch program, which would leave Configuration Manager open and running in the background.

The System Watch Demo Screen

A System Watch screen will open. You will see that RescueLogic is running in test mode, with the default sample database that most people use as a starting point for setting up their own RescueLogic system. Alarms are color-coded by type, and clearly labeled with their locations. Double -click on any item in the list to see it located on a floor plan. In this instance, double-click on the third item in the list, "Smoke Detector Elevator Lobby."

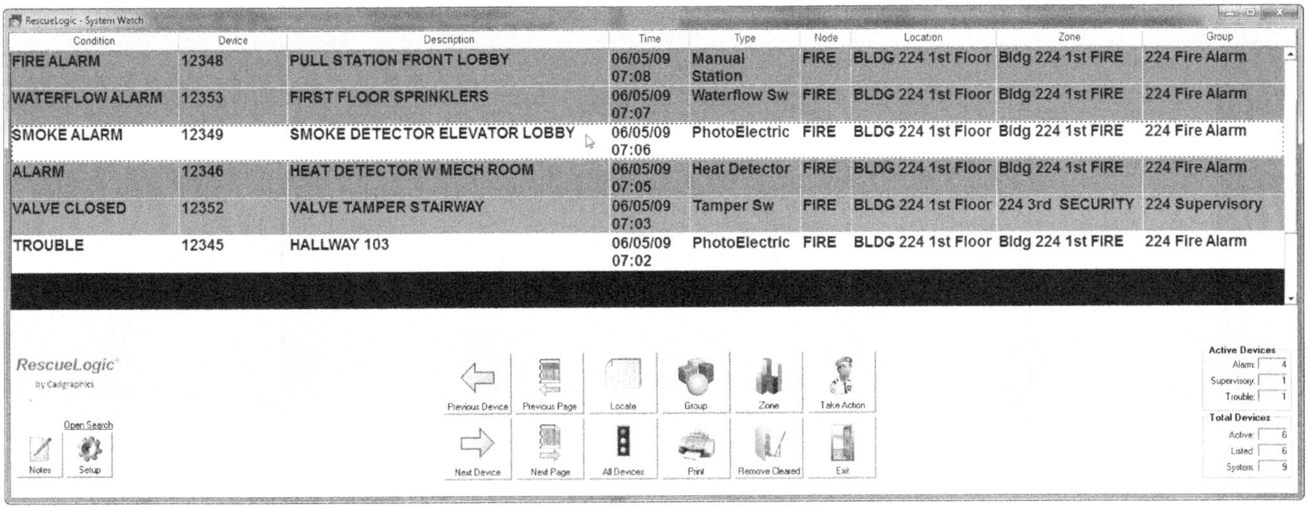

Zoom In

You will see the alarm blinking on the floor plan. Click the "Zoom In" button on the bottom of the screen.

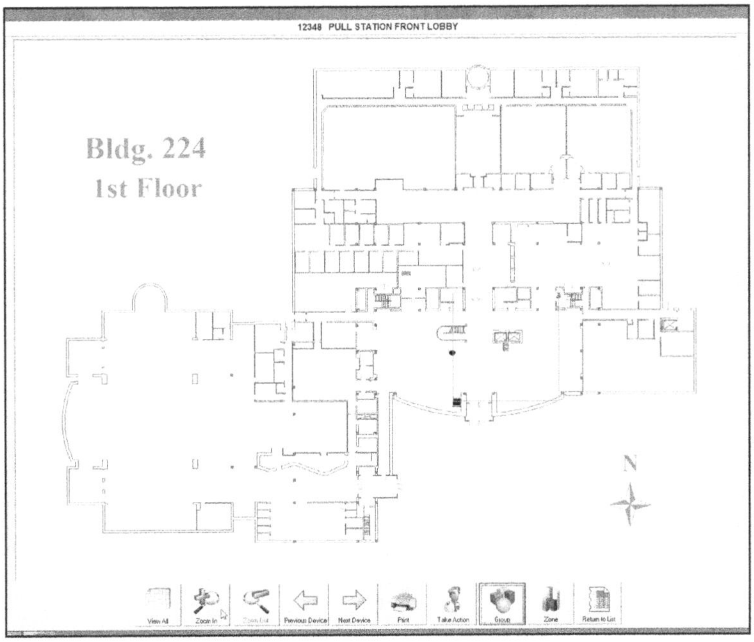

See Device Images

Once you have zoomed in, you will be able to see an image of the device that is in alarm. Click "Zoom In" again for an even closer view.

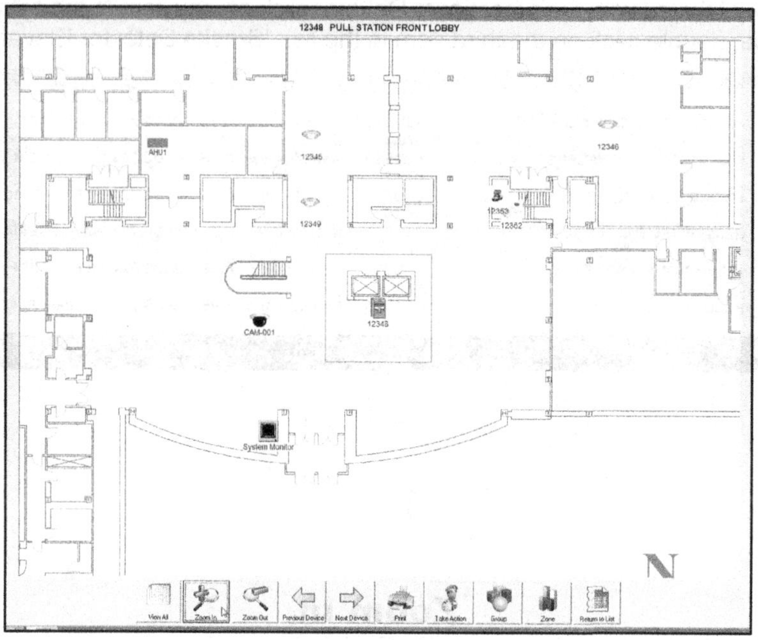

Maximum Zoom

Once you have zoomed in as much as possible, the "Zoom In" button will be grayed out. Now click the "Take Action" button to see the emergency message associated with the alarm.

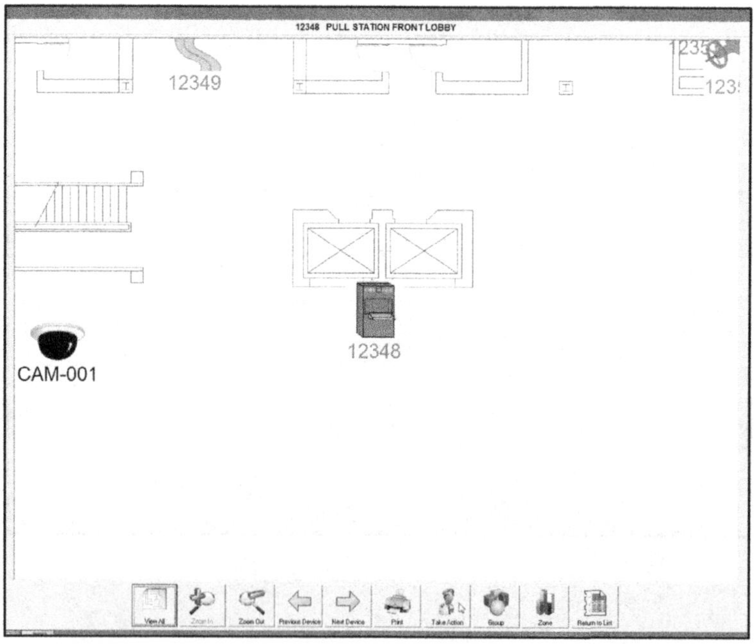

"Take Action" Messages

Read the "Device Action Message," and then click the "Close" button. You can click on the "Zoom Out" navigation button to return to the floor plan. You can click on "Next Device" or "Previous Device" to go directly to other devices on the floor plan. You can also click the "Return to List" button to go back to the color-coded list of alarms and devices.

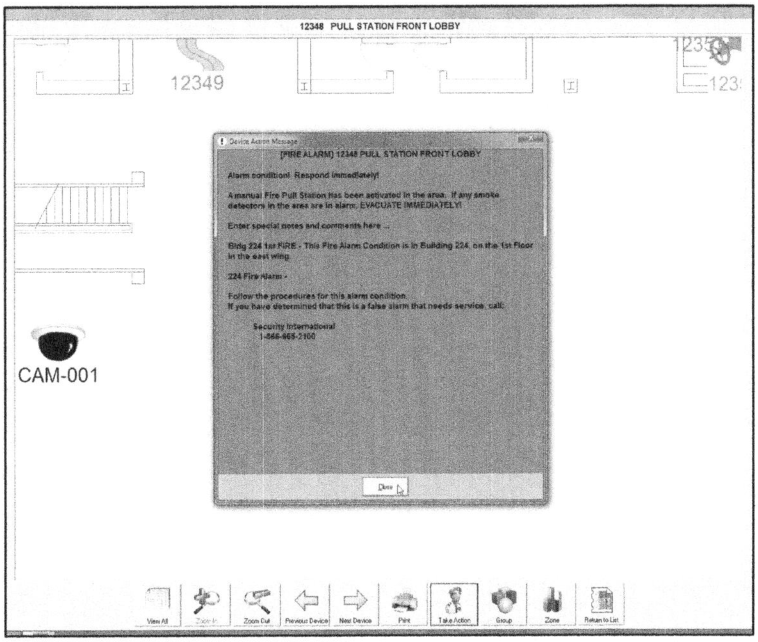

Helpful Hint: Whenever a device is in trouble or alarm, you will see it blinking on the floor plan. You do not need to click on the "Take Action" button to get the emergency message — you can also click directly on the image of the alarm, and the action message window will appear.

Chapter 4: Customize Your RescueLogic System

RescueLogic is easy to customize. You can adapt the software to meet your needs and change the look to suit your taste. This chapter will show you how to make the System Watch screen work for you.

The System Watch List

Most people start customizing RescueLogic by changing the appearance of their screens. The next few pages will show you how to change the appearance of your System Watch list.

After you have worked with RescueLogic for a while, and you are comfortable with the interface, you can customize your system even more. For details, see the System Watch chapter later in this guide.

For now, start customizing your RescueLogic system by opening the Configuration Manager program. Go to the "Test" drop-down menu and choose "System Watch."

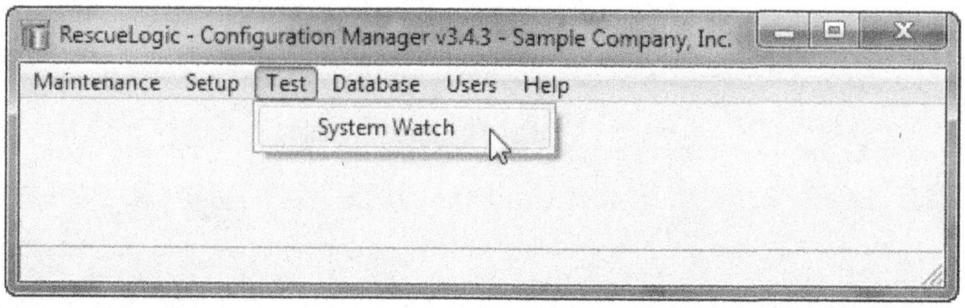

You will see System Watch running in test mode. Click the "Setup" button in the lower left-hand corner.

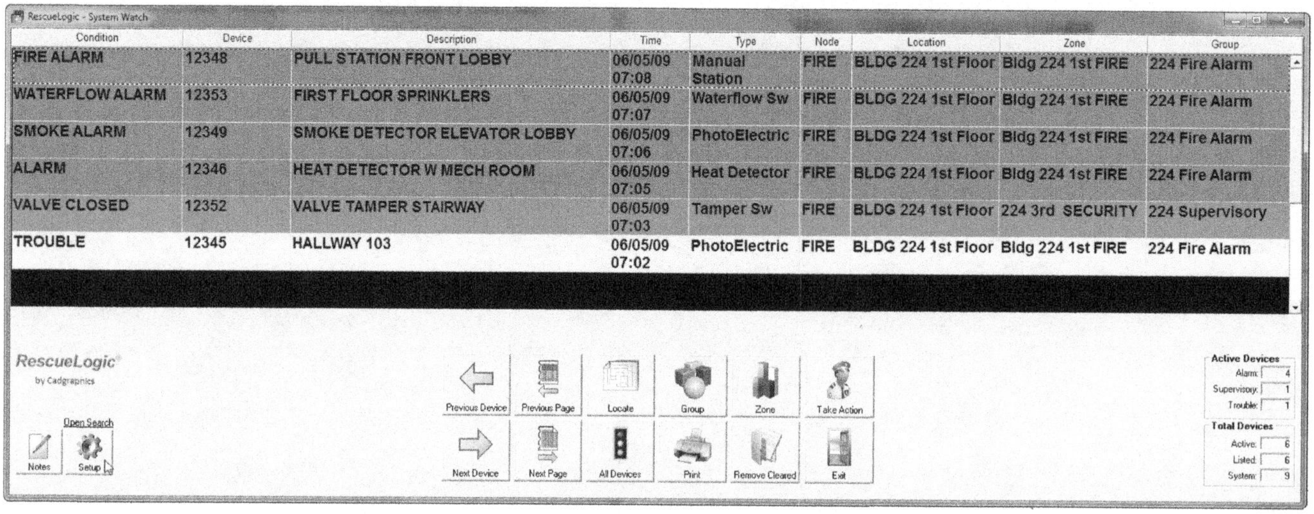

System Watch Settings

Once you click on the System Watch "Setup" button, the "System Watch Setup" window will open. The first tab, "Settings," includes a number of options.

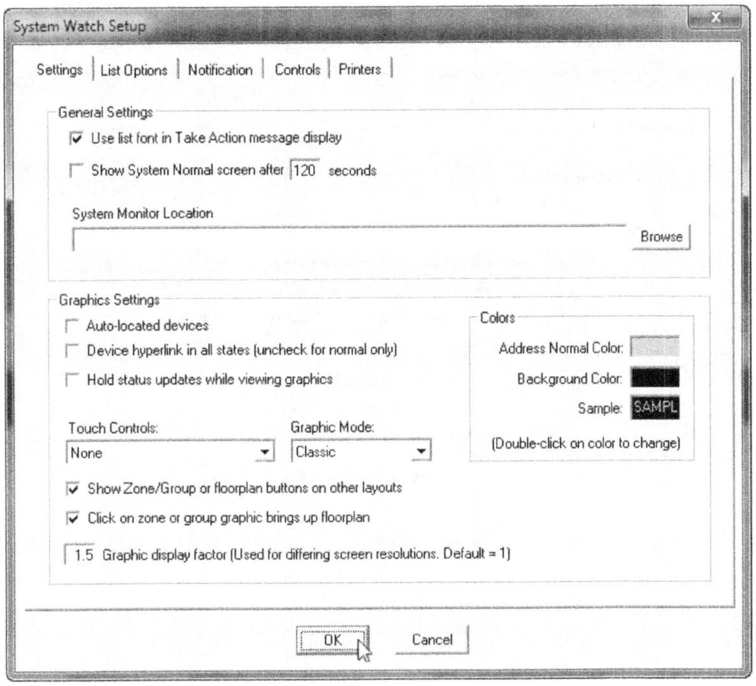

To get a feel for the changes you can make, look at the "Colors" section. Double-click on the "Address Normal Color" or "Background Color" to try new combinations. Black and white work well for most users.

When you are through with the "Settings" tab, click on the "List Options" tab.

System Watch List Options

The “List Options” screen has a check box to “Save column widths and other settings on exit.” Check the box to save your preferences when you close System Watch.

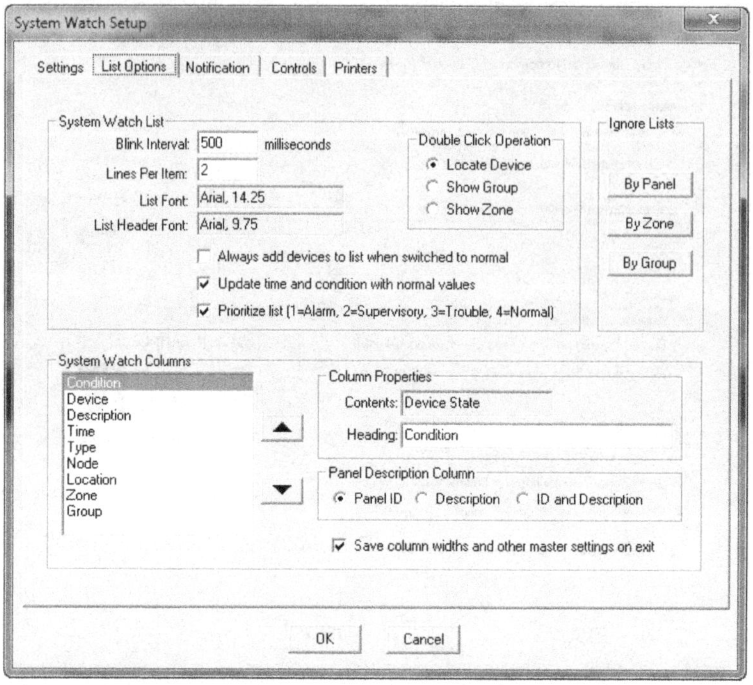

The System Watch Setup will also help you set the following preferences:

The “Blink Interval” setting determines how fast an active device will flash on screen.

The “Lines Per Item” setting controls the height of each box of text used to list a device. If you choose to use multiple lines of text, the lines will wrap automatically.

If you use a single RescueLogic station to monitor alarms from a number of buildings, you can set RescueLogic to ignore some alarms. You can filter alarms by Panel, Zone, and Group.

The System Watch “Column Properties” section allows you to change the order of the columns and the heading at the top of the list.

System Watch Fonts

To change the font for your System Watch list, double-click in the "List Font" and "List Header Font" fields.

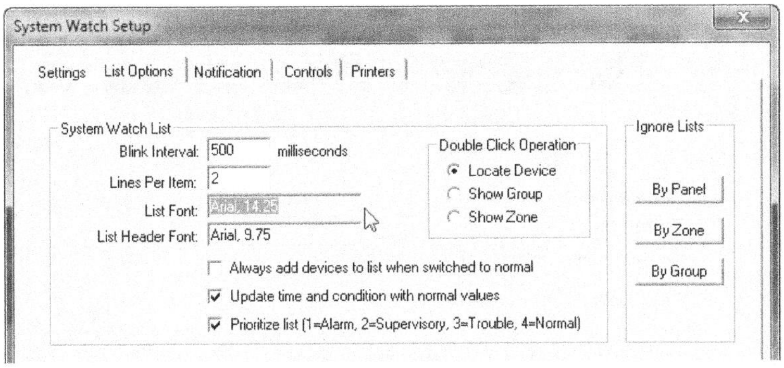

You may use any standard Windows font you like; we recommend Arial, bold, 12 point for items in your list, and Arial, 11 point for the header font. Choose new fonts for both your list items and your headers, and then click "OK" to close the "Font" window and return to the "List Options" screen. Then go back to the top of the System Watch Setup window and click the "Notification" tab to proceed.

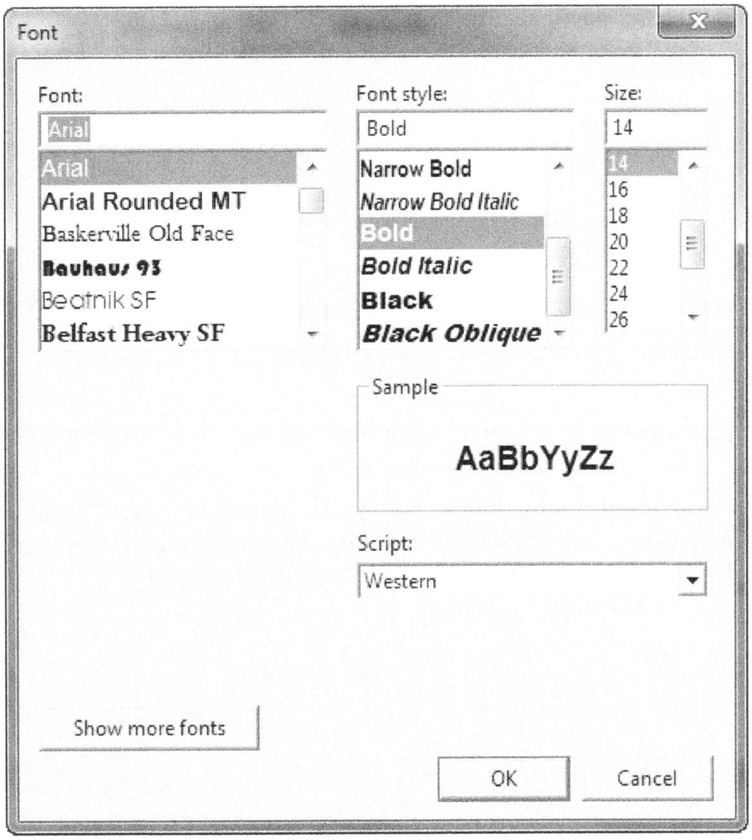

Helpful Hint: You might notice that you are not able to use this window to choose font colors. Color settings are determined by the state of each device.

Notification Options

You will use the "Notification" tab section to choose whether your system will play an audible alert during trouble and alarms.

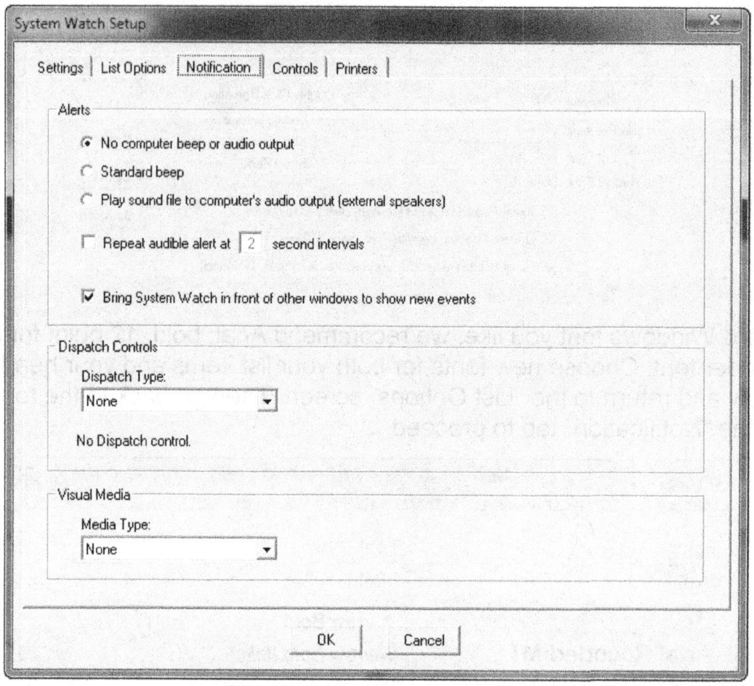

To hear an audible alert, click "Standard Beep."

To assign specific sound files to play when devices are in trouble or alarm, click "Play WAV file."

To repeat the audible alert until the alarm has been cleared, check "Continuous Alert." (UL 864 listed systems will be preset for continuous, audible alert.)

To force RescueLogic's System Watch screen to come to the forefront on a new alarm or trouble — interrupting other Windows programs — check "Bring System Watch to Top."

Dispatch Controls sets the type of control that the System Watch user has over email alerts. Emails may be sent automatically, and the System Watch user may need a way to pause and purge messages. If you select "None," the System Watch user will not see the overriding control for email messages.

Control Options

You will use the "Controls" tab section to allow selected levels of control for each System Watch station.

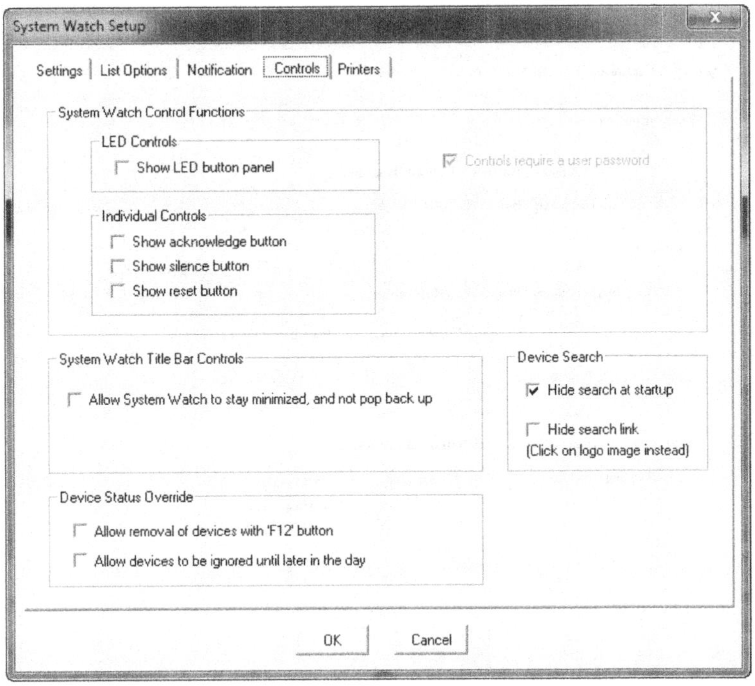

If you are an expert user, you may want to check "Allow System Watch to stay minimized." You'll probably want to minimize the screen while you set up your system. When you're through setting it up, however, uncheck the box to ensure that your RescueLogic computer will display full-screen as a monitoring station.

The "System Watch Control Functions" relate to UL-listed systems. Leave them unchecked for now.

The Device Search control allows you to hide the search window, which will leave more screen space for the main System Watch screen. An optional Search link can be shown as a reminder of that search function. In any case, the Device Search window will appear if the user clicks on the system logo.

Printer Options

You will use the “Printers” tab section to set your printing preferences.

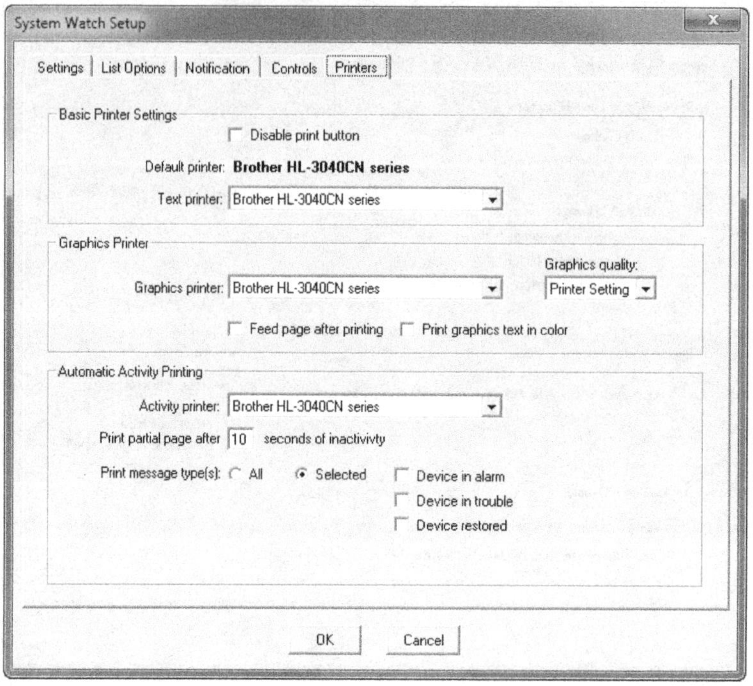

If your RescueLogic computer isn’t connected to a printer, you may want to check “Disable print button” as a reminder that nothing will print by pressing the button.

The Basic Printer Settings allow you to choose the printer that will receive text-based printouts such as the device list and reports.

The Graphics Printer option selects the printer that will print floor plans, zones, and group graphics screens. (It may be the same printer as the text printer.)

Automatic Activity Printing determines which printer will print event logs, which can often be lengthy.

When you have set up your printing preferences, click “OK” to close the System Watch Setup window and see the changes you have made to your System Watch list.

Chapter 5: General System Information

This is where the real fun begins. As you set up general system information, you will start customizing your RescueLogic system specifically for your site. If you are working with a RescueLogic demo program, the default demo database will provide a head start on system setup. The information you enter here will stay in your system, and be fully functional even after you activate your software. You will also be able to copy a database you've configured at your office onto a new computer, and put it into service at the job site.

General System Information

As you continue to customize your RescueLogic system, you will find yourself entering more and more details about your facility. You will enter some of those details by modifying your General System setup.

To modify your General System setup, make sure Configuration Manager is running. Open the "Setup" drop-down menu, and click on "General System Information."

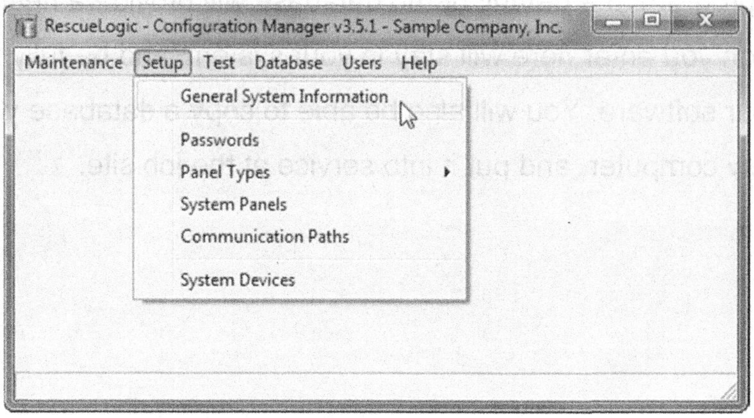

Company Name

Enter your company name exactly as you want it to appear throughout your RescueLogic system. You can change your company name until you activate your copy of RescueLogic. Once the software is activated, the name is permanent. (See Appendix A for activation instructions.)

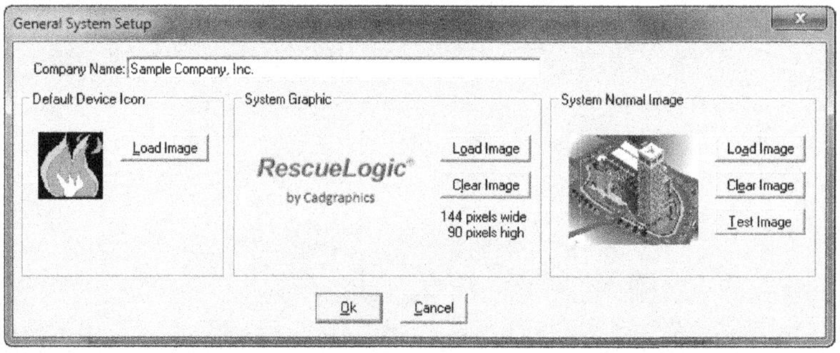

Default Device Image

The default image for devices in your system is a red square. Until you assign specific images for each type of device in your system — such as smoke detectors and intruder alarms — RescueLogic will use the default image to show devices on your floor plan. While most users do not change the default image, it is easy to replace. First, click the "Load Image" button.

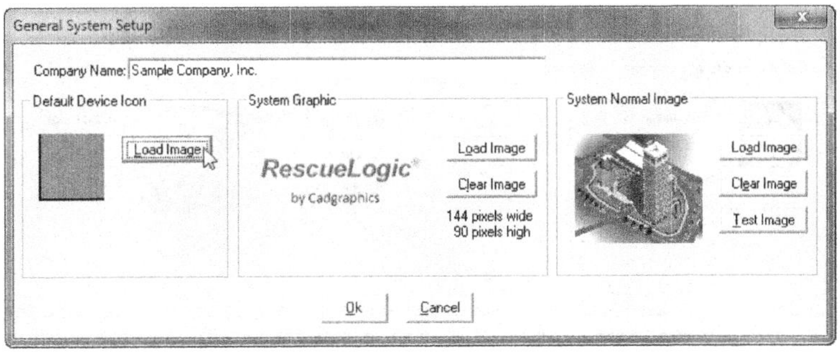

A "Select Device Image" window will open. You can browse to any Windows metafile image file on your computer, or choose a new default image from the RescueLogic "Device Images" folder. (We recommend that images be formatted as Windows metafiles, or WMFs.) Now you can select a new image from the Device Images folder. In this example, we'll choose the "flame" image.

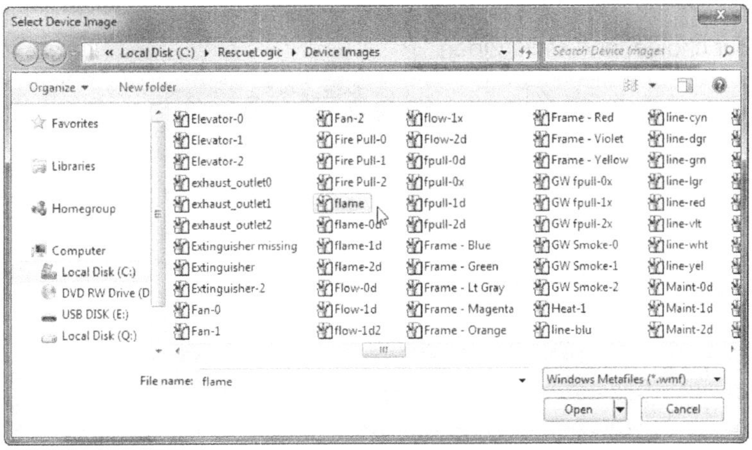

Your Company Logo

You can use the “General System Setup” screen to import your company logo, so it will be displayed on your System Watch screen. To insert your logo, click “Load Image.” (If you do not want to display a logo, click “Clear Image.”)

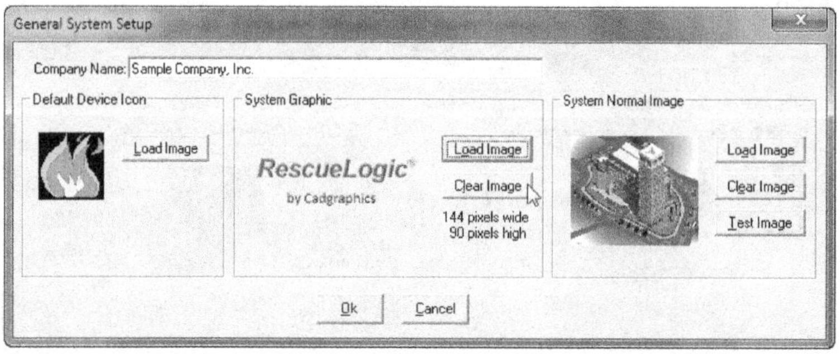

Helpful Hint: Logo files should be 144 pixels wide by 90 pixels high. You can create and edit logo files in most drawing and paint programs. Transparent outer edges usually look best against the various grays of Windows backgrounds.

Find the logo image of your choice, and click “Open.”

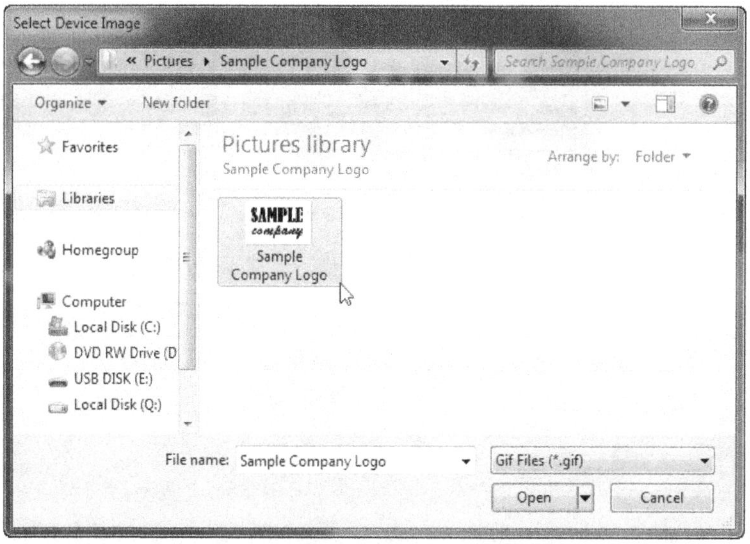

Your logo will appear in the “System Graphic” section of the setup window.

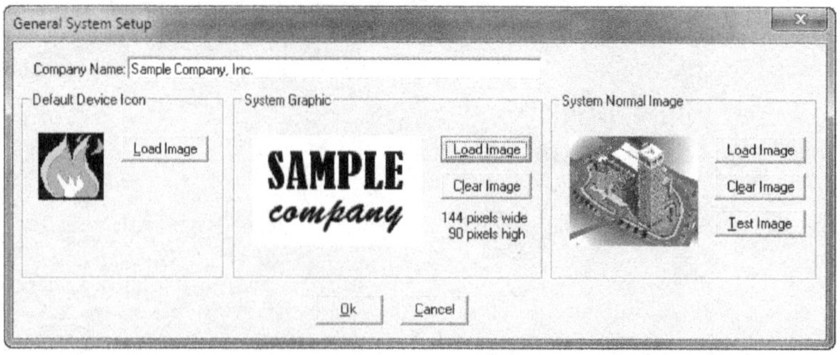

Your "System Normal" Image

You can choose a "System Normal" image to be displayed whenever there are no active devices in your system, just like a screen saver. First, click "Load Image." (If you do not want to display an image, click "Clear Image." Then, when your system is in normal status, the screen will simply be blank.)

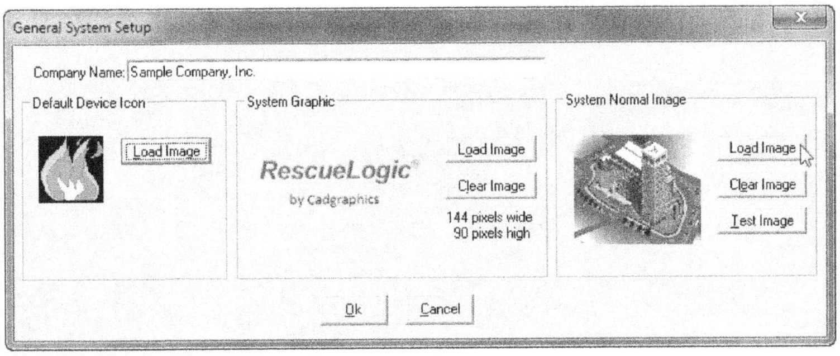

Browse to the picture you want to use and click "Open." You can use any digital photo or graphic you like. We recommend using a Windows metafile, because WMFs are generally smaller than other file formats.

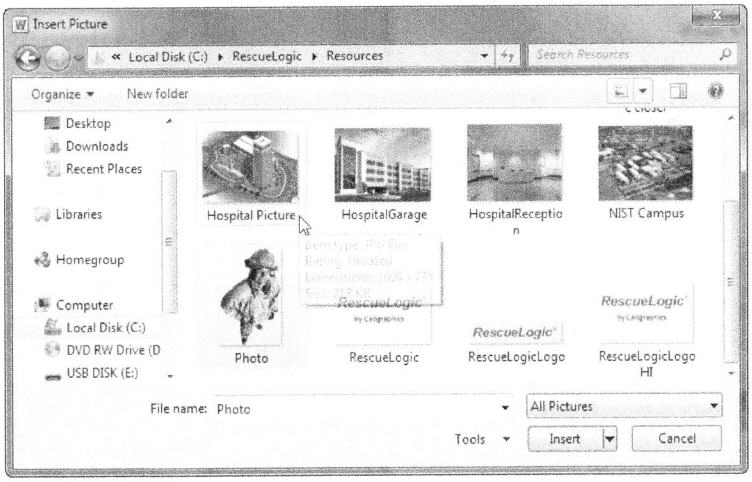

Once you have clicked "Open," a thumbnail image of the photo you have chosen will appear in the General System Setup window. Click "Test Image" to see how the photo will look on your screen.

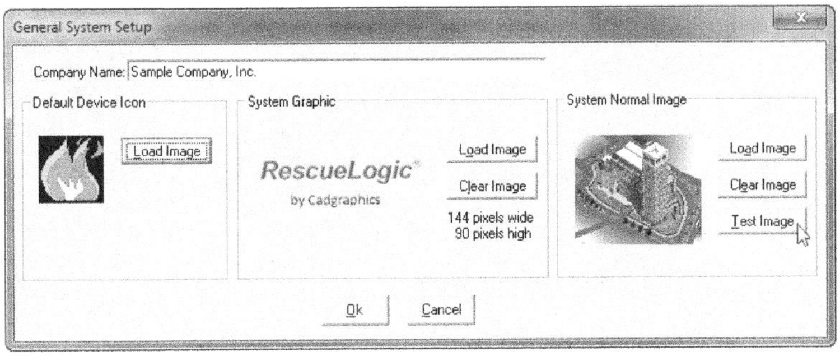

Your new "System Normal" image will fill your screen. Click the "X" in the top right-hand corner to close the test image.

Click "OK" when you are finished setting up your general system information.

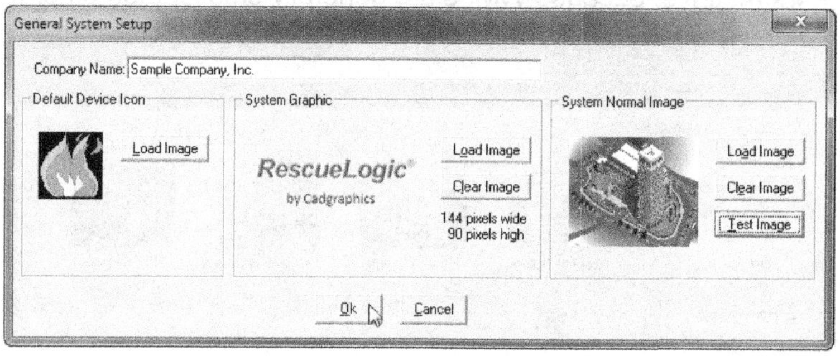

Chapter 6: Passwords

You will probably want to protect your RescueLogic system with passwords to prevent unauthorized users from changing your settings and personal preferences — or worse, shutting down your monitoring station to play games or surf the Internet. This chapter will show you how to establish your system passwords and keep them from getting lost.

Establish System Passwords

Your RescueLogic system is password protected, to help ensure that unauthorized users do not tamper with your settings or shut down your monitoring program. You can establish varying levels of passwords, to allow a wide range of users to access the information they need.

The default Level 1 password is the numeral **1**. The default Level 2 password is the numeral **2**. The default Level 3 password is the numeral **3**. In addition, the default administrative password is **password**.

As you customize your RescueLogic system, you will need to establish four separate passwords. Each password should be four to ten characters long.

The **Level 1** password will allow all authorized users to make cosmetic changes to the system and set individual preferences.

The **Level 2** password will enable some authorized users to add and delete notes to clarify the system for other users.

The **Level 3** password will enable a select few users to shut down the RescueLogic system. (Most users rely on RescueLogic to monitor the status of their fire alarm and security systems, so they never want the software to shut down accidentally. When they do choose to shut it down, it is typically for maintenance.)

The **administrative** password will enable system administrators or engineers to enter devices and modify their locations in the RescueLogic system. Until you change it, the Configuration Manager password is **password**.

Start by opening Configuration Manager. Go to the "Setup" menu and click on "Passwords."

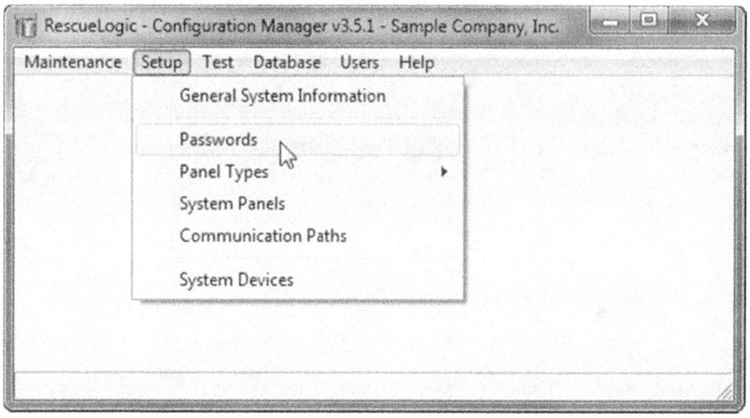

Enter the Default Password

You will be asked for the default administrative password, which is **password**. Enter it, and then click "OK."

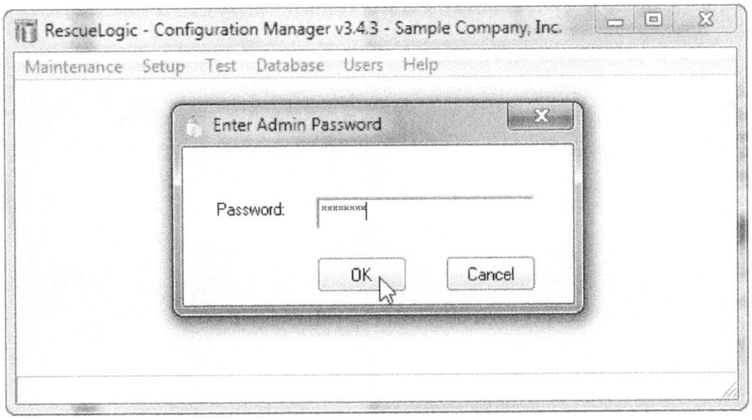

Use the "Password Setup" screen to enter new passwords in each field. Each password should be four to ten characters long. Passwords are not case-sensitive. You may change the password life, but most users never need to make adjustments. The default is five seconds. That means that once you enter your password, you can execute other functions within five seconds without having to re-enter your password. When you are done setting up all four passwords, click "OK."

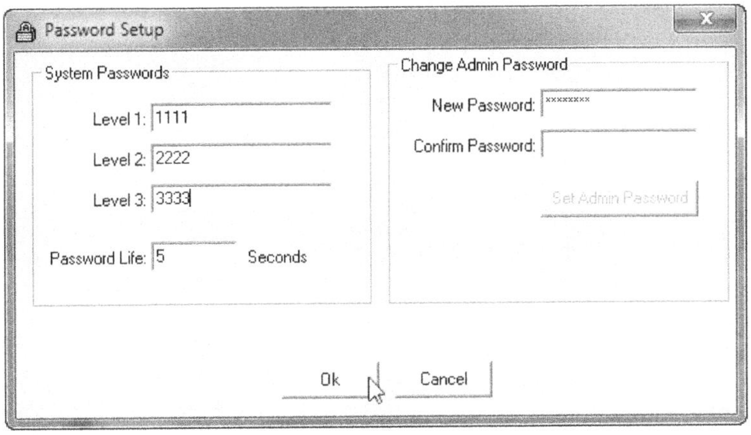

After you change your passwords from the defaults, use this space to write them down.

Password Level	Default Password	Your New Password
Level 1	1	
Level 2	2	
Level 3	3	
Administrative	Password	

Chapter 7: Add Devices

With RescueLogic, you can describe your alarms and devices in plain English, add emergency instructions and sound files, and position components on maps and floor plans. You can even add IP cameras and web-based information, so they can be monitored and seen from your RescueLogic monitoring station. This chapter will show you how to add a wide range of alarms and devices to your RescueLogic system, and how to categorize them by zones and groups.

List the Types of Devices on Your Site

Every device in your fire alarm or security system has an identification number, or address, that identifies it to the manufacturer's alarm panel. Devices are also labeled with abbreviations for device type, and a description intended to clarify their location. The result is an alpha-numeric code that can be difficult to interpret: the abbreviation "01L03D101 SMK MECH MEZZ," for example, might represent smoke detector #101, located in the mechanical room on the Mezzanine Level, and reporting to Panel 1, Loop 3.

Are you ready to convert your device addresses from codes to plain English? Start by opening Configuration Manager. Go to the "Maintenance" drop-down menu and click on "Device Types."

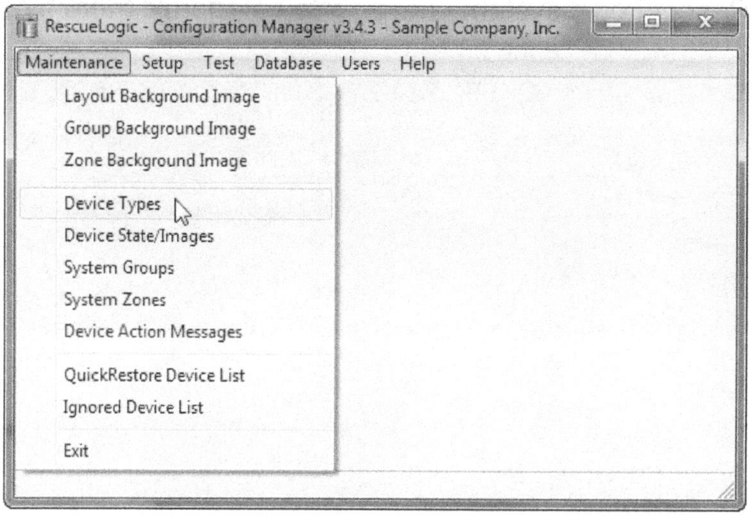

You will see a list of device types, ranging from panels and heat detectors to keypads and proximity sensors.

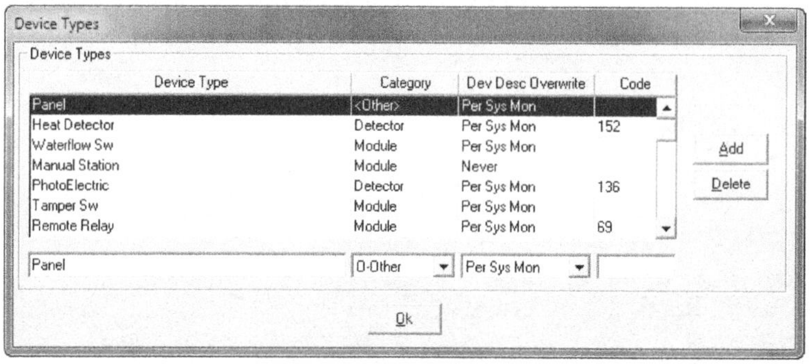

Each device type has a corresponding category: "Detector" indicates that the device is a smoke, heat, or fire detector. "Module" indicates that the device is a control or input device, such as a manual pull station or a water flow switch. The "Other" category is used if the Detector or Module categories do not apply. The list is part of RescueLogic' default database. It may include most of the types of devices in your alarm system.

The column on the right titled "Code" was created for specific systems, and is reserved for future use. You can normally disregard the Code column.

Review the list, because you will want it to include every unique type of device in your system.

Edit Device Properties

You can highlight any item in the list to edit its properties in the box beneath the list.

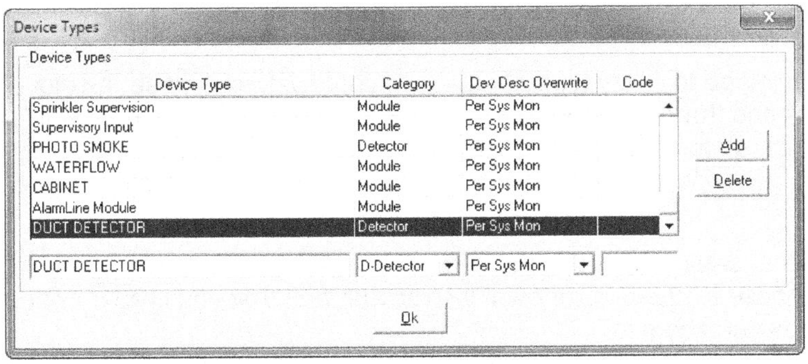

Add New Types of Devices

If you have devices on your site that are not included in the list, click the "Add" button.

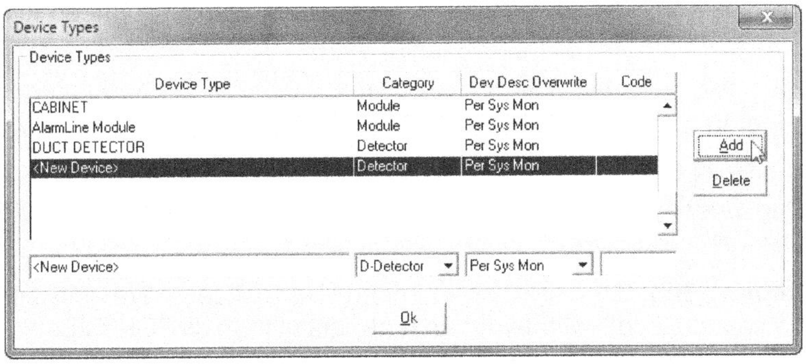

Use the edit box at the bottom to type in the name of each new device — a **Duct Smoke Detector**, for example. Simply type over the entry that says <New Device>. The devices you enter are automatically added to the list.

Click the "Add" button to continue adding new types of devices. Click "OK" when you are through.

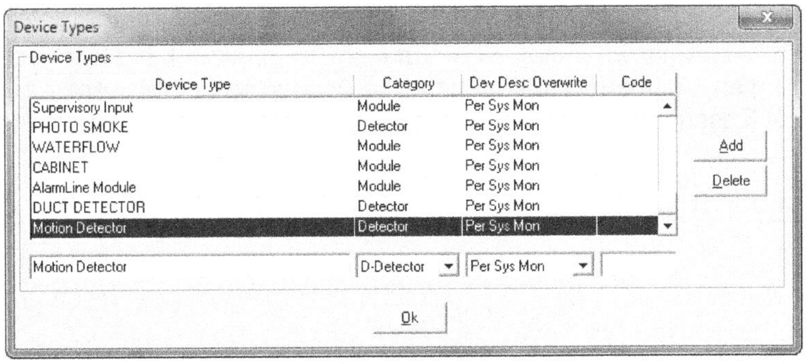

Helpful Hint: The name you enter for each device should exactly match the name it has been given on your fire alarm panels. If your panel lists a device as a "smk.det," you should list it as a "smk.det" in your RescueLogic system, too. If your system includes similar devices from two manufacturers but their names vary — "smk.det" and "smoke detector" — be sure to include both variants in your list. If the names do not match up, you will discover the mistake during your first test of the system, because each device's corresponding "Device Type" in your System Watch list will be blank.

Device Images

RescueLogic can display images of every device on your site, shown in their correct location on maps and floor plans, and color-coded according to their status. By default, when devices are in normal standby mode, they are green. Devices that are reporting trouble are yellow, and devices that are in alarm are red.

You will need to assign an image to every type of device in your system, and set a color scheme for them. You will establish three images and three separate color schemes for every type of device in your system. The three sets of images will depict the status of every device: normal, trouble, and alarm. Typically, devices are depicted in red when they're in alarm, yellow when they are in trouble, and green when they're in normal mode. Security devices in alarm are blue.

Many standard images are already included in your RescueLogic database. You can also create your own custom graphics. If you choose to create your own, we recommend that you create Windows metafiles (WMFs) for the greatest clarity when you zoom in.

A Note about Image File Formats

RescueLogic will work with most image file formats. Most CAD packages, photo editing programs, and drawing software can convert image files from one format to another. Usually, you simply need to select to save a file in another format.

AutoCAD Drawing (DWG): DWGs are the native AutoCAD drawing format. Every CAD program on the market can open DWGs. You will Export portions of DWG files as the WMF format for use in RescueLogic.

Bitmap (BMP): BMPs are uncompressed images. They are relatively large files compared to JPEGs and GIFs. They can be black and white, grayscale, or color — as few as 16 colors, in fact. Microsoft Paint, which comes with Windows operating systems, can edit BMPs.

Graphics Interchange Format (GIF): GIFs are color-mapped files that can have anywhere from two to 256 colors. GIF files are always compressed, but they retain more detail than JPEGs. GIFs are usually used for line art and graphics, not photos, and they are the predominant image file format for the World Wide Web.

Joint Photographic Experts Group (JPEG): JPEGs are compressed image files, with less detail than GIFs. JPEGs are primarily used for photos. The more you compress a JPEG, the more pixilated it will look. JPEGs are either true color or grayscale. JPEGs are the smallest image files, so they are a good format for photos that are to be sent as e-mail attachments or posted on web pages.

Windows Metafile (WMF): The Windows Metafile Format is the original 16-bit native vector file format for the Microsoft Windows operating environment. WMF files can be used to store both vector and bitmap graphics. We recommend WMFs for most RescueLogic images, because they show the most detail when users zoom in and out.

Assign Device Images

To assign standard images to new devices, start by opening Configuration Manager. Go to the "Maintenance" drop-down menu and click on "Device State/Images."

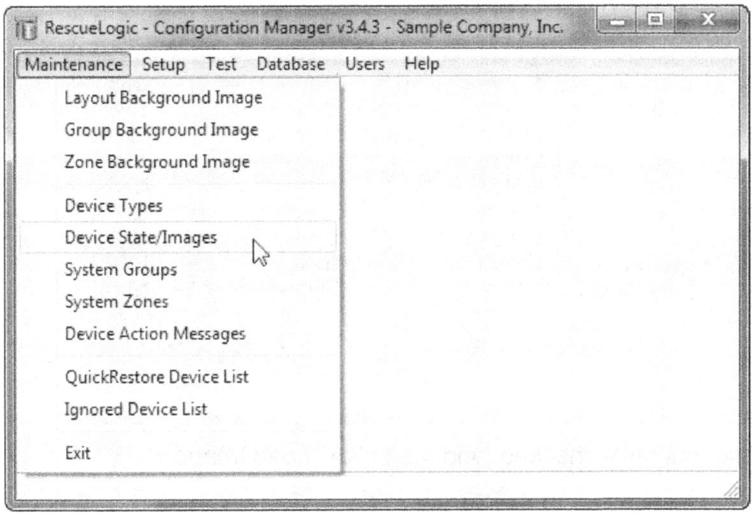

The "Device State/Image Maintenance" window will open. You will notice that a drop-down list includes all of the device types in your system.

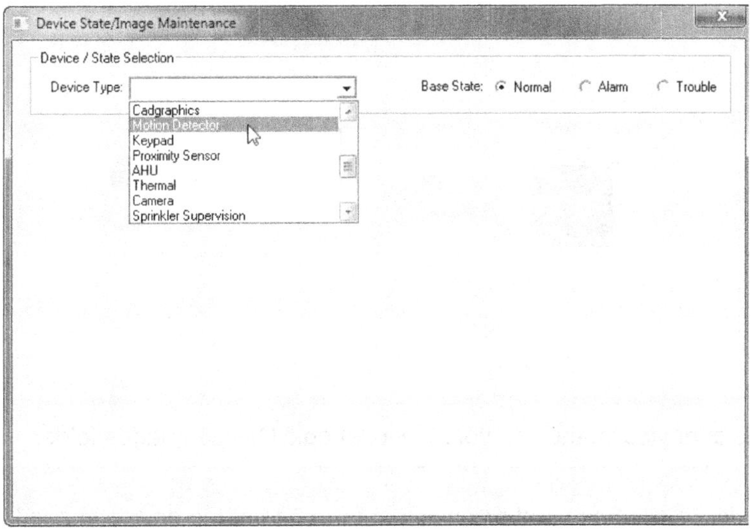

Begin by loading an image for the duct smoke detector when it is in normal status.

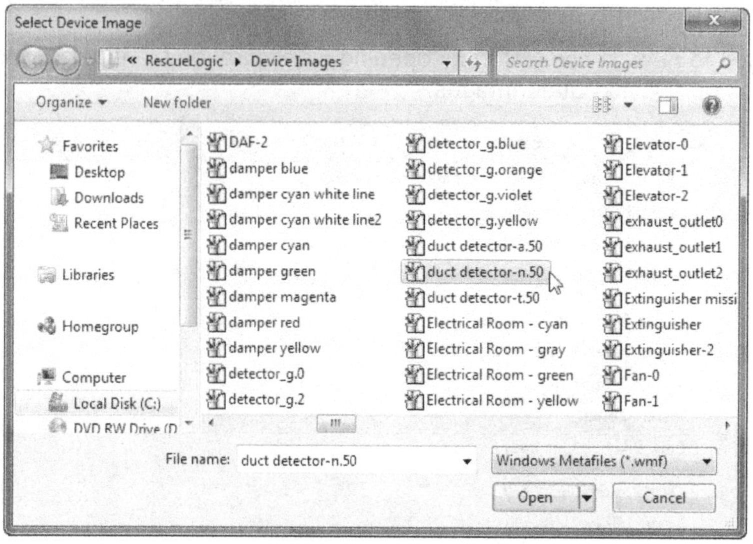

Make sure that the “Normal” button is checked, and then click “Load Image.”

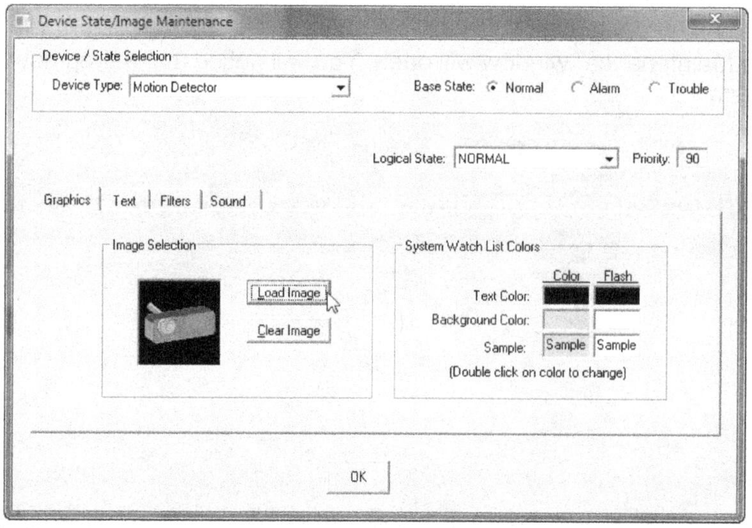

You will find a wide range of device images on your RescueLogic Device Images folder.

Helpful Hint: RescueLogic’ developers used a consistent format to name device image files. Images of devices in normal status are labeled with the suffix “-0.” (Likewise, images of devices in alarm are labeled with the suffix “-1.” Images of devices in trouble are labeled with the suffix “-2.” If you create your own image files, you should use the same naming convention. Remember, you will have three different pictures for each device.

Assign Images for Devices in Normal Status

Once you have selected an image for a duct smoke detector in normal status, your Device State/Image Maintenance window will look like this. By default, the "System Watch List Colors" are green. You can double-click on the colors to change them, but we recommend that you leave them set to green.

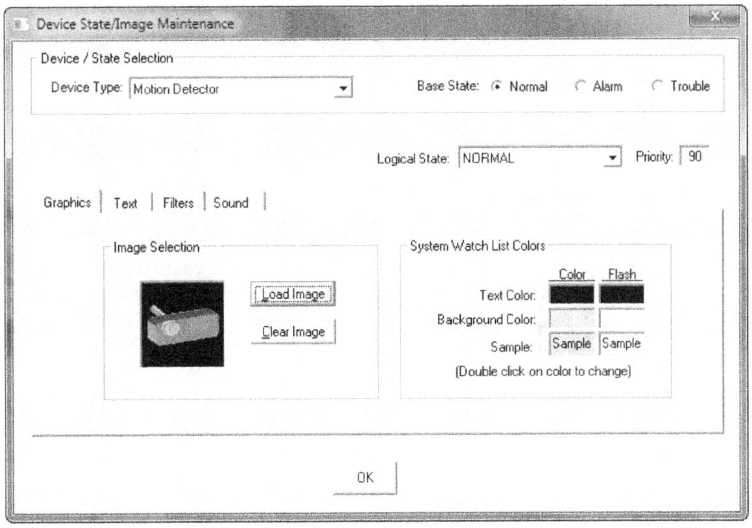

Assign Images for Devices in Alarm

Follow the same procedure to select images for devices in alarm and in trouble status. In this example, we'll work with a heat detector in alarm. Make sure that the "Alarm" button is checked. The "System Watch List Colors" are red, by default. You can change the color, but we recommend that you leave it set to red. That way, when a device is in alarm, it will flash in red.

Helpful Hint: While the "Basic State" is set to "Alarm," you should choose the appropriate "Logical State" for the device. Choose "FIRE ALARM" for fire alarm devices and "SUPERVISORY ALARM" for non-fire alarm devices such as tamper switches and security alarms.

Assign Images for Devices in Trouble

Follow the same procedure to select images for devices in alarm and in trouble status. You'll notice that "System Watch List Colors" are yellow, by default. You can double-click on the colors to change them, but we recommend that you leave them set to yellow. That way, when a device is in trouble, it will flash in yellow.

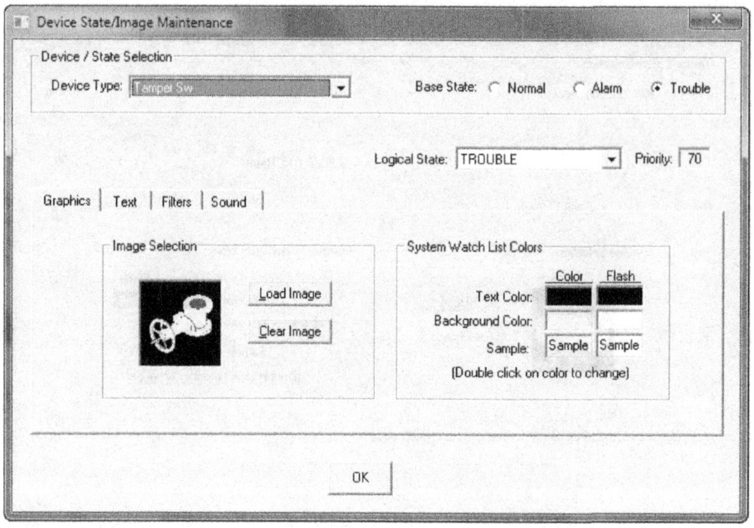

Helpful Hint: When you are done assigning images for devices in normal, alarm, and trouble status, you can quickly check your work by highlighting any device in the "Device Type" in the drop-down menu. Then you can use your keyboard's up and down arrow keys to scan all device type properties, and make sure you didn't leave any blank.

Assign Unique Text Alerts

You can customize text alert messages for devices in each state. Simply click the "Text" tab to modify the alerts that will appear on screen.

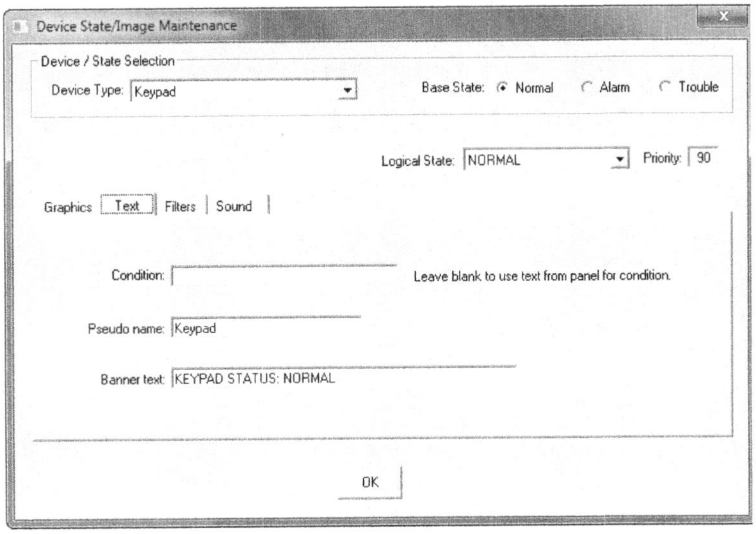

Filter Alerts

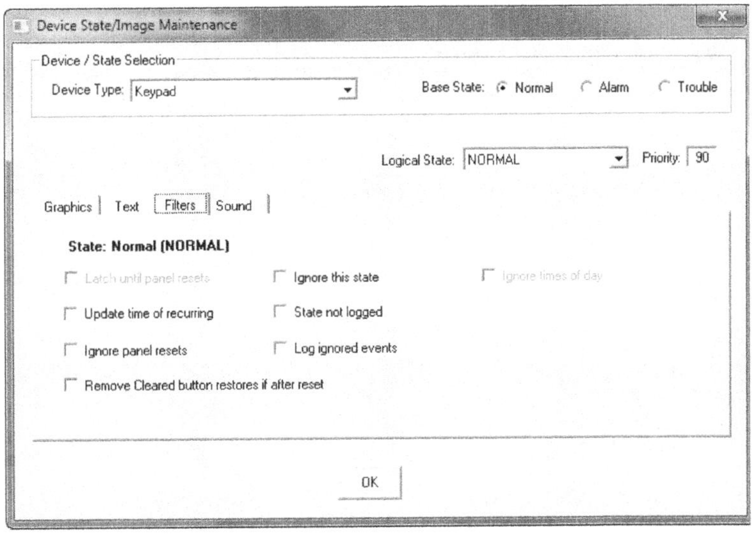

When you have a variety of alarm panels connected to your RescueLogic system, you may find it necessary to vary their behavior to make alarms consistent for your users. You can use filters if the default behavior settings don't meet your needs. Basically, the filters are overrides to ensure that alarms stay on screen when they need attention, and clear out when the situation is normalized.

Helpful Hint: You may choose to ignore some security alarms during certain hours of the day. To ignore a "SUPERVISORY" device state, check the "Ignored" box of your choice and select the time. "FIRE ALARM" device states cannot be ignored.

Assign Sound Files

You can establish a unique alert sound for devices in each state. In this case, we will assign a sound to play when a smoke detector goes into alarm. Choose "Smoke Detector" from the device type drop-down menu. Set the Base State to Alarm. Then, on the Sound Tab, click Select.

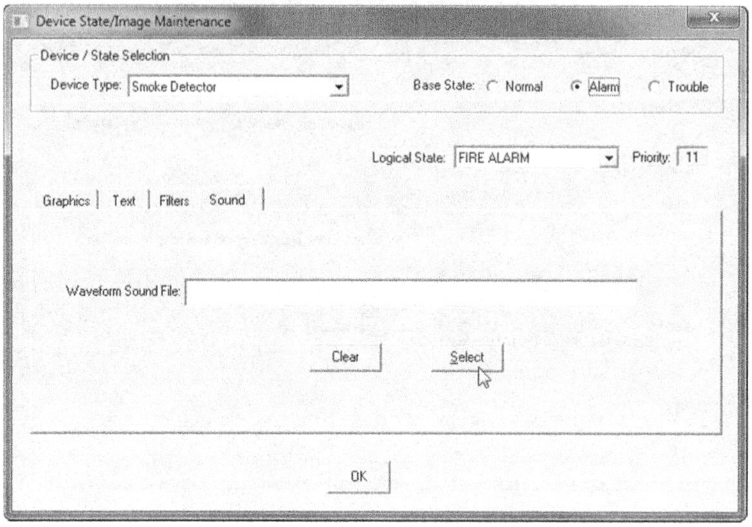

Choose a WAV sound file from the RescueLogic "Sound Files" folder on your hard drive.

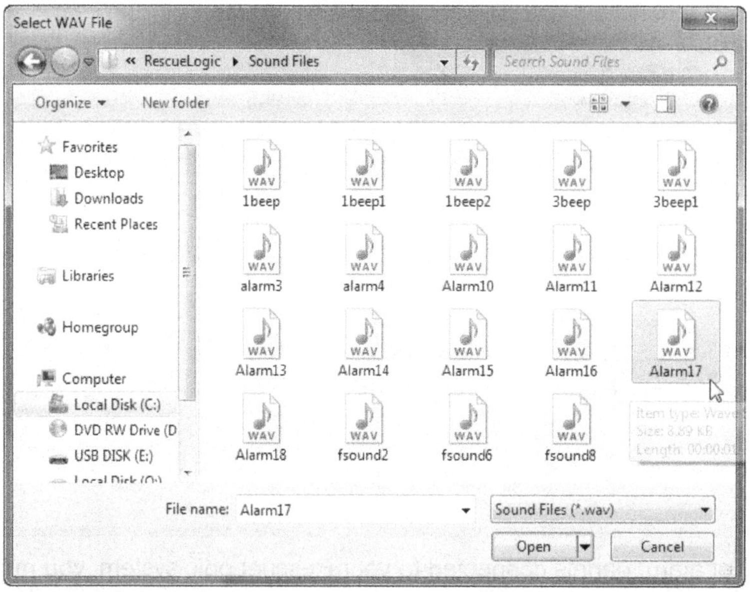

Helpful Hint: You can create sound files with text-to-speech software. Any text you enter will sound as though it's being read aloud by a familiar voice. Save the result as a .wav file.

When you finish assigning sound files to each device type in alarm, and possibly trouble, click "OK."

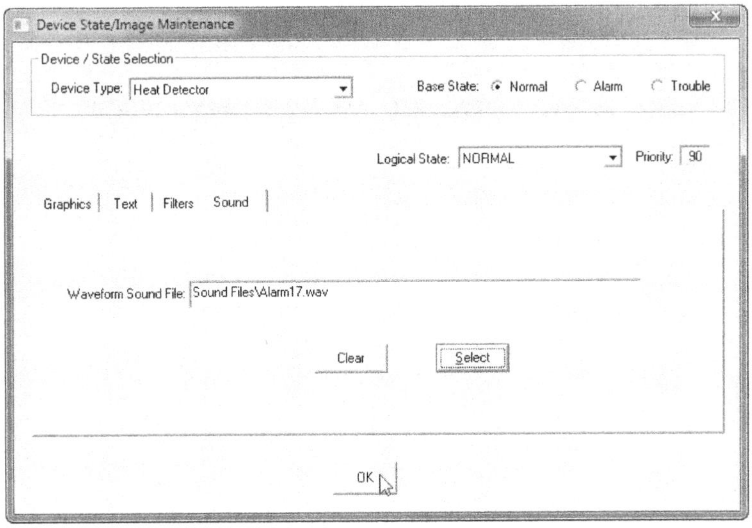

Add Individual Devices to the Database

When a control panel reports anything about a device for the first time, that device will automatically be added to the RescueLogic system. Device types are usually assigned automatically. While model and manufacturers of system components may vary, the basic categories of information that RescueLogic tracks remain the same: device type, panel, address, and description. You can view your device list in database form and make changes to the description of any device. You can also add notes and comments to clarify each location for your security team.

To make changes to your database of devices in your system, make sure that Configuration Manager is open. Go to the "Setup" drop-down menu and click on "System Devices."

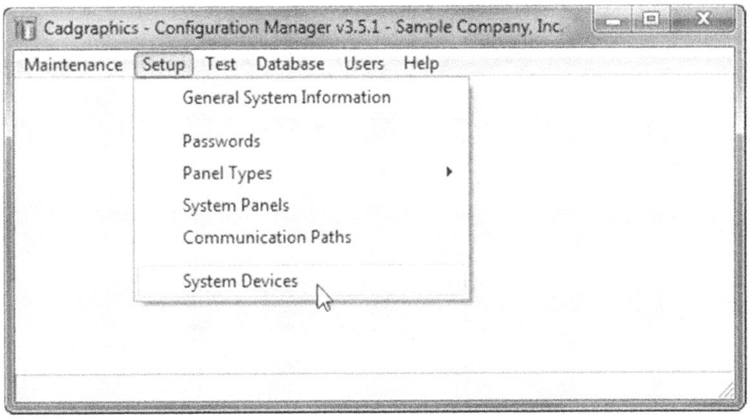

You will see a list of devices in your system.

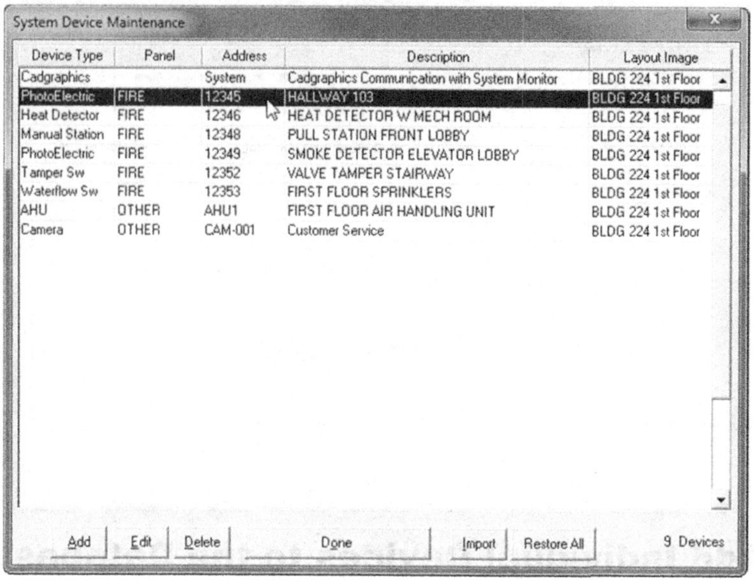

Click "Add" at the bottom of the screen to create a new device. Then, double-click on it, or any other item in the list to view and change its properties.

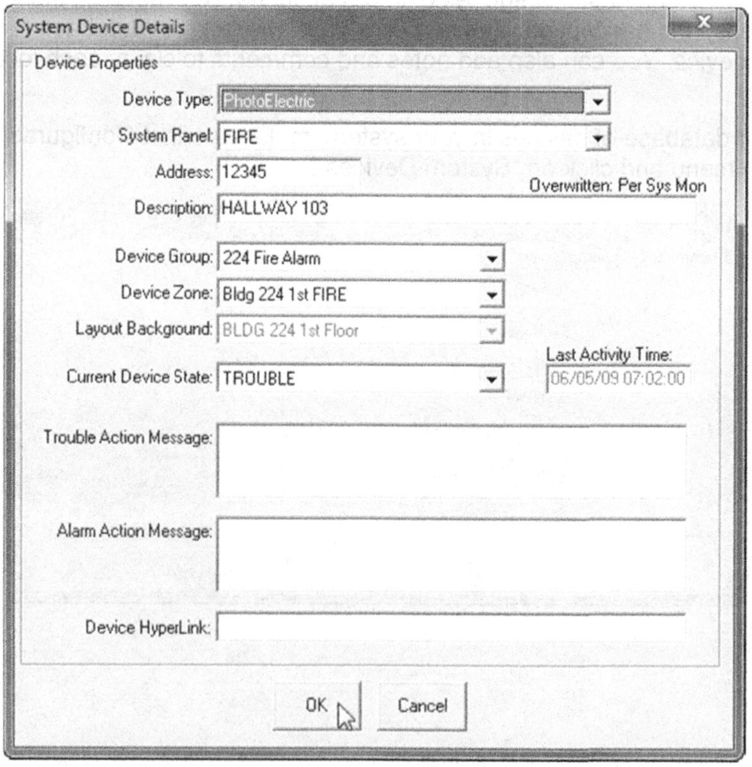

Click "OK" when you are finished editing the properties of this device.

Import Devices Automatically

You can import every device in your system automatically, if they are all listed in your alarm panel's data file or in a spreadsheet file. Check with your alarm system installer to determine what device information files are available.

Format a Device Data File

You can use Microsoft Word, Notepad, or any word-processing software that will allow you to cut and paste text, and allow you to save your data file as a simple text (.txt) file.

If your data file is in spreadsheet form, save it as a comma-delineated file with a .csv extension. We recommend that you open your comma-separated file with Microsoft Wordpad, because it includes a handy search-and-replace function that will help you format your data.

You must name the formatted data file "CGImport.txt" and save it in your hard drive's root folder, which is normally drive C. The complete file path should be **C:\CGImport.txt**.

Format your data file with a header line at the top, which will identify the data that will be included, as well as the order in which the data will appear:

ADDRESS | DEVICE TYPE | DESCRIPTION | PANEL | ZONE | GROUP |

Separate each data field with a vertical bar, and end the header line with a vertical bar, too. The vertical bar (|) is located on the same key as the backslash. Enter it by hitting SHIFT \.

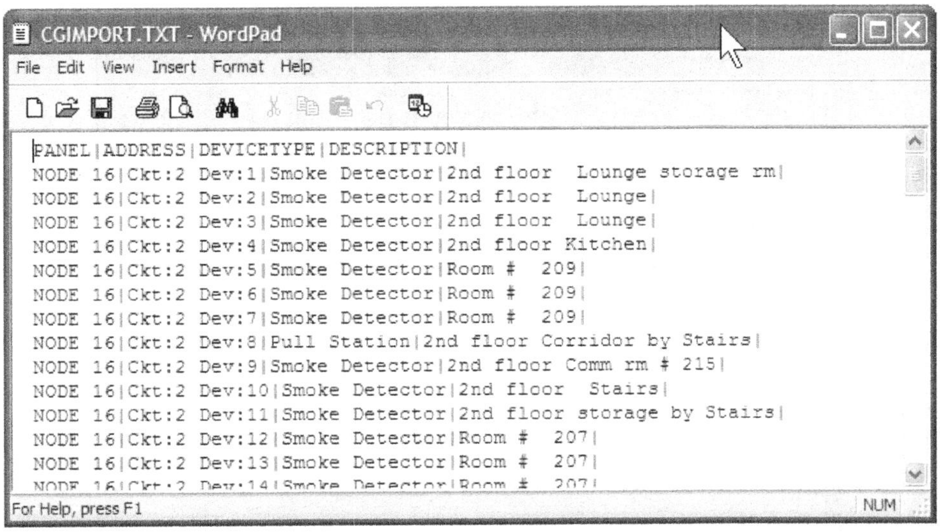

Helpful Hint: It doesn't matter how you list your data fields, as long as you are consistent. Your alarm panels may list panel data first, for example, or they might not even include panel information. Similarly, you do not need to include information in every field. If you do not have zone and group data, simply omit the zone and header fields from the top line. In fact, the only required field of data is the address field.

Import the Device Data File

Once you have prepared your data file, open Configuration Manager. From the "Setup" drop-down menu, click "System Devices."

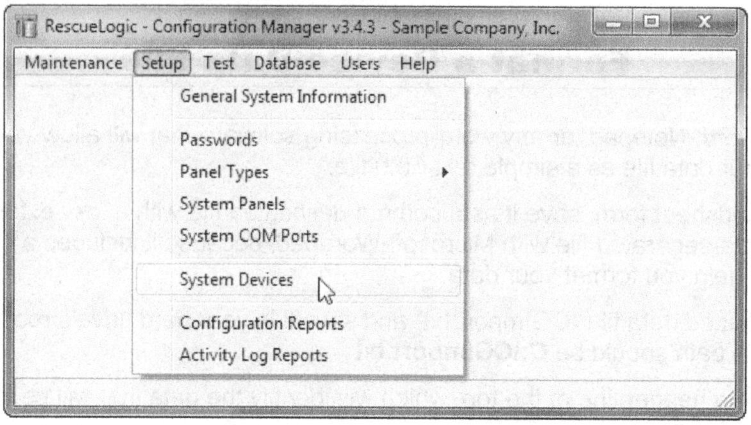

Delete Default Devices

The "System Device Maintenance" window will open, with a list of devices from RescueLogic' default database. Delete them, and then click "Import."

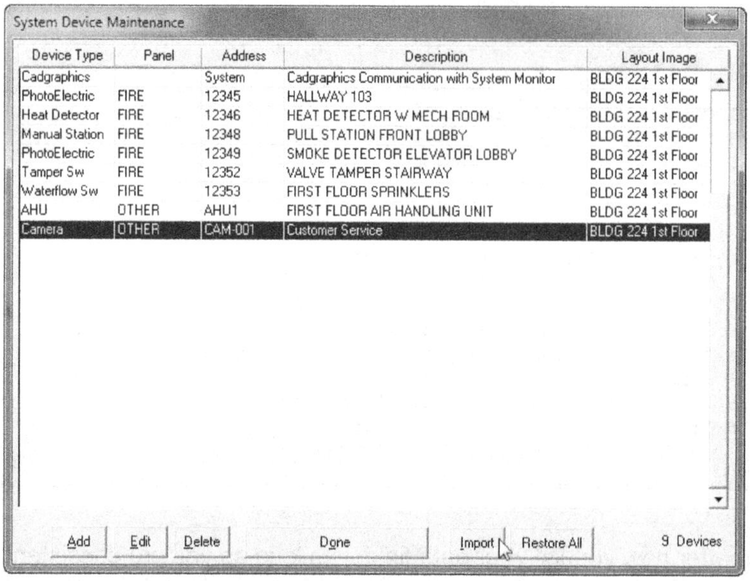

Importing Panels

The "System Device Import" window will open. The "Create Import File" is designed for panel manufacturers to use, so ignore it and look down at the "Import File/Import Panel" information at the bottom of the window. Make sure that the "Import Panel" in the drop-down menu is the same panel that has all of the devices listed in your CGImport.txt file. (By the way, if your CGImport.txt file has panels allocated for each device, you can disregard the "Import Panel" information.) Click "Import File."

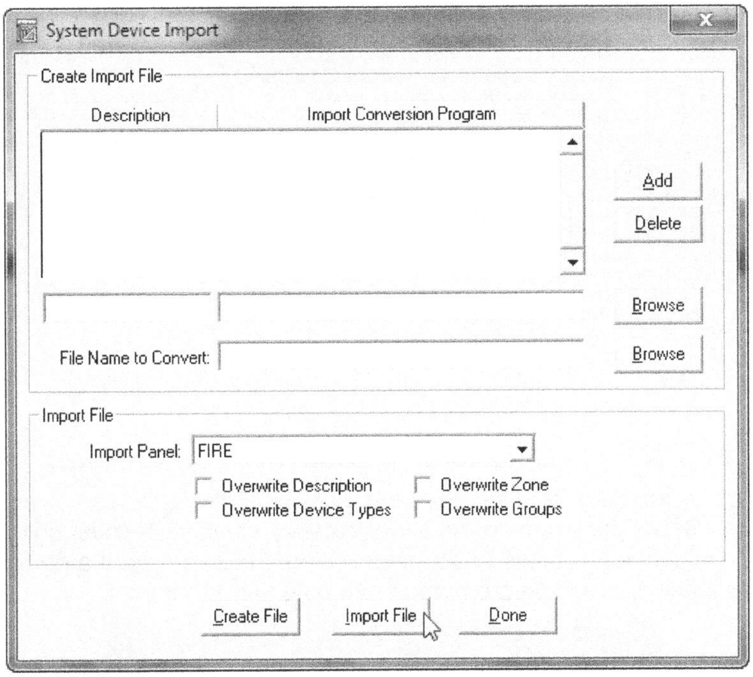

Helpful Hint: Because this is the first time you will be importing devices from the panel, you can leave the four "Overwrite" boxes unchecked. Later, if you want to modify the devices — for example, if you want to assign them to different zones — you can import them again, and overwrite the category you are modifying, but selectively preserve the information that is already in the database.

You'll see a preview of the data file that RescueLogic is prepared to import. Make sure it is the correct file, and click "Proceed." RescueLogic will begin importing devices from your data file.

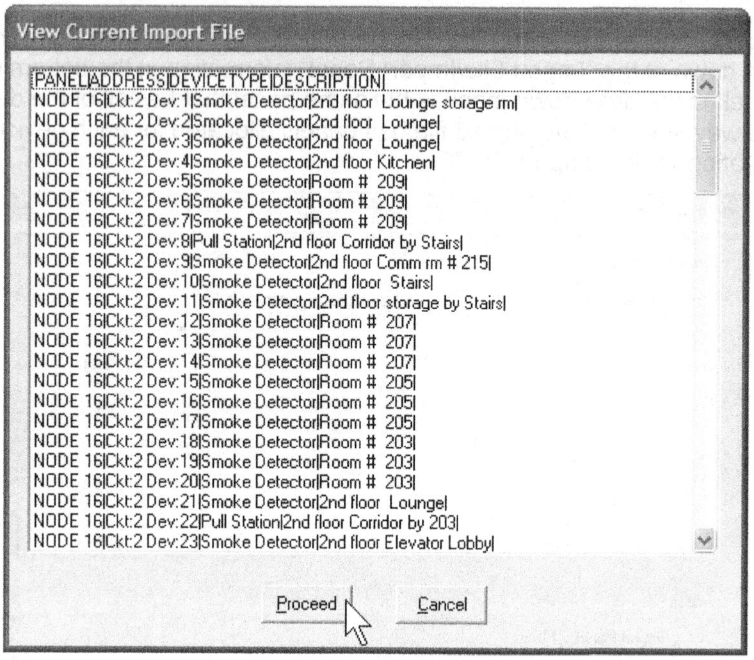

RescueLogic will scroll through the data file. As it adds each device to the database, it will display the status of that device: "Adding device 1S101," for example. As it imports each device, RescueLogic will also format related areas of the database. You might be prompted to add information. For example, if a particular group in the import file is not already in the database, you will be prompted to add the group name.

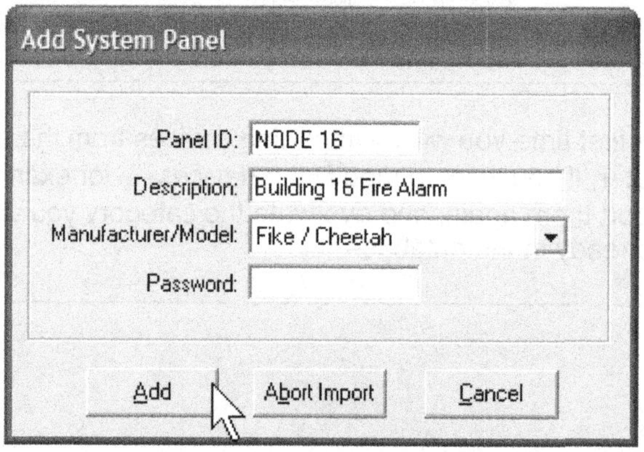

If a device type is not in the database, you will be prompted to complete a "Device Type" entry so that RescueLogic can add the new type. Choose a new category from the drop-down list, and click "Add."

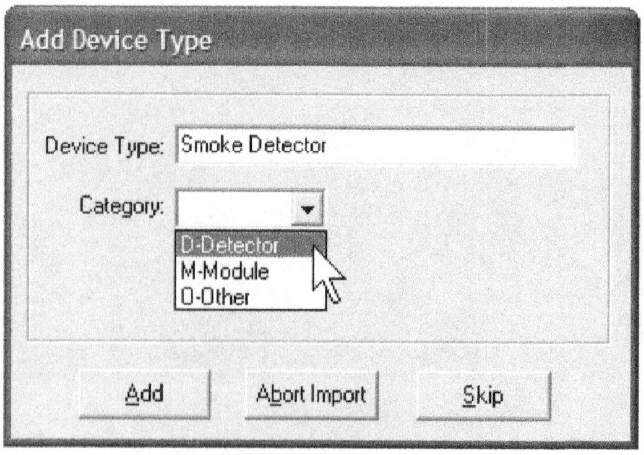

When the import is complete, click “Done.”

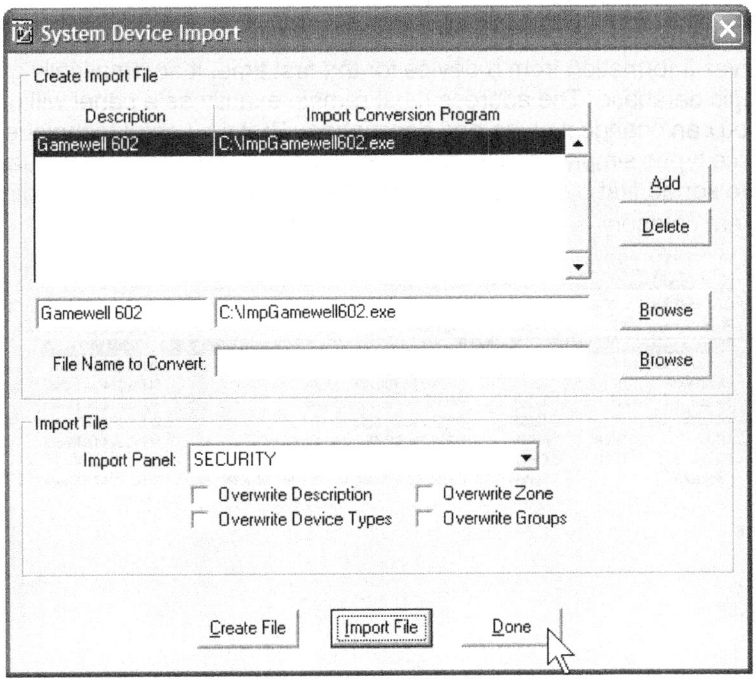

The new device list will now show the devices you just imported.

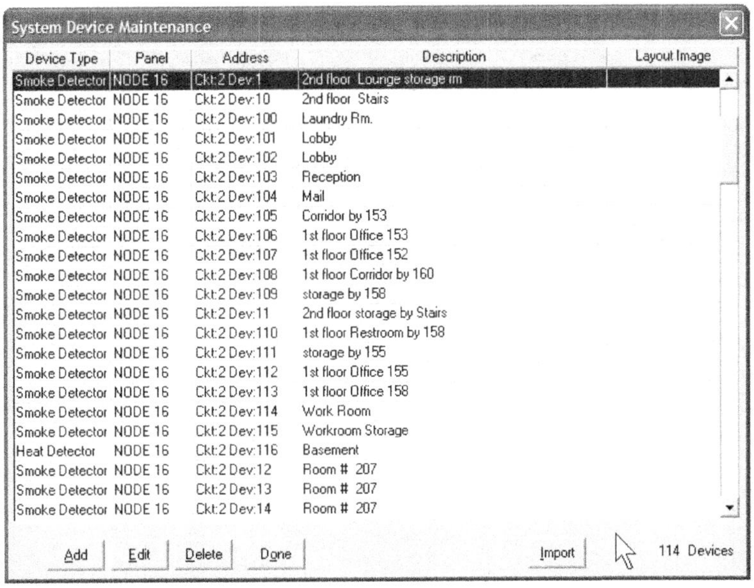

Change Information about System Devices

When RescueLogic receives information from a device for the first time, it automatically gives the device an address in the RescueLogic database. The address must remain exactly as a panel will report it, but once a device is in the system you can change its type and description. That's a useful technique if, for example, your control panels report device types simply as "contacts," which could refer either to manual pull stations or to water flow switches. Devices are sorted first by panel, then by address. Click on the gray heading at the top of a column to sort devices by a different category — by address, for example.

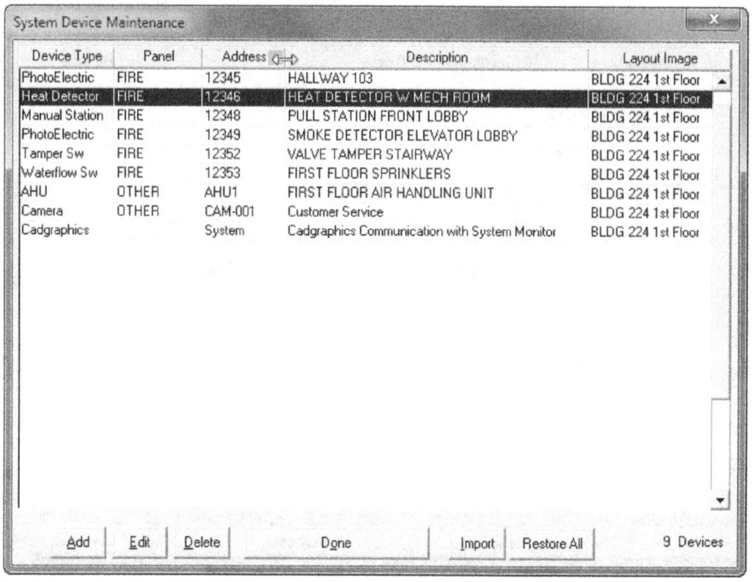

Highlight any item and click "Edit" or double-click on the line to view or change its description or other values.

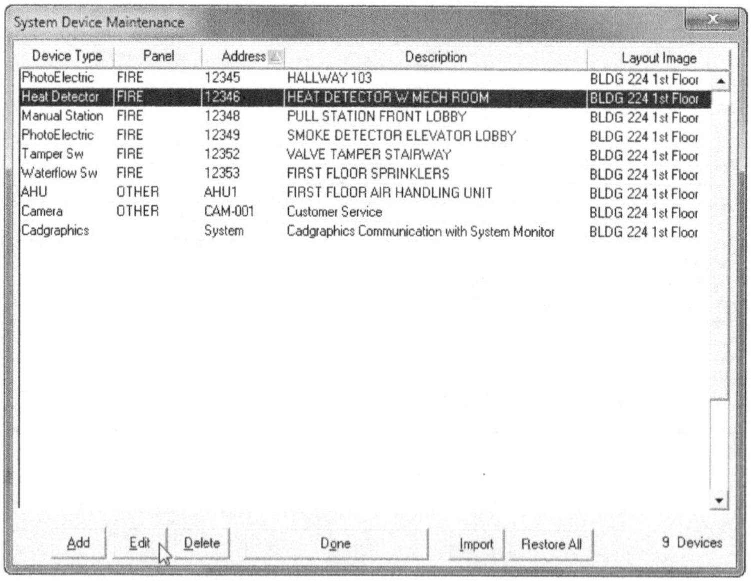

Change Device Types and Device Descriptions

RescueLogic assigns device types based on database matches. For example, if a control panel sends a message about a device called a “smoke detector,” and you have listed “smoke detector” in your database, the software will automatically assign the picture and color scheme you have selected for all smoke detectors. You can use the drop-down list to change device type classifications.

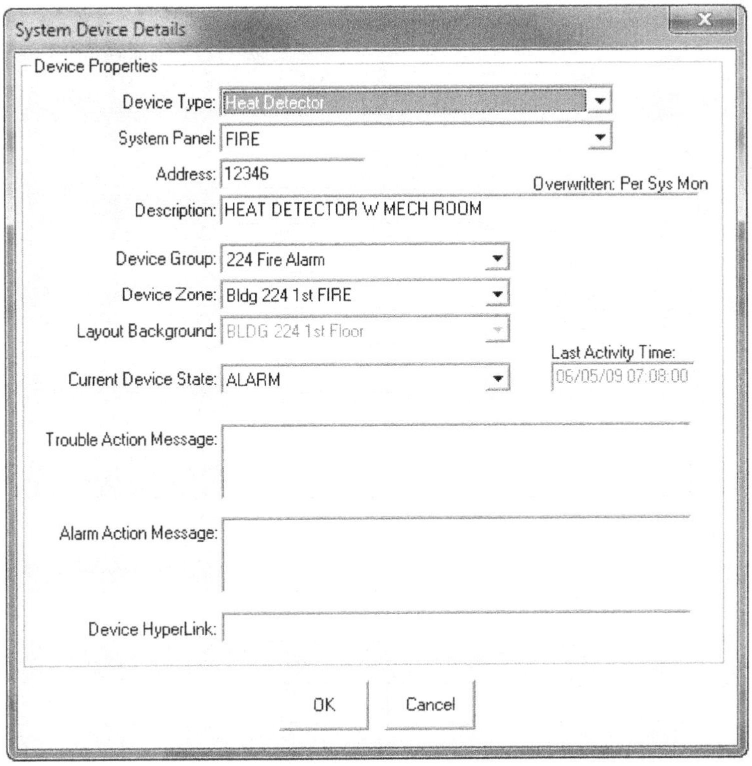

You may change device types and modify or append descriptions as you like. The System Panel, however, is automatically defined. You should not have to change it. Likewise, RescueLogic assigns an address to each device the first time it encounters or receives information from a device. Addresses are key information that should be changed only if an error occurred when the device was first imported.

Please note that to the right of the description, there is a status indicator that says “Overwritten: Per Sys Mon.” That description you enter on this screen may be overwritten if System Monitor sees a different description from your control panel.

Helpful Hint: If you want to test your system, manually change the “Current Device State” to force a device into alarm or back to normal.

The Device Type value is assigned automatically only when the device is first discovered. After it is already in the database, the device type will not be changed automatically, because if you change it manually, you'll want it to remain as you set it.

You'll see your change reflected in the list.

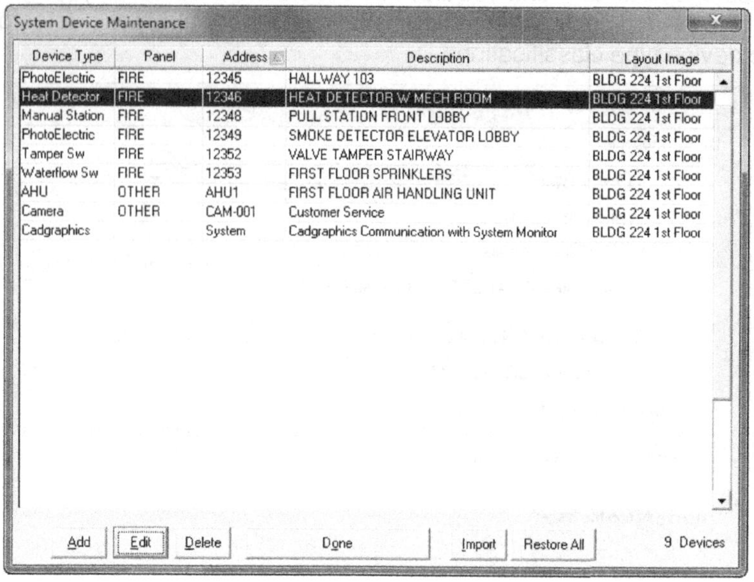

Chapter 8: Hyperlinks

With RescueLogic, you will be ready to connect to any TCP/IP address on your site or on the Internet. A quick click on your background map or floor plan will link you to web pages, IP cameras, or HVAC building controls — each in its own dedicated window. In this chapter, you will learn how you can get online with RescueLogic.

Link to Video

You can connect security camera images to your RescueLogic system simply by adding the TCP/IP address of your camera to the "Device Hyperlink" field.

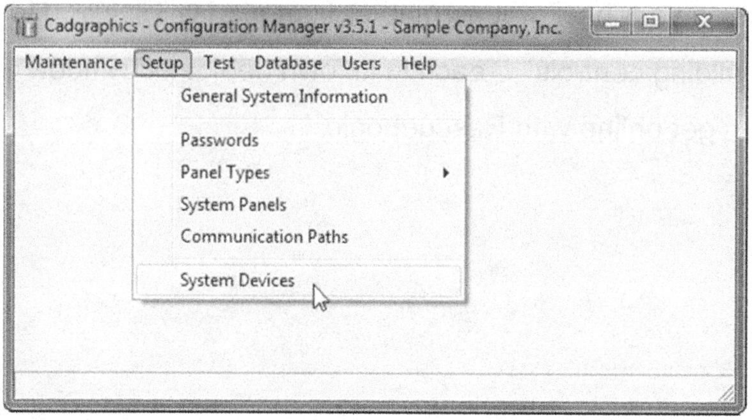

Choose the camera you'd like to connect.

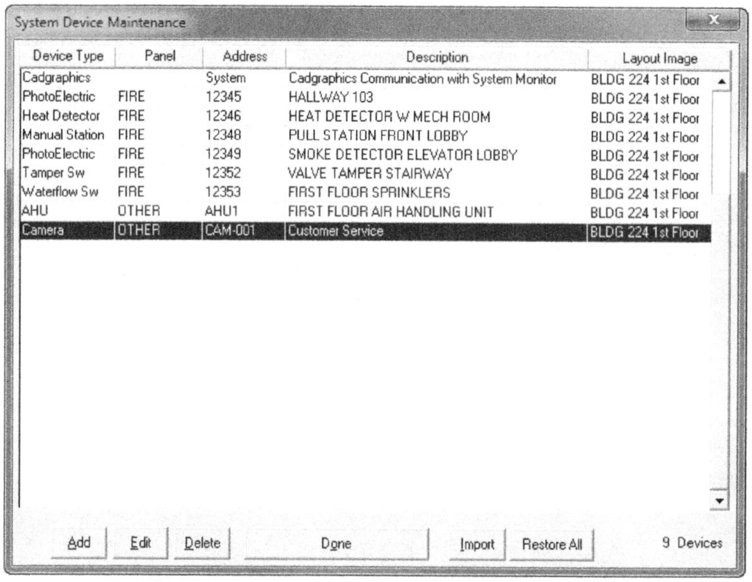

Enter the IP address in the "Device HyperLink" field.

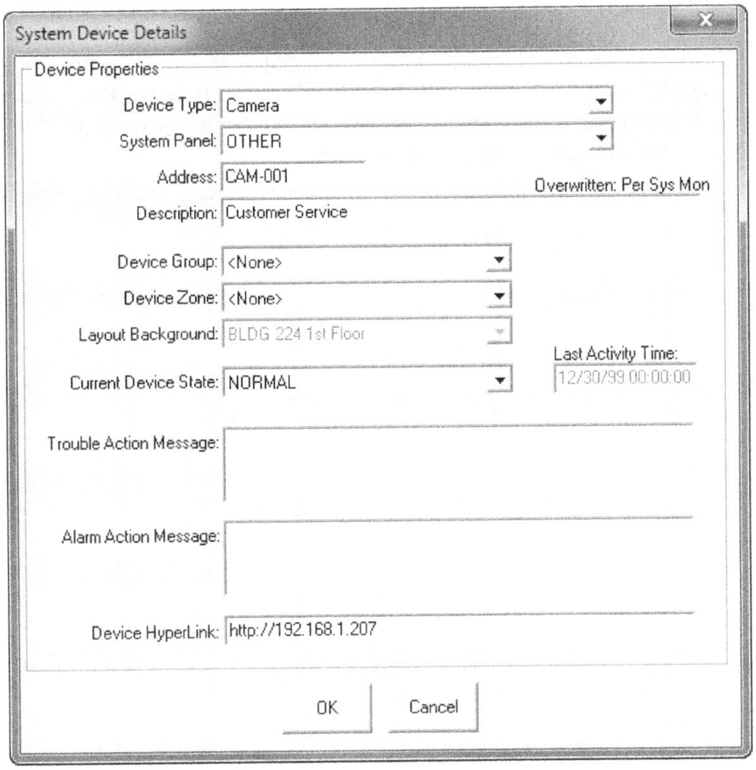

With the device hyperlink in place, you can monitor any information at the TCP/IP address you specify. In the System Watch program, you will simply click on a device image — the icon of a CCTV camera, for example — just as you would click on the image of any other device for more information. A new "Hyperlink" window will open on screen, and you will see your TCP/IP data, streaming live and in real time.

Link to HVAC Controls

You can use the same method to display building and industrial controls, such as heating, ventilation, and air conditioning. With a device hyperlink in place, you can monitor any information at the TCP/IP address you specify. You will simply click on a device image — the icon of an air-handling unit, for example. A new "Hyperlink" window will open, and you will see your HVAC data, live and in real time.

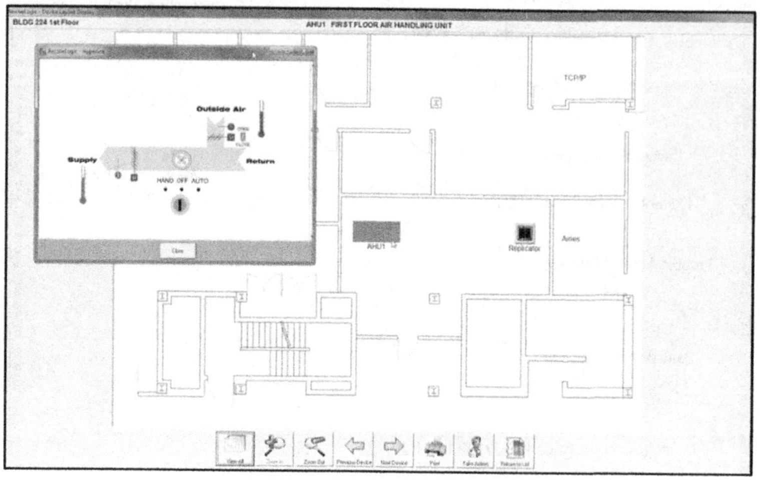

Link to Web Pages

You can also make hyperlinks that will allow RescueLogic users to go directly to important web sites: corporate web pages, for instance, news sites, or web sites with emergency management information and contact lists. By linking through RescueLogic, you can control which pages users will be able to access.

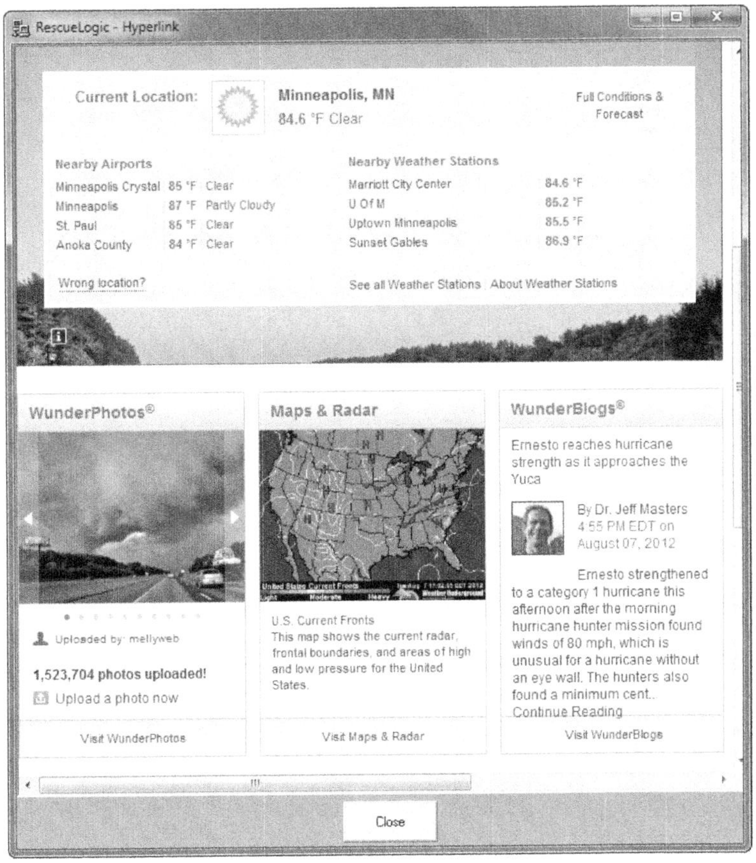

Chapter 9: Groups and Zones

When you group alarms and devices — or assign them to zones on your site — you will make it even easier to save time, save property, and save lives. This chapter will show you how to set up groups and zones for your facility.

Create Groups and Zones of Devices

You may find that you want to create groups of devices, to make it easier for your staff people to locate alarms and trouble conditions. You might want to use RescueLogic to depict an aerial photo of your entire site, for example, and then group every device in a single building.

Each device in your system can only be assigned to one group at a time. If you want an additional graphic view of groups of devices — such as an elevation view that shows a cross-section of all of the floors in a high-rise — you can create zones of devices. In effect, zones are a useful way to zero in on related devices. Typically, users create a group to show a building on a site plan, and a zone to show an area of that building.

Whether you are setting up groups or zones, the step-by-step process is the same. On the following pages, we will show you how to set up system groups. When you move on to establishing system zones, you will repeat the same steps — but you will use the "zone" menu items instead of the "group" selections.

Creating a Group

To create a group of devices, start by opening Configuration Manager. Go to the "Maintenance" drop-down menu and click on "System Groups."

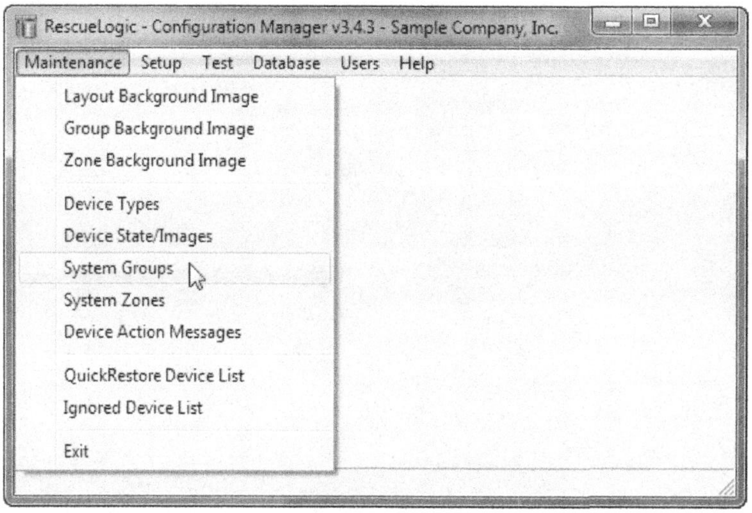

Click "Add" to begin adding device groups to your system.

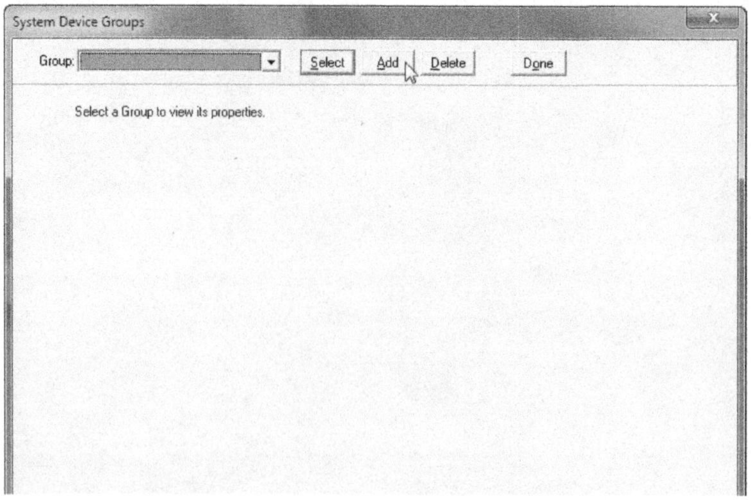

Name Your Group

Make sure you're working in the "General" tab at the bottom of the window. Give your group a name and enter a device help message. (See the chapter on "Action Messages" for more information about developing emergency instructions for first responders.) When you are through, click on the "Devices" tab.

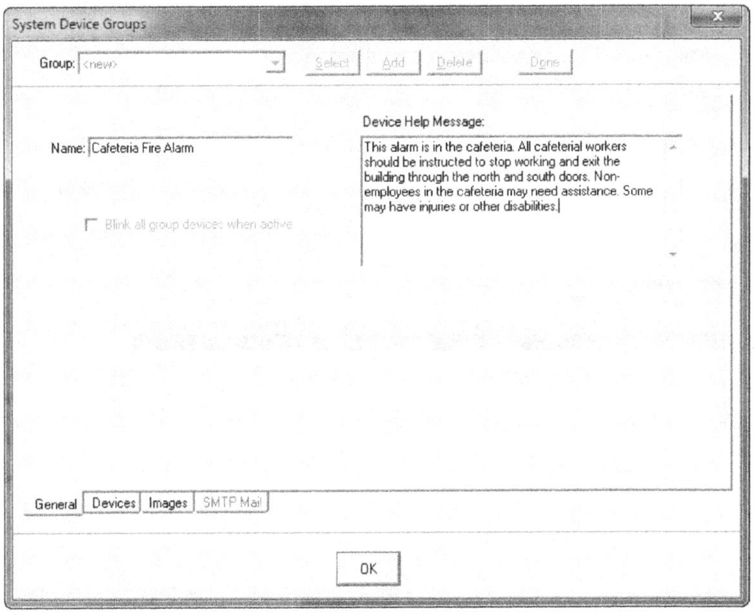

Helpful Hint: You can create a paragraph return in your "Device Help Message" box by clicking the CONTROL and ENTER keys simultaneously.

Assign Devices

Click the "Devices" tab at the bottom of the window. Add devices to your newly created group. Highlight them in the bottom list, and then click "Add." When you are through, click on the "Images" tab.

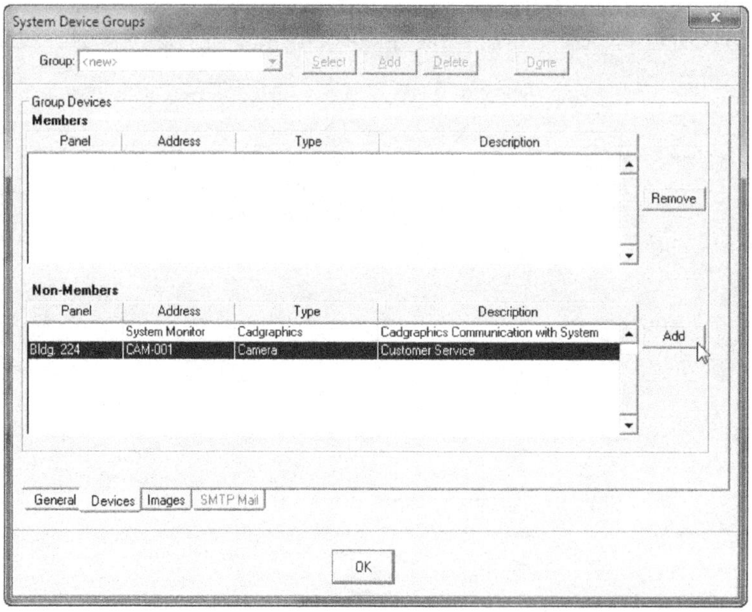

If you'd like to add many devices to the list, hold down the ENTER key to add them faster.

Simply click the gray header title to sort the list.

Assign Images

Click the "Images" tab and use the "Group State" drop-down menu to start assigning three separate images for your group — one for normal, one for trouble, and one for alarm. We recommend solid green for normal, solid yellow for trouble, and solid red for alarm. Select your "Group State" first, and then click "Load Image."

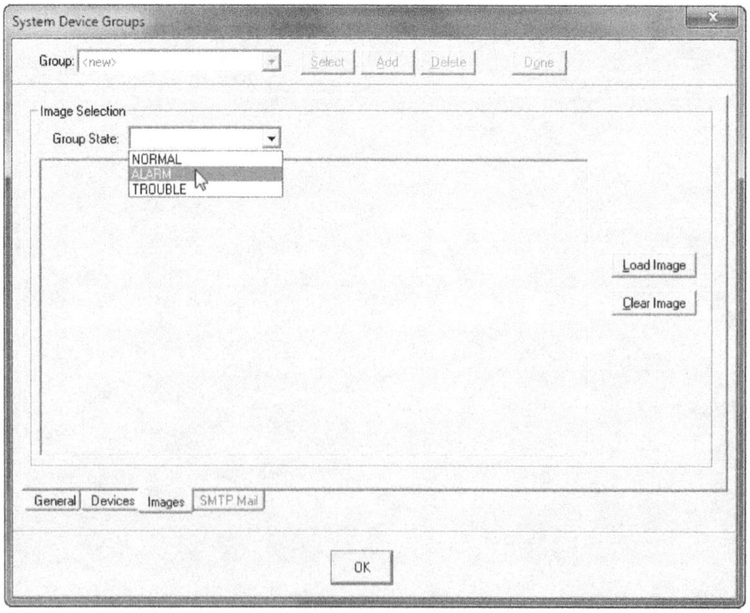

You can find the solid color images in the RescueLogic folder, in "Device Images."

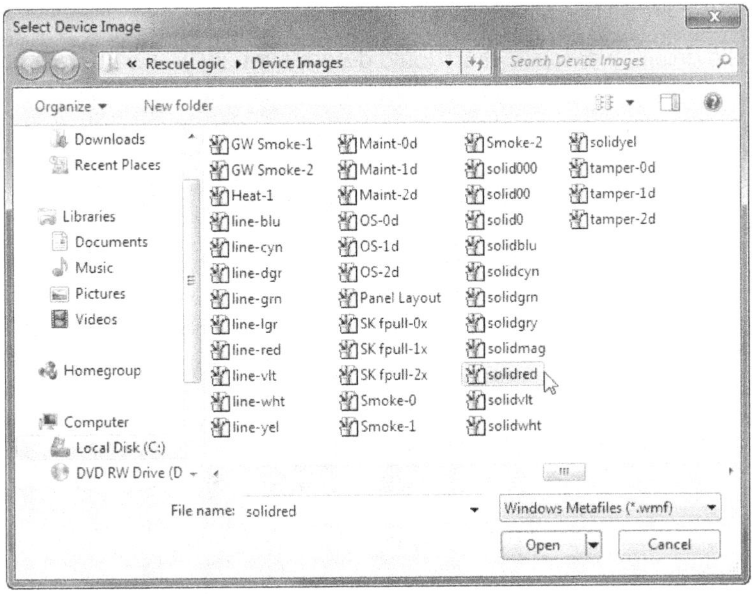

Helpful Hint: Use solid green to help you locate a group as you set it up on a background map, but remove it when you are through. That way, a group in normal status will be clear, but it will flash in red or yellow when it is in trouble or alarm. The next chapter will give you more information about background maps and floor plans, including those associated with zones and groups.

Preview Your Image

Once you have loaded each image, you will see it in the preview window. Follow the same procedure to assign images to your group in all three states: normal, trouble, and alarm. When you are finished, click "OK."

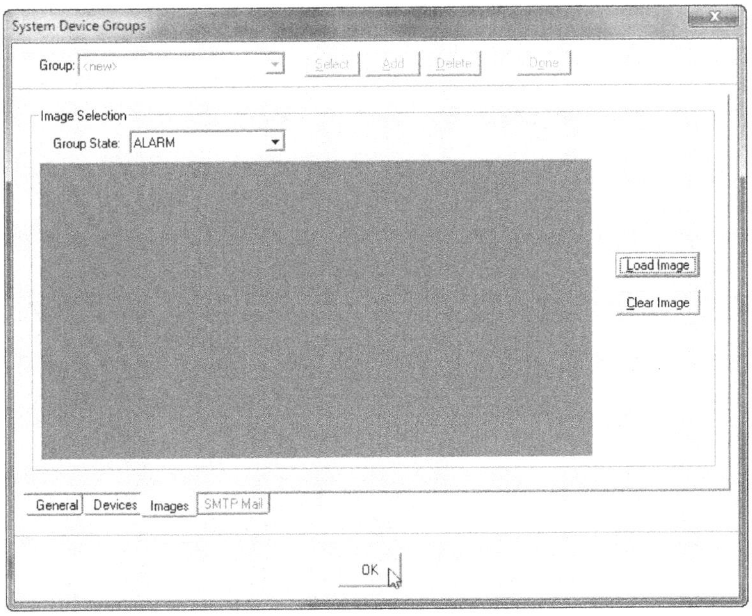

Establish System Watch Settings for your Group

Once you have configured a group or a zone, you should determine how you want users to see it from the System Watch screen. Start by opening the Configuration Manager program. Go to the "Test" drop-down menu and choose "System Watch."

When the System Watch screen opens, click the "Setup" button in the lower left corner.

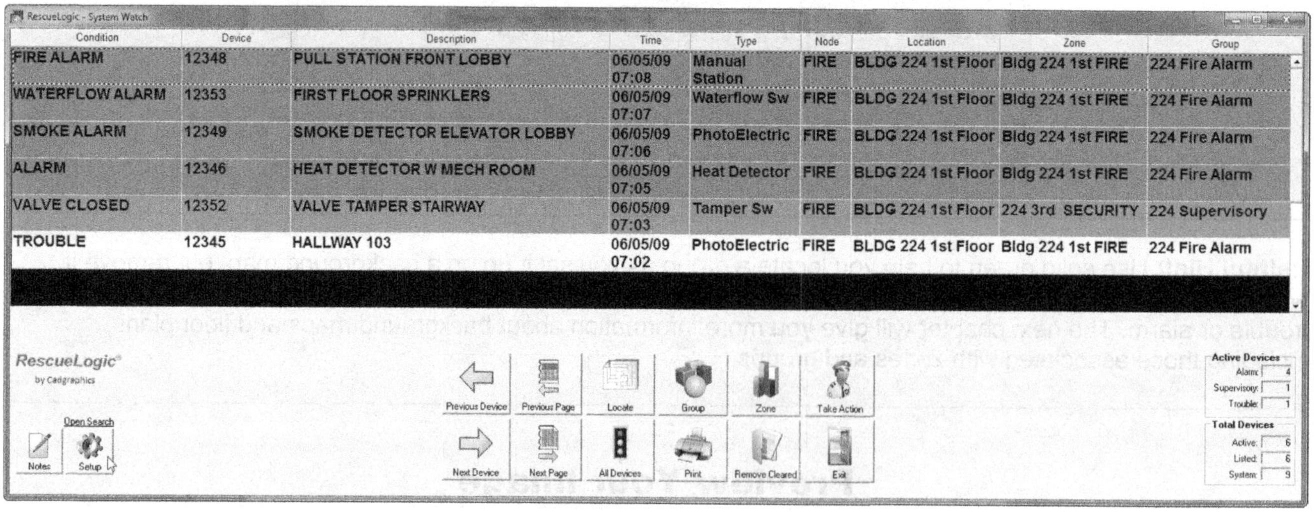

Note that the column on the list always shows the group — which in this case, is 224 Fire Alarm.

Zone, Group, and Floor Plan Buttons

Use the System Watch "Settings" tab screen to determine whether you will show "Zone" and "Group" buttons at the bottom of the System Watch screen, and whether clicking on them will display a floor plan for the user.

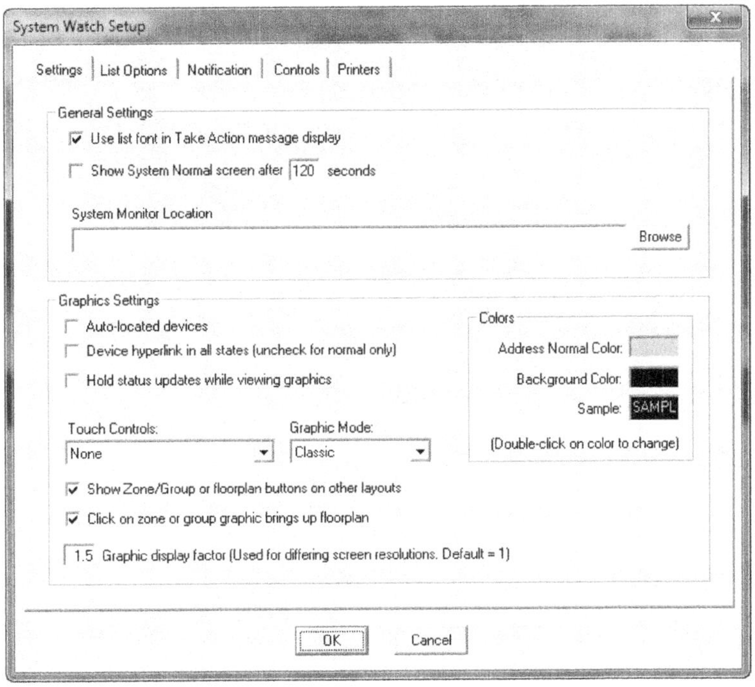

Use the System Watch "List Options" tab screen to determine whether double-clicking on any list item will locate a device, or show its group or zone first.

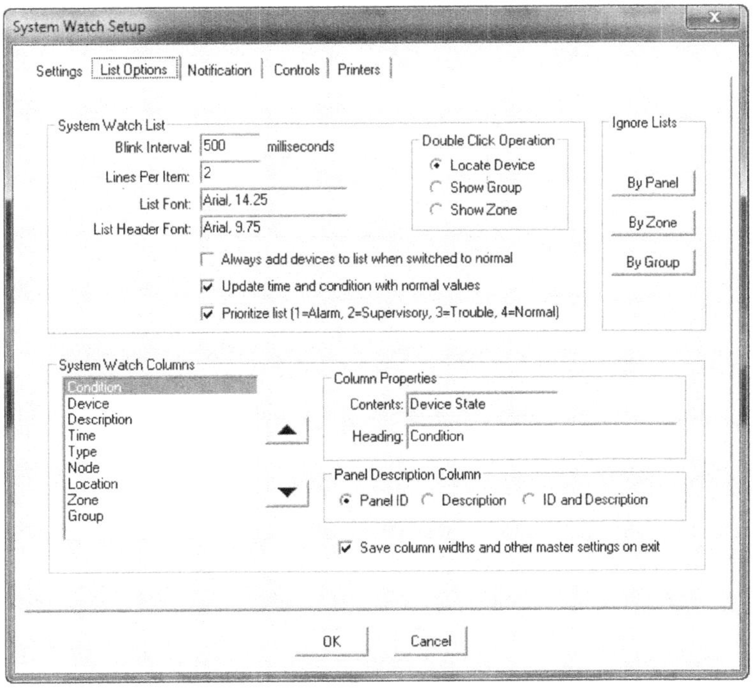

Chapter 10: Background Maps and Floor Plans

Background maps and floor plans are the main reason RescueLogic was created. Pictures help responders find alarms and trouble conditions quickly and easy. RescueLogic's background maps and floor plans are flexible, too. You can use practically any digital image file or photo to display devices, zones, and groups. This chapter will show you how to work with maps and floor plans — the background images that make up the backbone of your RescueLogic system.

Background Maps and Floor Plans

RescueLogic makes it easy to display alarms, detectors, and security devices on a floor plan or map of your facility. This chapter will teach you how to set up your graphic backgrounds.

Start by opening Configuration Manager. Go to the "Maintenance" drop-down menu and click on "Layout Background Image."

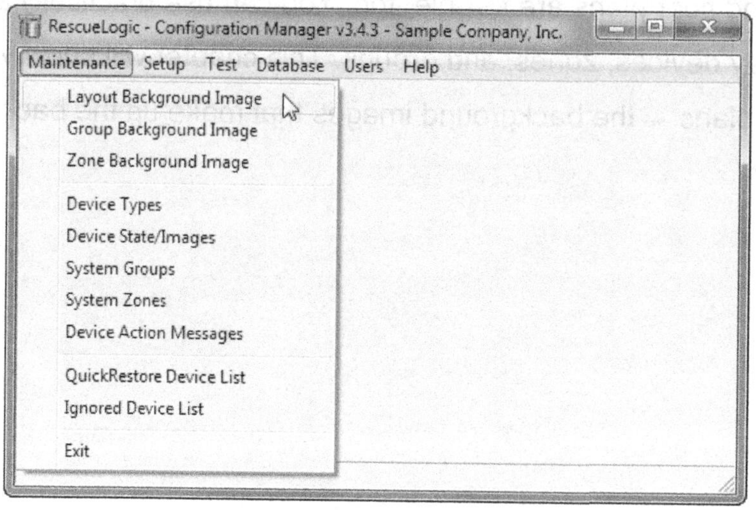

Select a sample background map or floor plan from the drop-down list.

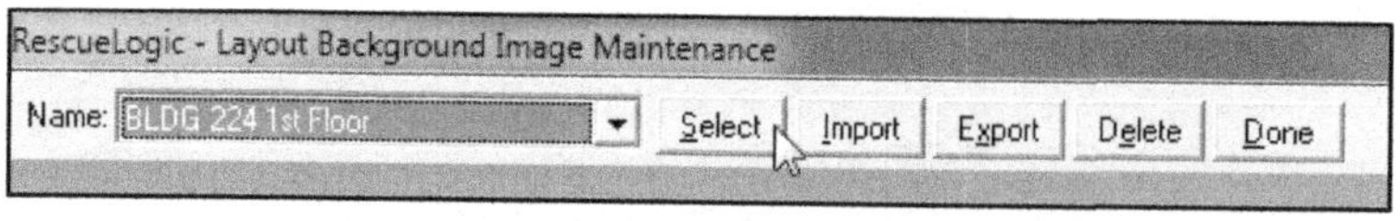

See a Sample Floor Plan

You'll see a sample floor plan, ready for customization.

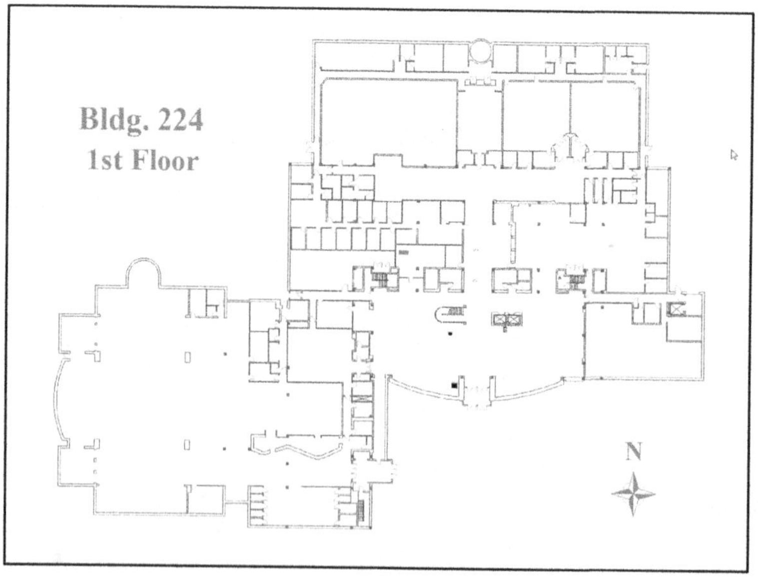

Zoom in to Edit

Click any area of the image and drag the automatic rectangle to zoom in on that portion of the image.

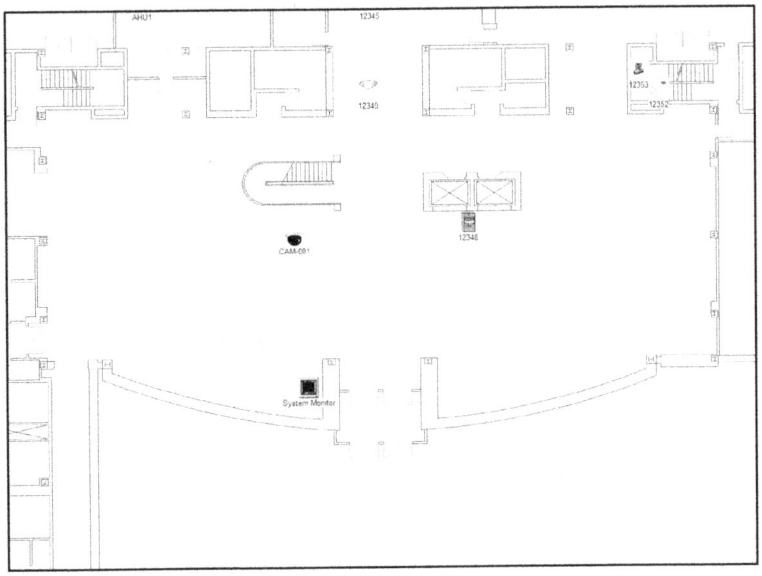

Edit Device Images

Zoomed in, you can see device images clearly. Right-click on any device image and you'll see a pop-up menu. You can use the pop-up menu to edit a device, delete it from the floor plan, or make a device transparent. To go quickly to edit mode, you can also double-click on a device.

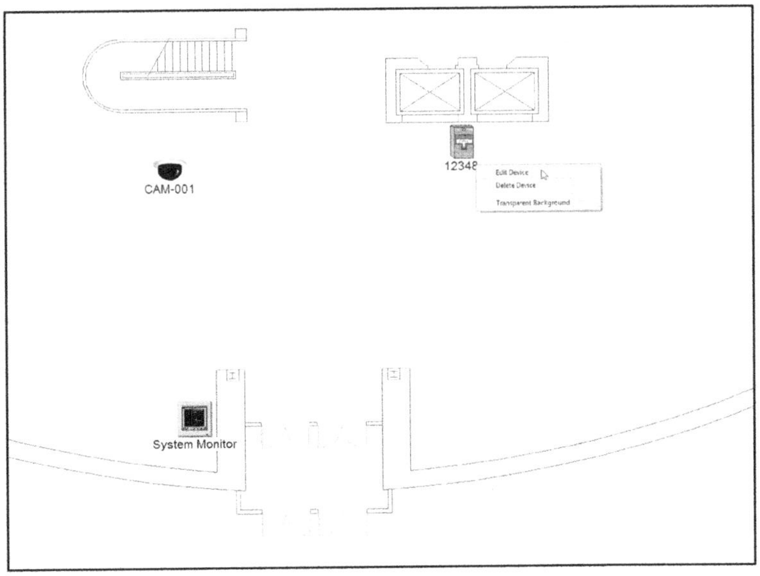

Change the Size of a Device Image

You may want to change the size of a device to make a floor plan more readable. Start by double-clicking on the image of the device you want to change. When you are in the edit mode of a device, you will see four corner "handles" or "grips" surrounding the device. Click on one of the handles and drag in or out it to resize the image.

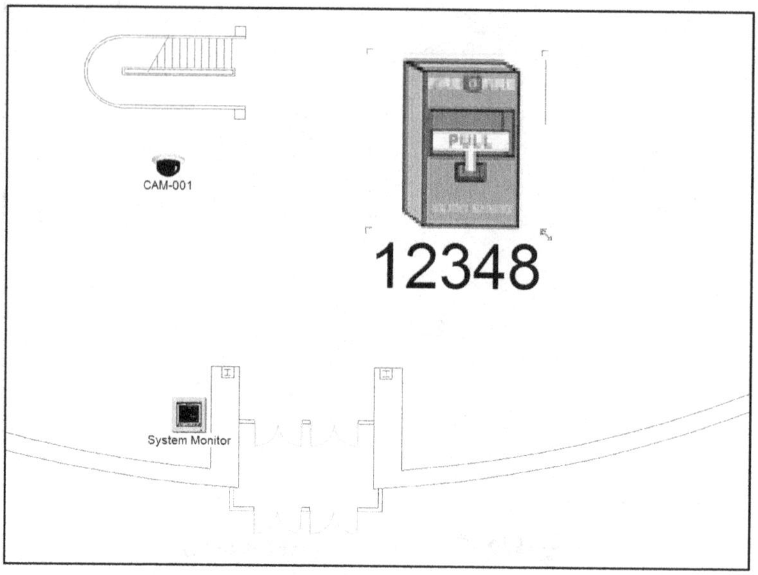

Make a Device Transparent

Choose "Transparent Background" if you want to see through the device image to the walls on the floor plan. Transparent backgrounds are useful if you are placing a device in a small area, like a utility closet.

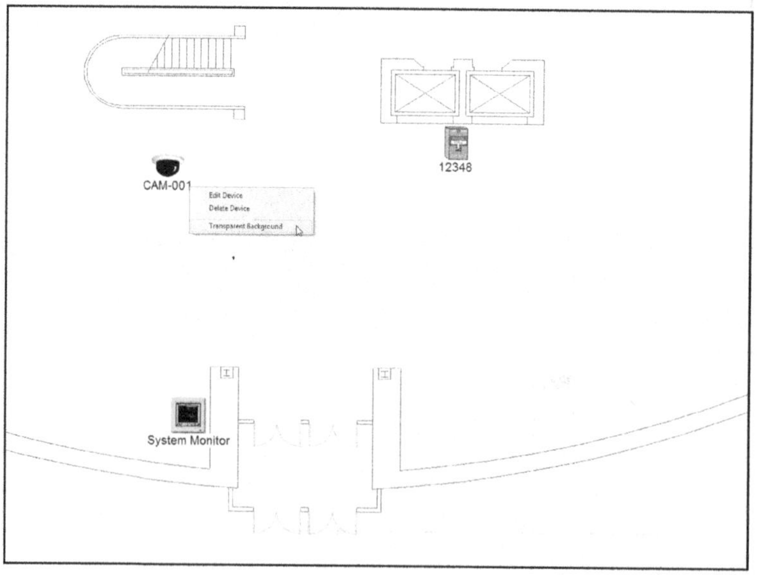

Move a Device to a New Location

You can move a device image to any location by double-clicking it and dragging it to a new location.

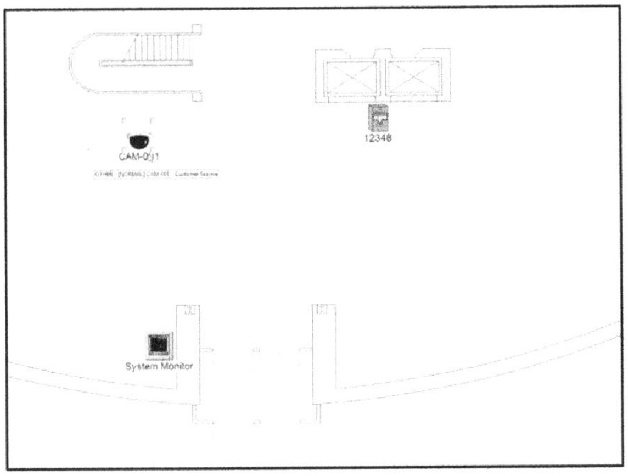

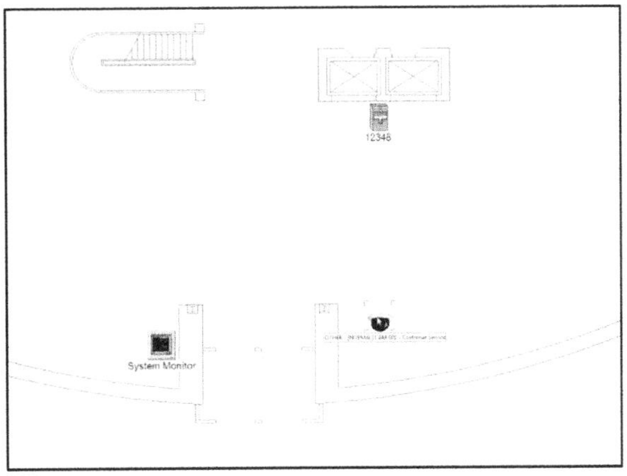

Move a Device to a Different Floor

If the image is on the wrong floor, click "Delete" to place it back on the list of items to be placed later. (It will not be removed from the database until you specifically remove it using the "System Device Maintenance" function in Configuration Manager.)

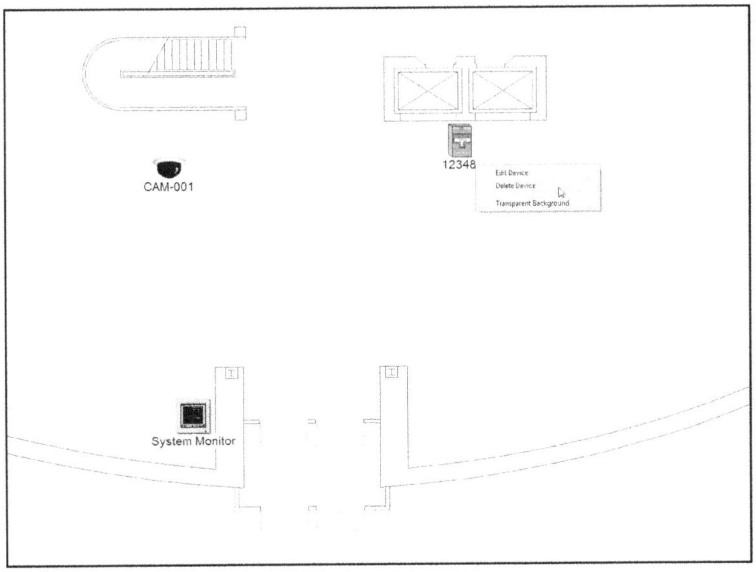

Helpful Hint: By checking the "Devices" buttons on the bottom of the screen, you can choose to resize all of the devices on the background, or only one. The size you set while for "All non-custom devices" is selected will be the default when new devices are dropped onto the floor plan. By checking the "Sizing" buttons, you can choose your anchor — either the edge or the center.

Change Text

To change the text of any label, right-click it and select "Edit Label" from the pop-up menu.

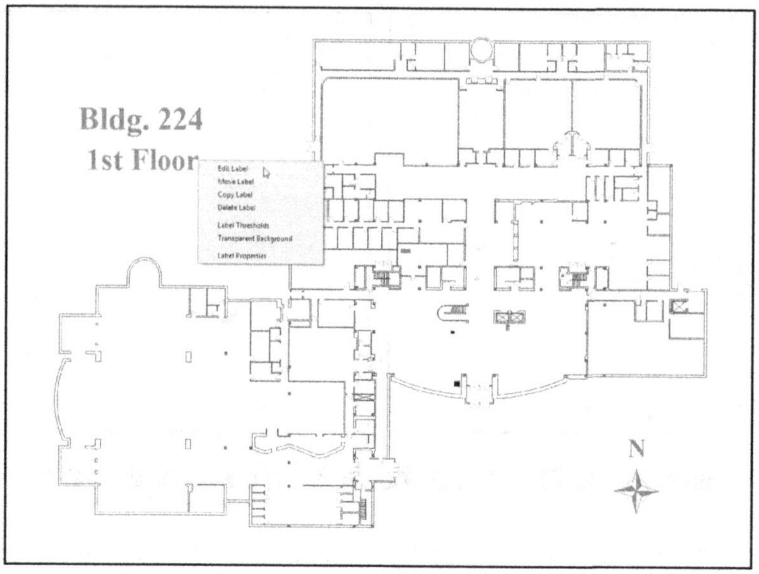

Change the text of the label and hit the ENTER key on your keyboard.

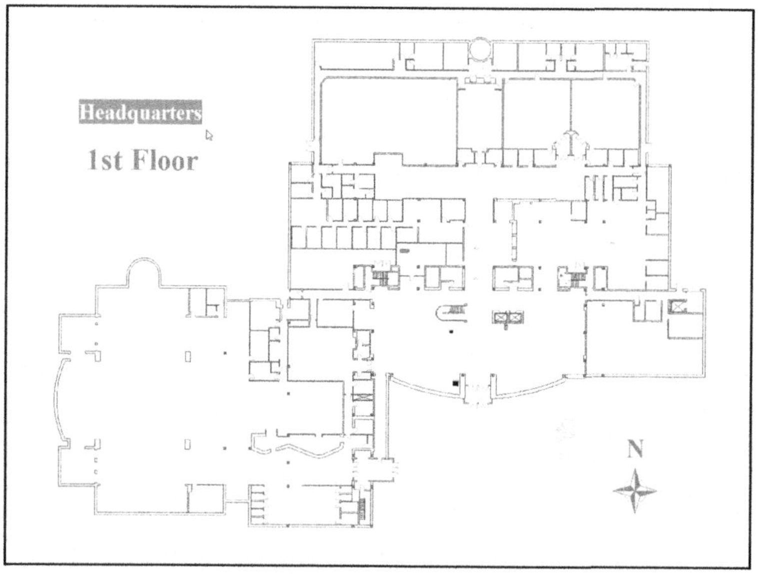

Label Fonts, Styles, Colors, and Sizes

You can format your labels in any Windows font, style, color, or size. To change the appearance of a text label, right-click it and choose "Label Properties" from the pop-up menu.

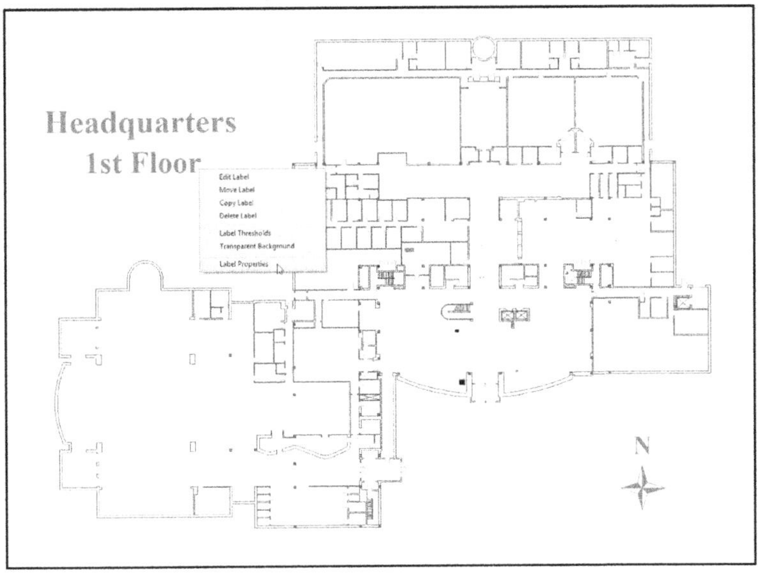

Choose the font, style, size, and color you want. For this example, we have chosen Arial Bold, in black.

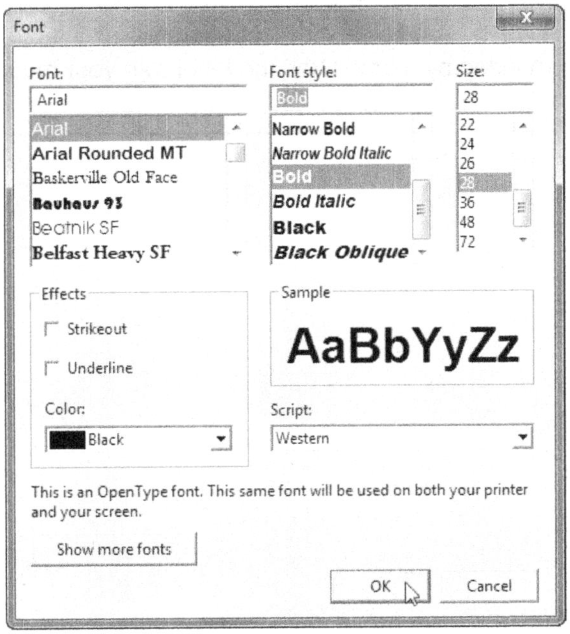

Helpful Hint: When you edit label properties, the changes you make will apply to any new labels you create.

Move Labels

Once you have changed the font for your labels, you can move them around the floor plan. First, right-click on the label you want to move. A pop-up menu will appear. Select "Move Label."

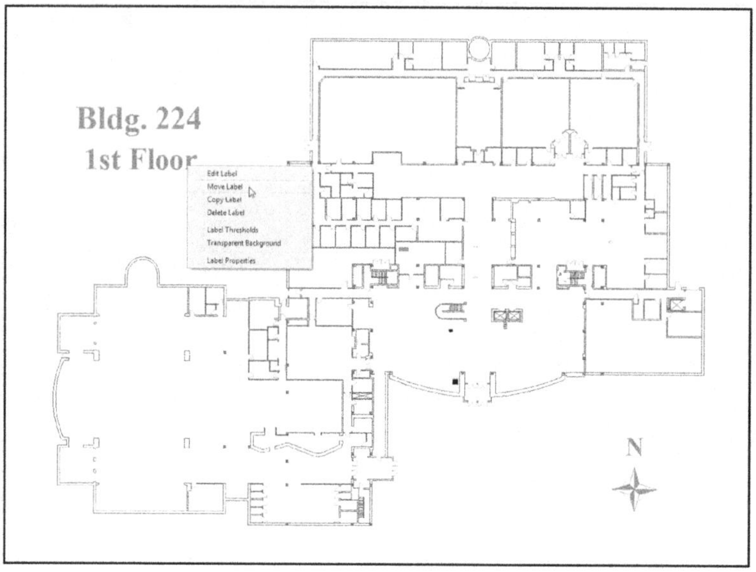

Drag and Drop Labels into Place

The label you selected will be surrounded by a box. Grab the label with your mouse, drag it to a new location, and drop it into place.

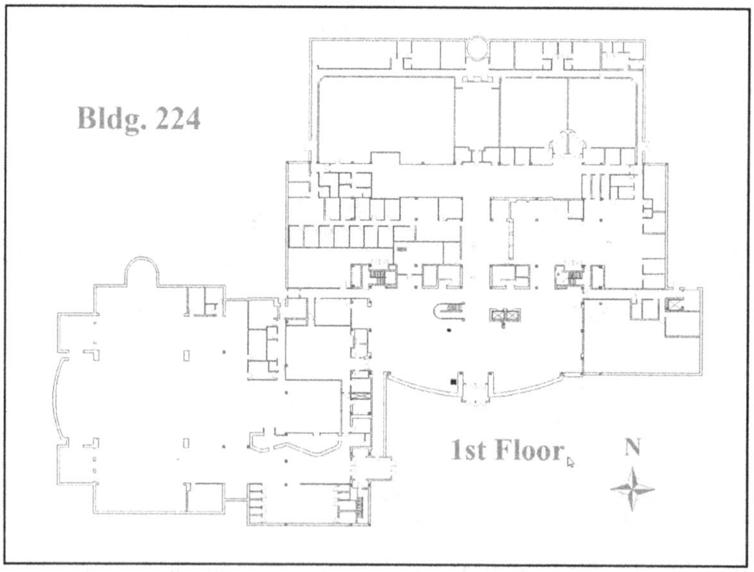

Insert Labels

To insert labels on any background image, right click a blank area and choose "Insert Label" from the pop-up menu. A cursor will appear wherever you clicked. Type your desired text.

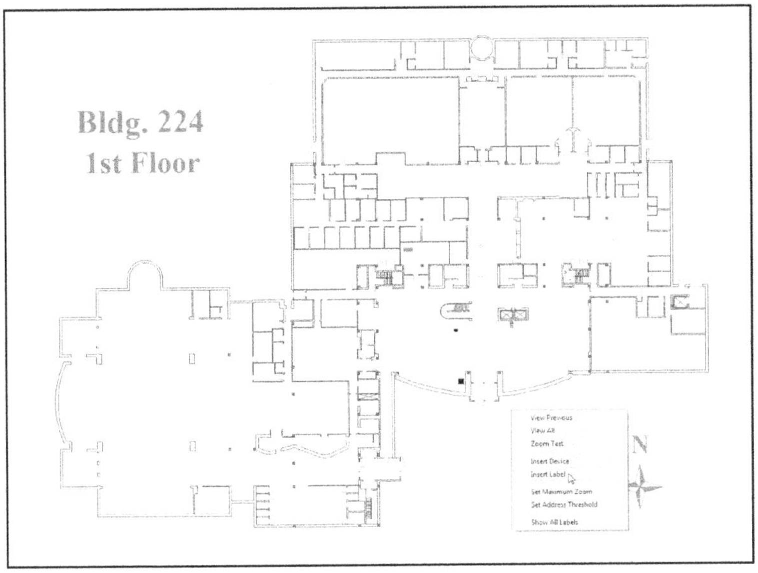

Copy Labels

The easiest way to add a new label is to copy an existing label — especially if you have already formatted your existing labels with the font, size, and style you like best. Your new label will have the same properties as the original. To copy a label, right-click it and select "Copy Label" from the pop-up menu. Once you have dropped a new label into its new location, right-click on it. Choose "Edit Label" from the pop-up menu and change the text. You can also double-click on a label to edit the text.

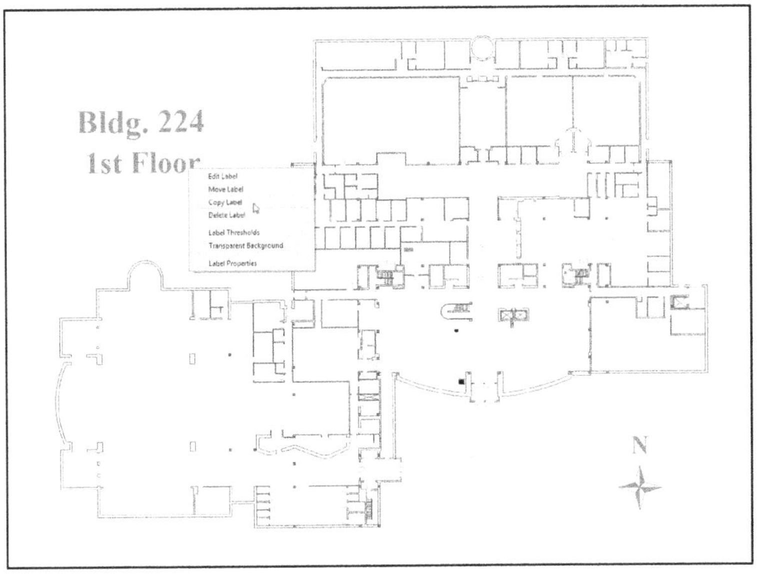

Show All Labels

When you start zooming in to work on floor plans, you will probably notice that you can't see any labels. That 's because RescueLogic is designed to hide full-size labels when you zoom in. If the labels were enlarged along with the rest of the floor plan, they would look huge. Likewise, when you look at an entire floor plan, details like room numbers are usually too small to read — but when you zoom in, you'll notice that there is plenty of space to add additional information such as room names and numbers. As you work with background images, you will be able to place a separate set of labels for each zoom level. Most users establish two sets: one for full screen, and one for maximum zoom.

To see every set of labels on your floor plan, right-click anywhere on the floor and select "Show All Labels."

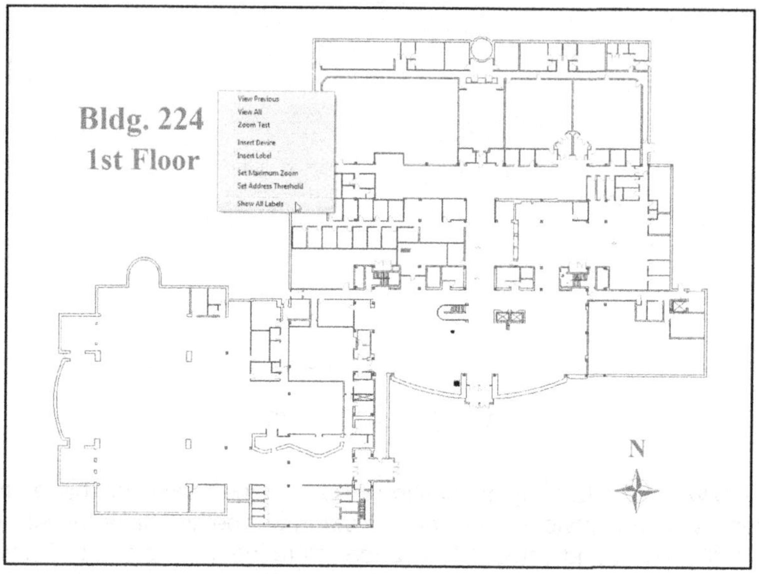

Helpful Hint: Remember that when you mouse over a device, you will automatically see its panel, its address number, and its description appear. As a result, you might choose to rely more on that information and use fewer labels on your floor plan.

Change Label Thresholds

By setting label thresholds for each floor plan, you can make large labels disappear when you zoom in, and add smaller, more detailed labels for close-up viewing.

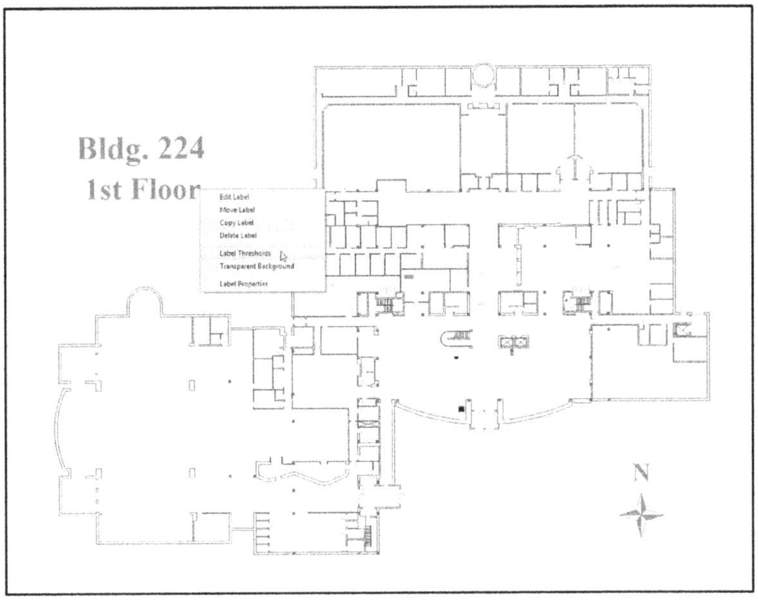

Set Zoom Thresholds

You can choose any zoom threshold between 100 percent and 3300 percent. Most people choose a zoom of 100 percent to 200 percent for large area labels, and 200 percent to 500 percent for smaller, detail labels that show when the floor plan is zoomed in the first time. Set thresholds from 500 to 3300 percent for the second-level zoom.

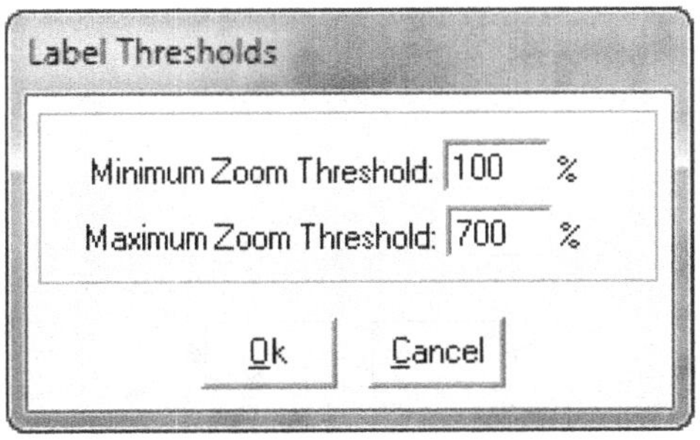

Helpful Hint: Feel free to experiment with your label thresholds, and find the parameters that look best on your background maps and floor plans. You can use the "Zoom Test" and "Show All Labels" functions shown on the next pages to check your results.

Zoom to Test Your Label Thresholds

Look at the "Current Zoom" indicator on the top right corner of the screen that says, "Current Zoom: 100%." Whenever you zoom in on any area, the indicator will show how much the picture is enlarged. When you see the same floor plan in System Watch, you will be able to click a "Zoom In" button to enlarge the image.

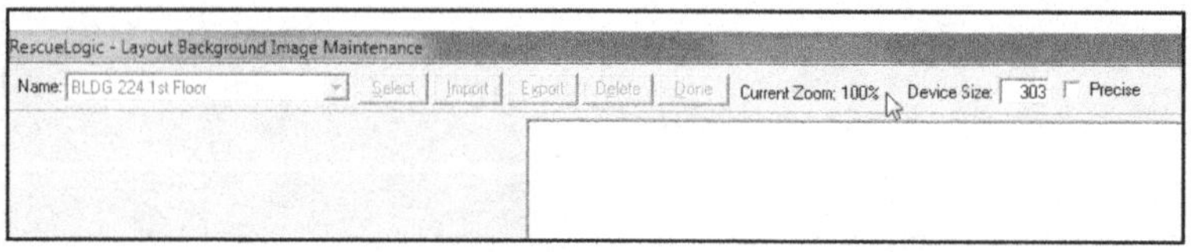

You can use the fields at the bottom of the screen to customize that "Zoom In" function.

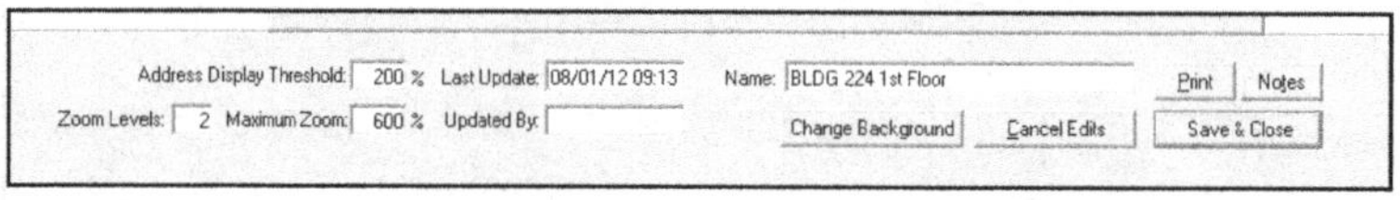

The "Address Display Threshold" field, which in this case is set to 200 percent, means that address labels will not begin to appear until the System Watch user zooms in to at least 200 percent.

The "Zoom Levels" field determines the number of times a user must click the "Zoom In" button to reach maximum zoom.

The "Maximum Zoom" field represents the maximum percentage that an end user can zoom in on a floor plan.

To see the effect your changes in any field make for the end user, right-click on the floor plan. Select "Zoom Test," to see the System Watch screen's preset zooms.

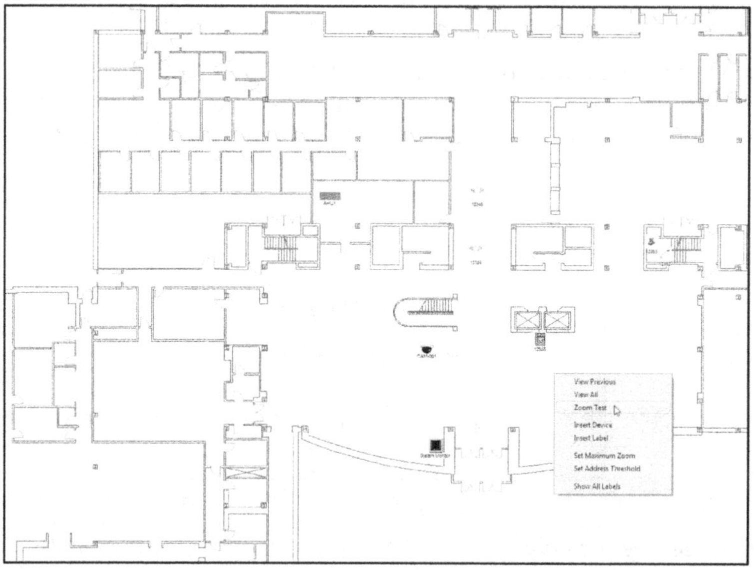

Insert Devices

If you have devices in your database that have not been placed on a floor plan, you can position them quickly and easily. Simply right-click on a blank area of your floor plan and select “Insert Device.”

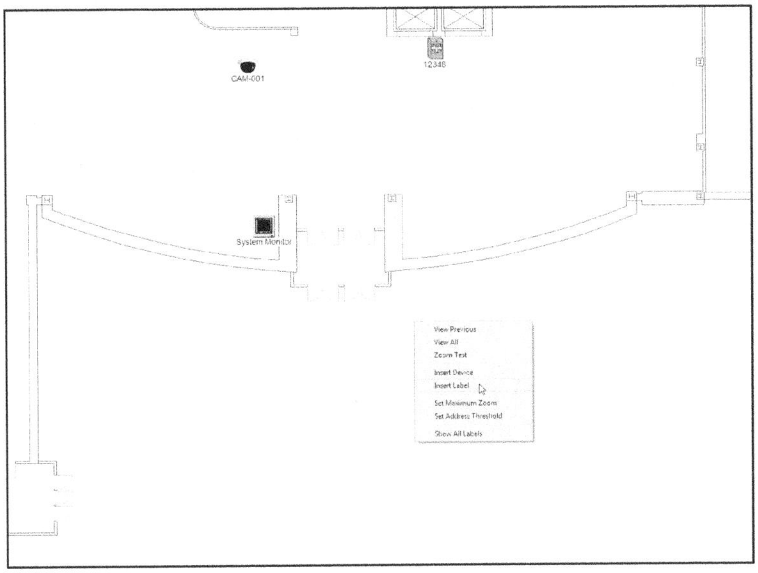

You will see a pop-up list of every device in your system that hasn't been placed on a floor plan. Highlight any device in the list, and its description will appear in the bottom window. You will also notice that the total number of unplaced devices is noted at the bottom of the screen.

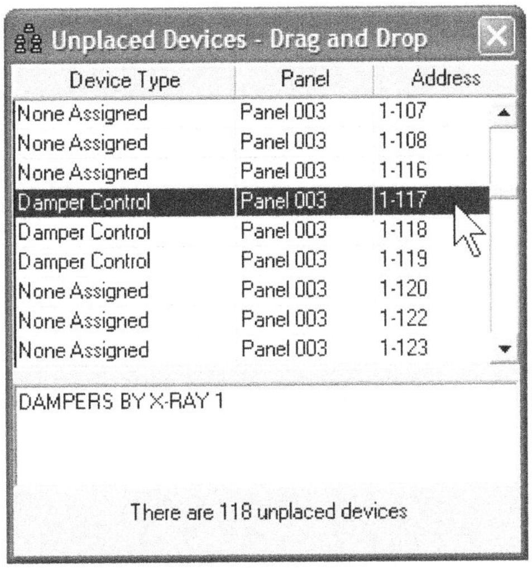

Drag and Drop Devices

Click and drag the item to its proper location on the image. As you drag the device line out of its place in the window, it will turn into a small box.

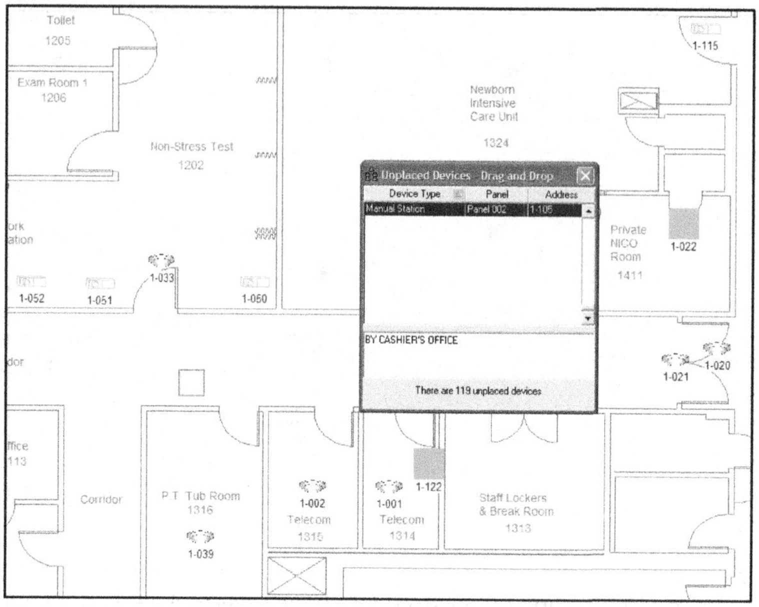

Once you drop each device into place on the floor plan, it will look like the device it represents.

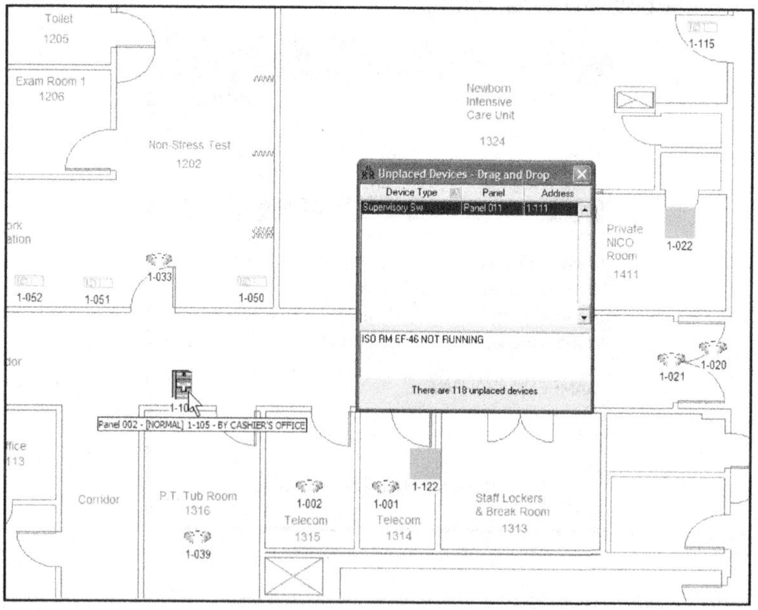

Helpful Hint: As you drop devices into place, you do not need to worry about exact accuracy. You can always double click on a device to move it or change its size. Right click for the menu to delete it..

Import Your Own Background Maps and Floor Plans

Here is how you can import your own background maps and floor plans. First, collect the CAD files you plan to use. Most architects use CAD software to design buildings; their CAD drawings are usually kept on file by building owners or facility managers. If you don't have CAD files, create them from architectural blueprints, or even your own sketches. Use CAD software to convert all of your CAD images to WMFs. (See "Tricks of the Trade" later in this chapter for information about how we optimize CAD files for background maps and floor plans.) Also, gather the digital photos you plan to use as background images.

Next, create a new "Background Images" folder in your RescueLogic folder, and use it to store all of your background images, maps, and floor plans.

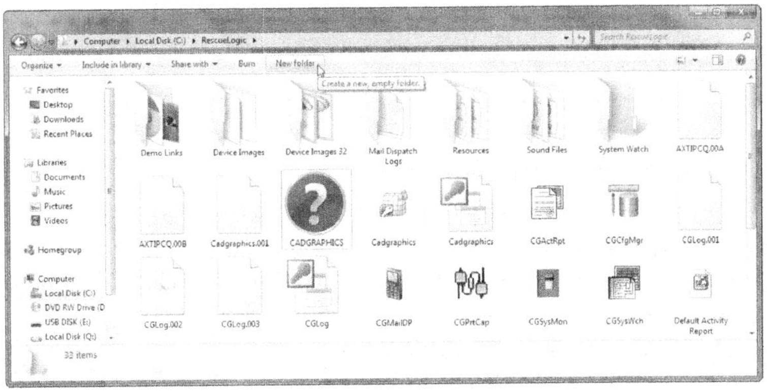

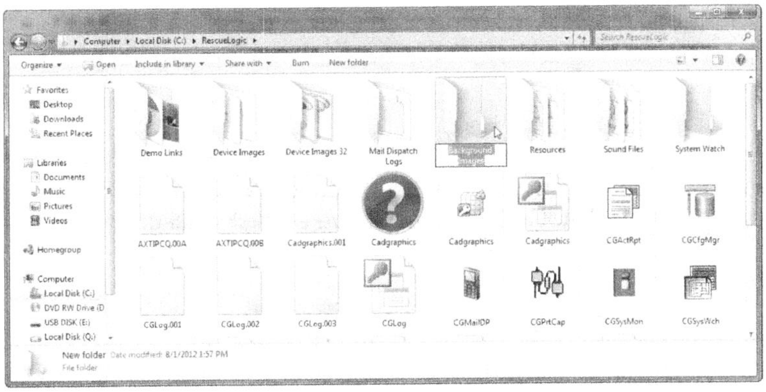

Open Configuration Manager. From the "Maintenance" drop-down menu, select "Layout Background Image."

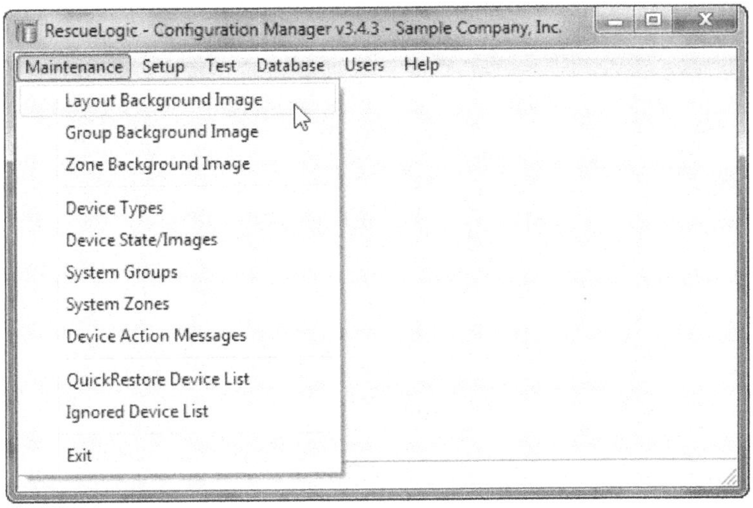

Open the "Background Images" folder.

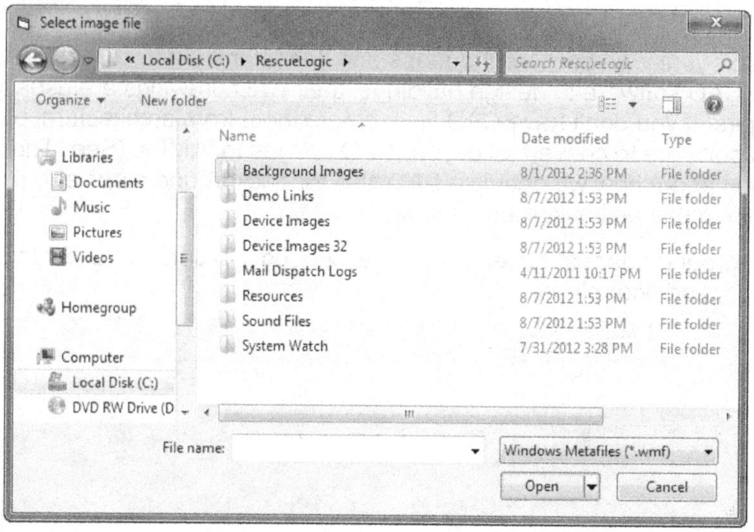

Find the image you want to use. Make sure the file type selection matches the file type you're searching for — such as a .wmf or a .png — or you might not be able to see it in the folder. Click "Open" to import the image.

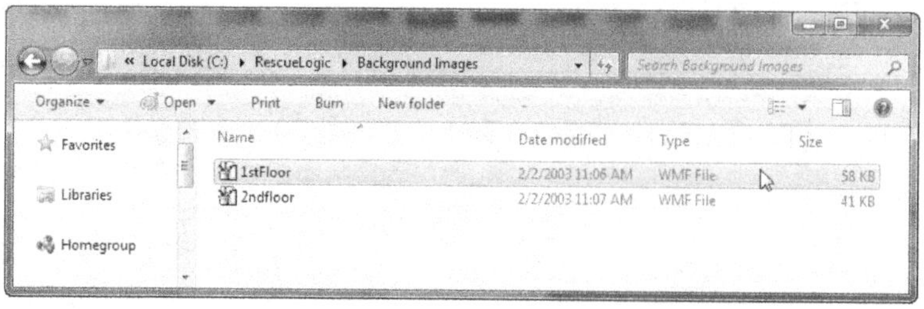

You will see a popup message asking if you want the background transparent. Choose Yes to use the default color for System Watch backgrounds. AutoCAD files may have a black background, which could make printing difficult.

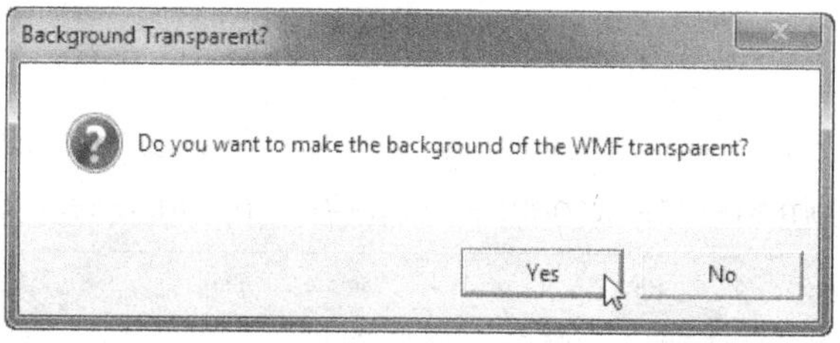

Your new background image will appear. At the bottom of the window, give it a name, adjust the "Address Display Threshold" and "Maximum Zoom" levels, and initial the "Updated By" field. Format your background image with any labels, notes, groups, and zones you like. You can also drag and drop alarms and devices. Click "Save and Close," and RescueLogic will add the new background image to your database.

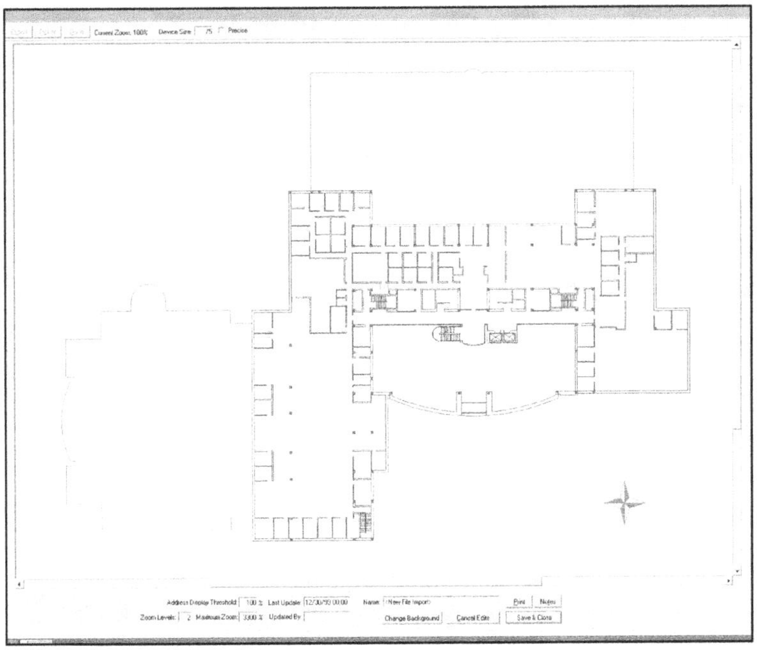

Add a Group Background Image

You can add a group background image so that you can see when any device in a group goes into trouble or alarm. Start by opening Configuration Manager. From the “Maintenance” drop-down menu, select “Group Background Images.”

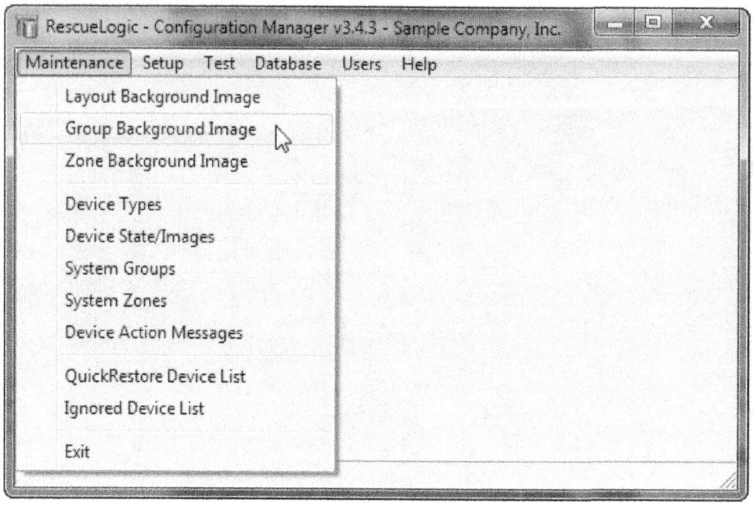

The “Group Background Image Maintenance” window will fill your screen. Click “Import.”

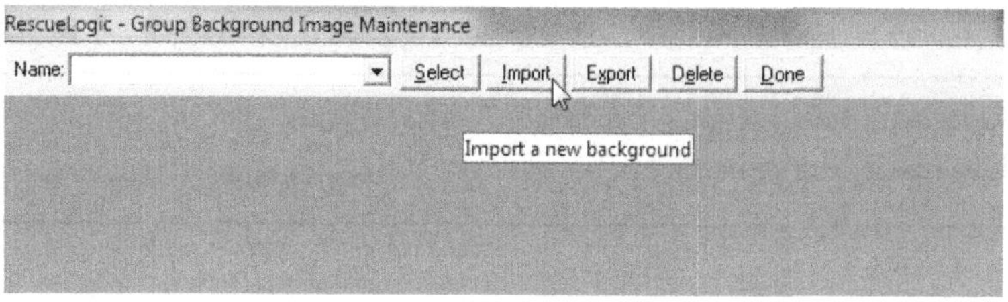

Find the image you want to use. (It must be either a WMF or a JPEG.) In this instance, we’re going to find an aerial view of a university campus. Click “Open” to import the image.

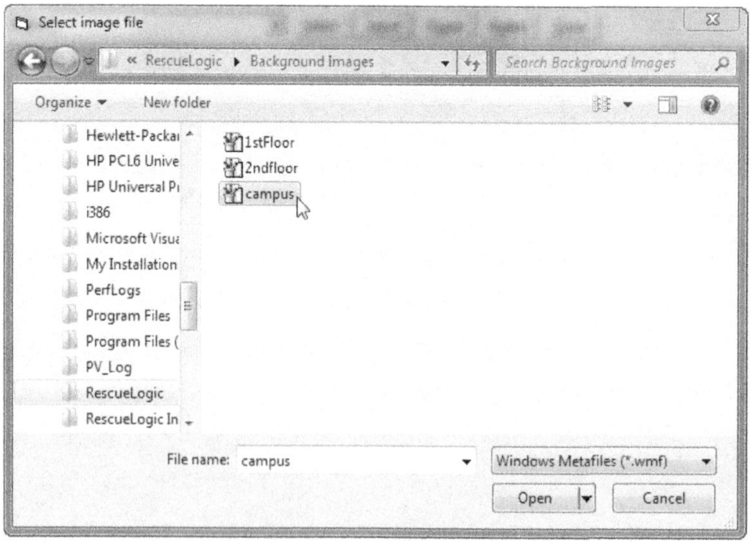

Click "Yes" to make the background transparent.

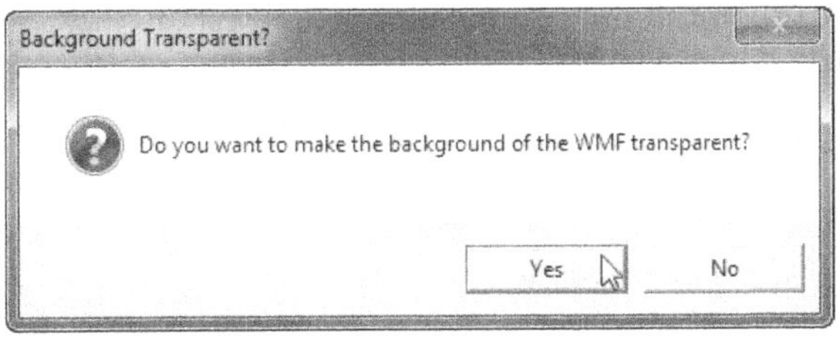

Give your new background image a name. (We are calling it "Campus.")

Right-click anywhere on the image and choose "Insert Group."

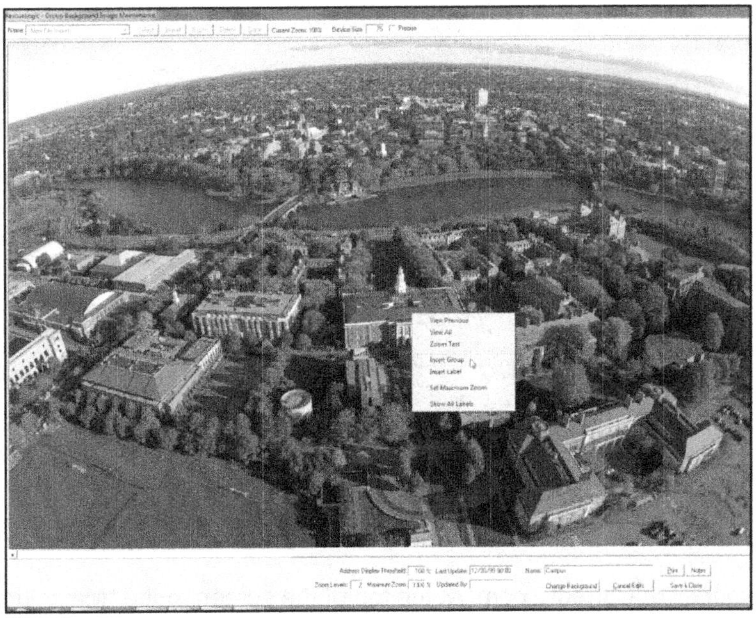

A “RescueLogic Group Selection” window will appear. Highlight the group you are working with, and start sliding it out of the window. As you move the line out of the selection box, it will turn into a colored box. Drag it into position on the background image and drop it into place.

You can click and drag anywhere on the background image to zoom in. To adjust the size of the box, either double-click on it or right-click on it and select “Edit Group.” When you are done, click “Update.”

Helpful Hint: Compare your own “Current Zoom” at the top of the screen to the “Maximum Zoom” listed at the bottom of the screen. If your picture is still relatively clear — like this one is — you should modify your “Maximum Zoom.” In this case, we will change the “Maximum Zoom” setting from 3300 percent to 700 percent.

Add Background Notes

When you are setting up background maps and floor plans, you can add background notes for future reference. Just click the "Notes" button at the bottom of the "Layout Background" screen.

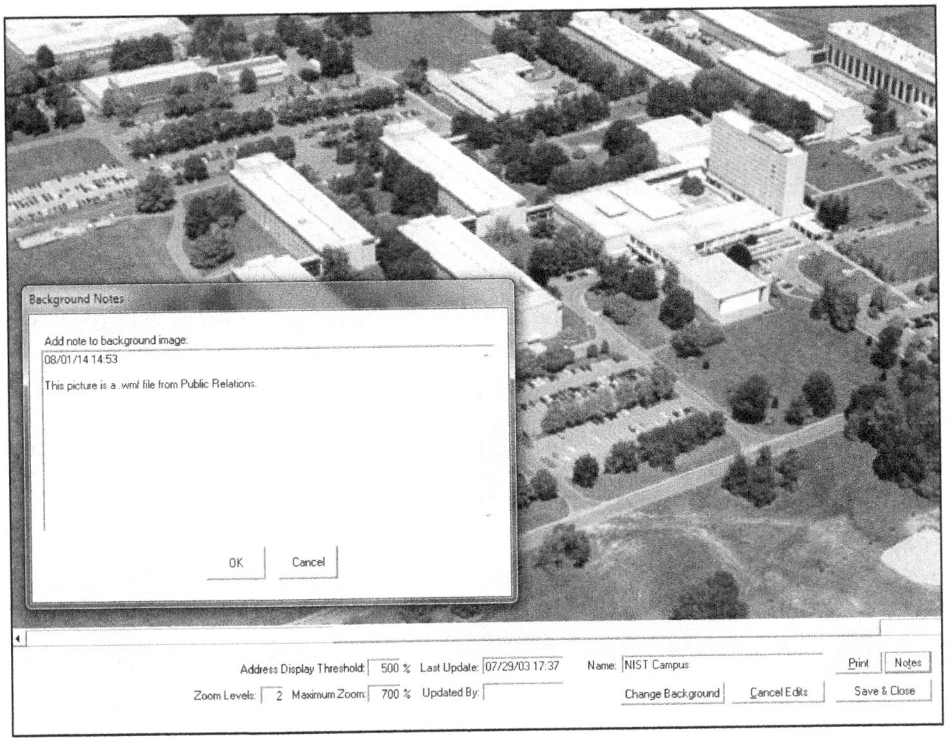

Helpful Hint: You might want to note the source of your background image, its current folder and file location, and any other information you might need later, just in case you need to revise a background map or floor plan. The comments you enter in background notes will not appear elsewhere in your RescueLogic system; they are strictly for your own reference.

Background Map and Floor Plan Checklist

Here is a list of things to double-check once you have finished setting up background maps and floor plans.

- ☐ Double-check names and street addresses; make sure that they are complete and capitalized correctly.
- ☐ To avoid confusion, spell out any abbreviations. Use "Street," for example, not "St."
- ☐ Include each building's full name. If your staff people or local residents use any other names or nicknames for some buildings — such as the "Old Gym," for example — include them in addition to the official name.
- ☐ Orient each map or floor plan with north at the top. Use a compass rose to point to north, south, east, and west.
- ☐ Use large labels for major building areas, such as "North Wing" or "Intensive Care Unit."
- ☐ Use smaller labels for more specific building areas — typically, room numbers or office names, such as "Engineering" or "Supply Room."
- ☐ Double-check the readability of your labels and addresses at various zoom levels.
- ☐ Check all devices using Configuration Reports, which will list every device. The left column of the printout includes the name of every device. The right column will list the name of each device's background. If that field is blank, it means the device is not placed on a floor plan.
- ☐ One other tip: You can also use Configuration Reports to tell if you've put a device on the correct floor. If all the devices are listed as being on the first floor, but in the middle of the list one is alone on the third floor, double-check it. Device addresses are sequential, and they are usually grouped by floor.
- ☐ Put your initials in the "Updated by" field.

Tricks of the Trade: How We Make Backgrounds

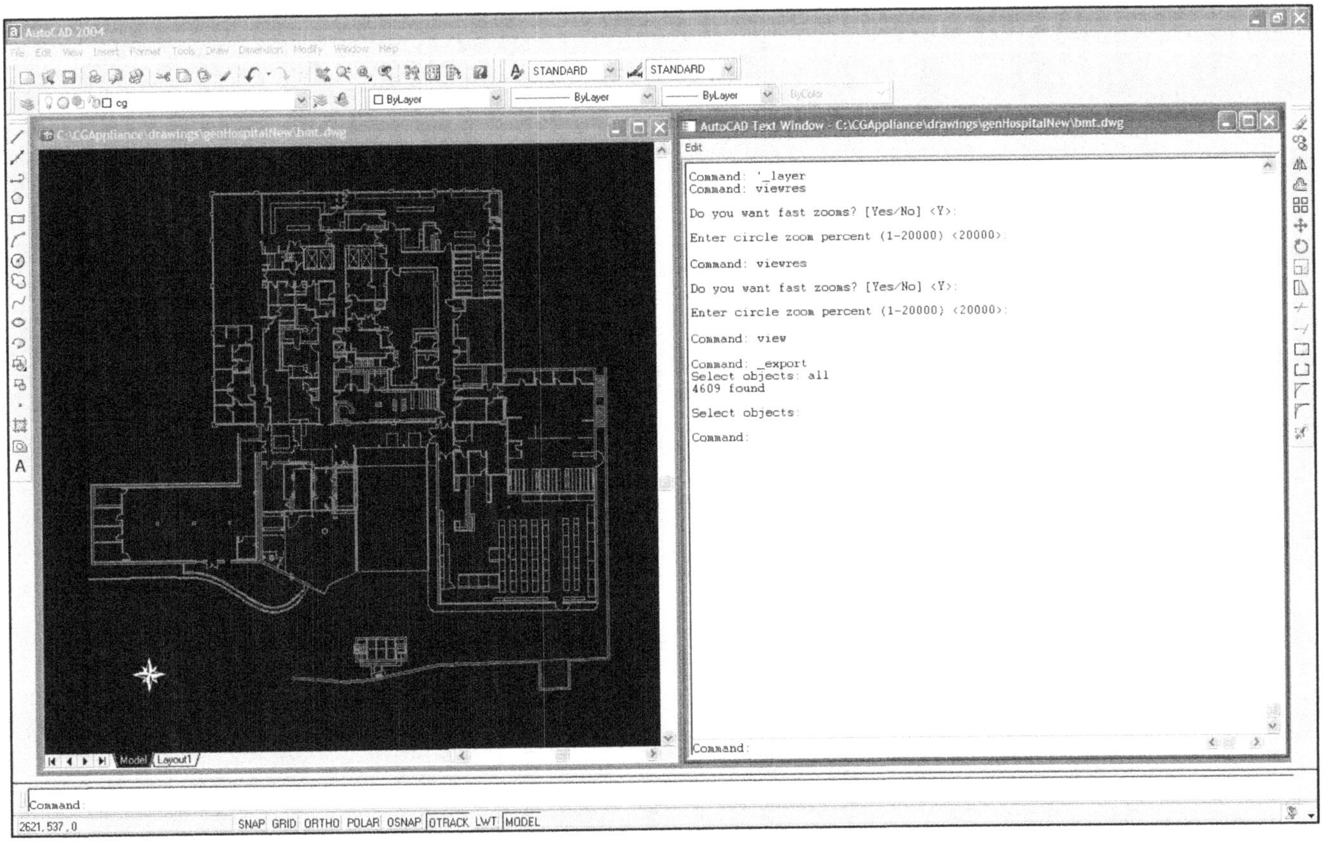

If you have AutoCAD software, it's easy to save CAD files as Windows metafiles for your RescueLogic system. Just make sure AutoCAD is open and running on your computer, and open your CAD drawing file (DWG). Open the "File" drop-down menu, click "Export," and locate the folder on your hard drive. By default, your new file will be listed in the same folder, with the same name, and a WMF extension. Click "Save." You will be asked to "Select Objects." Click on the entities or window around the drawing to select everything you want to include in your WMF. Click "Enter" and AutoCAD will save the file as a .wmf.

At RescueLogic, we go through a few extra steps when we convert our customers' background maps and floor plans to WMFs. First, we usually change the colors — because it's not uncommon for architects' doors and windows to be red, yellow, and bright blue, which detract from locating alarms in RescueLogic. We usually change walls to Windows Color 132 (cyan), and we change doors, stairways, and fixtures to Windows Color 8 (a dark gray). That color scheme looks best on a black background. If you prefer a white background, dark blue is best for walls, with black doors, stairways, and fixtures.

We use the command "VIEWRES" and set AutoCAD for fast zooms, to make sure that the finished WMF will be the highest possible quality when RescueLogic users zoom in. We set the resolution value to its maximum of 20,000. Otherwise, when users zoom in on curved lines, they see jagged edges, and circles actually look more like stop signs.

We also adjust the visible area of the .wmf and save it as a named view. We frame the image on screen to make it more aesthetically pleasing, and to create a size that we can duplicate exactly if we need to revise the floor plan later. We like to see space evenly distributed around all four sides, with enough space on the floor plan itself for labels and addresses. Then we zoom in on that rectangle and adjust the size of the edit window to move the border to the very outside edge of the screen, so it almost disappears from view. Then we select the visible image and save it as a .wmf.

Chapter 11: Action Messages

With RescueLogic "Take Action" messages, you can give first responders specific, real-time information about alarms on your site — including notes about hazardous materials, vulnerable building occupants, and management contacts. You can even offer "Take Action" suggestions in Spanish! In this chapter, you will learn how to use RescueLogic to give security guards, police officers, and fire fighters the emergency information they need.

Customize Your Action Messages

Every alarm and security device in your system will be linked to a color-coded message about its condition. The color-coding will match the colors you choose for your System Watch list; messages about devices in trouble, for example, will pop up on a yellow background. Messages about devices in alarm will pop up on a red background.

Start customizing your action messages by opening Configuration Manager. Go to the "Maintenance" drop-down menu and click on "Device Action Messages."

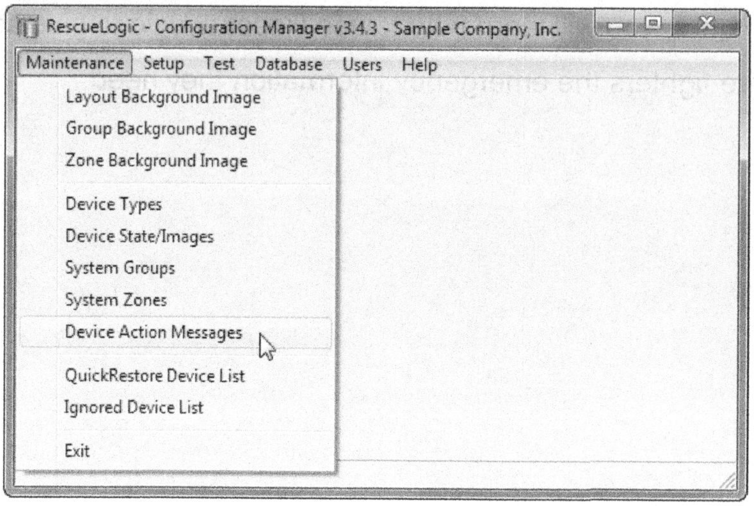

The Device Action Message Setup window will open.

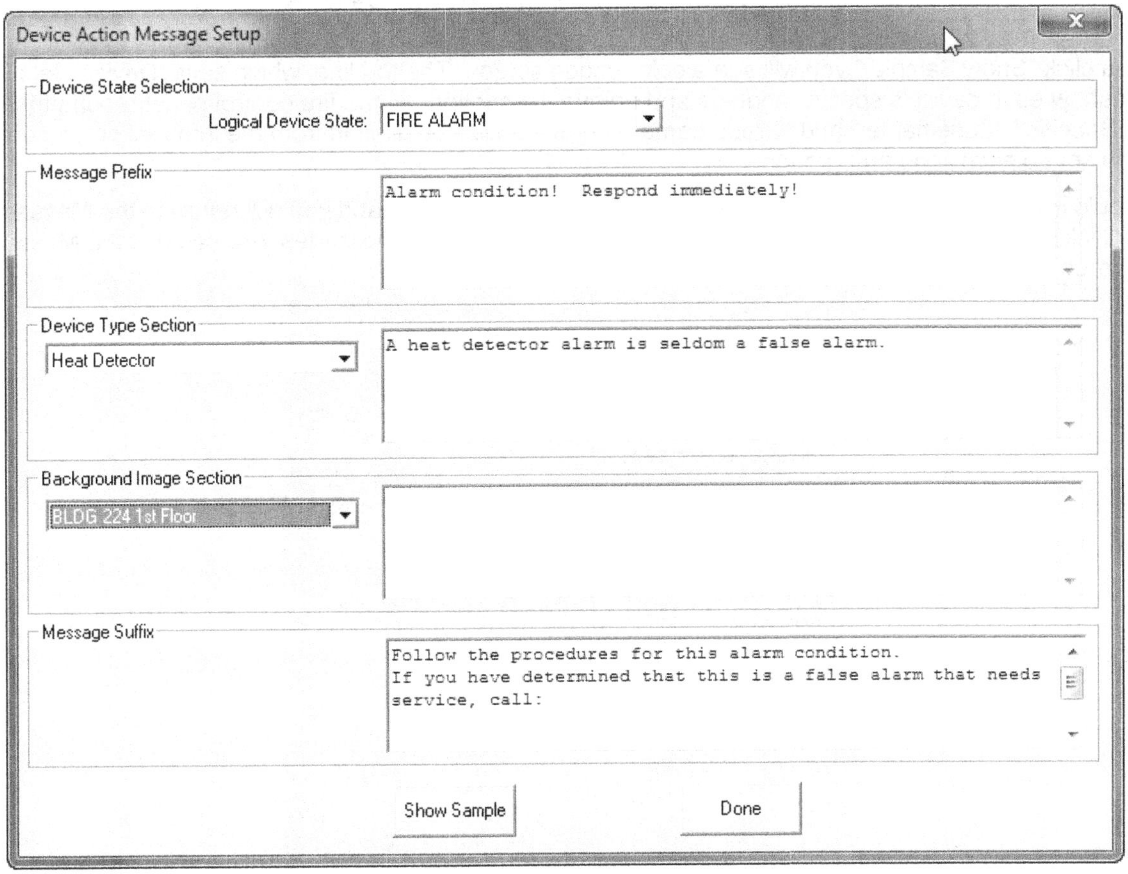

- Use the drop-down "Device State Selection" field to determine whether you are establishing messages for devices in fire alarm, supervisory alarm, or trouble.
- Write two separate "Message Prefix" notes: one for when devices are in trouble and one for when devices are in alarm.
- Use the "Device Type" section to write action messages for each device type in your system.
- The "Background Image" section: will indicate which floor or area of the building each device is located.
- The "Message Suffix" will bring up standard "boilerplate" information that applies to any trouble or alarm.
- Click "Show Sample" to continue.

Helpful Hint: You will probably find yourself writing two action messages for every type of device in your RescueLogic system. That makes this a good time to review and standardize your site's emergency policies and procedures and update your emergency contact phone list. You may even want to consolidate all of your action messages to develop an emergency operations handbook.

Preview Your Finished Work

Once you click "Show Sample," you will see a color-coded screen. The top line, which says "Device Help Test," will later show each device's specific address and unique description, as the fire control panel reports them. Your "Device Specific," "Zone name," and "Group name" information will be filled in from the information you enter when you set up each zone and group.

If you would like to make changes to your action message, click "Close," and you will return to the Message Setup screen. Click "Done" when you are finished setting up all of your action messages.You can use the Message Setup screen at any time to make changes or add information.

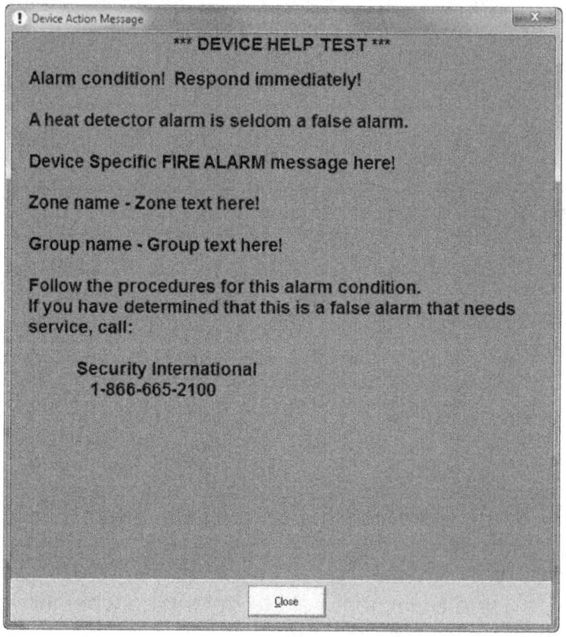

Helpful Hint: The preview screen may have a white background when the "Logical Device State" is set for "Fire Alarm." If you were expecting to see a red background, don't be confused: the device type you've selected is actually a supervisory alarm. The "Logical Device State" must match the type of your alarm device. Simply change the "Logical Device State" to "Fire Alarm," and the background will be red.

Chapter 12: Setting Up Ports and Panels

With RescueLogic, you can monitor a single alarm panel or an entire network of controls — even if your system is made up of panels and devices from one manufacturer, RescueLogic may connect to them all through a single port on your RescueLogic computer. This chapter will show you how to configure your RescueLogic system to recognize and receive data from the panels on your site.

Port and Panel Basics

In order for RescueLogic to receive information about alarms and devices on your site, you will need to connect your alarm panels to your RescueLogic computer. While every panel formats data in its own way — depending on the manufacturer — most come equipped with a COM port that can be connected to a printer. With RescueLogic, you can also use that COM port to connect an alarm panel to a computer.

In fact, with RescueLogic you can actually monitor an entire network of control panels through a single COM port. You can hard wire your panels directly to your RescueLogic computer, or, if your RescueLogic computer is more than 50 feet from the panel, you can use your IP network, twisted pair copper wire, fiber optic cable, or a wireless transmitter to connect the two.

Alarm panels and your RescueLogic computer share a common language: ASCII data. RescueLogic translates that data into plain English, and displays it on color-coded lists, graphic images, and maps and floor plans.

RescueLogic also combines panel data in ways that make it more user-friendly. In most alarm systems, every device has a panel address number: 1001, 1002, or 1003, for example. If your facility has three alarm panels on site — three *nodes*, in other words — each node might assign those same three numbers to three separate devices. Ultimately, you could have several devices that are all assigned the same panel address. RescueLogic eliminates the confusion by combining node numbers and addresses, so each device is distinct.

Configure Panels for your Site

The RescueLogic database contains information about the types of panels on your site. You can specify information about each panel in your system. If, for example, your facility has three panels — all of the same make and model — you will create three system panels with one panel type.

Open Configuration Manager. Go to the "Setup" drop-down menu and click on "System Panels."

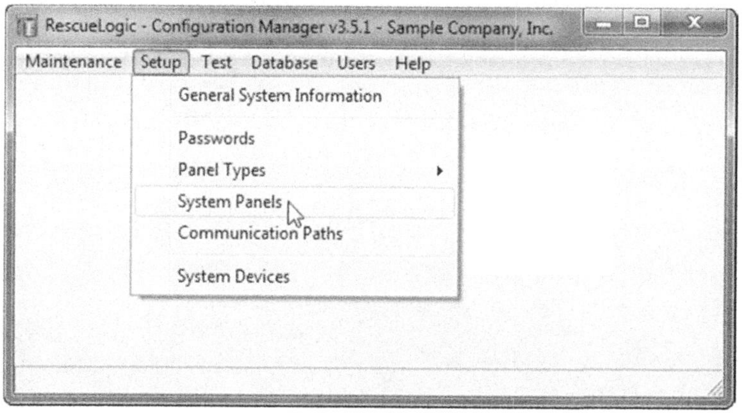

Create a List of Your Panels

The “System Panel Maintenance” window will open. You will see two default panel examples, named “Fire” and “Security.” The example setup has two Silent Knight alarm panels, one dedicated to fire alarm functions, and another panel dedicated to security functions. In this example, we will look at the fire alarm panel. Choose the first one, labeled “Fire” from the drop-down list. Then click “Select.”

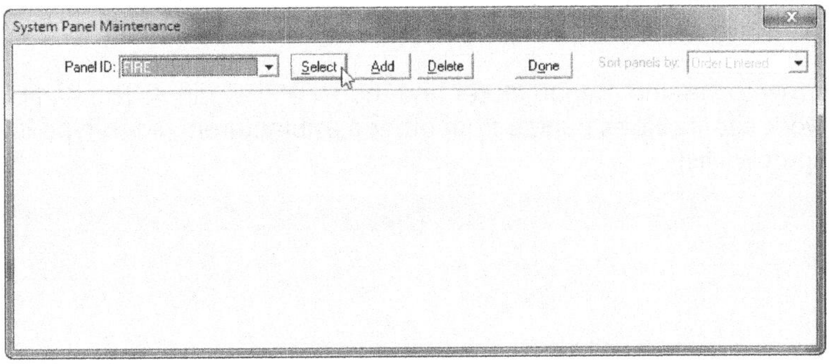

The Panel ID is labeled FIRE in this example to distinguish it from our other example panel used for security alarms.

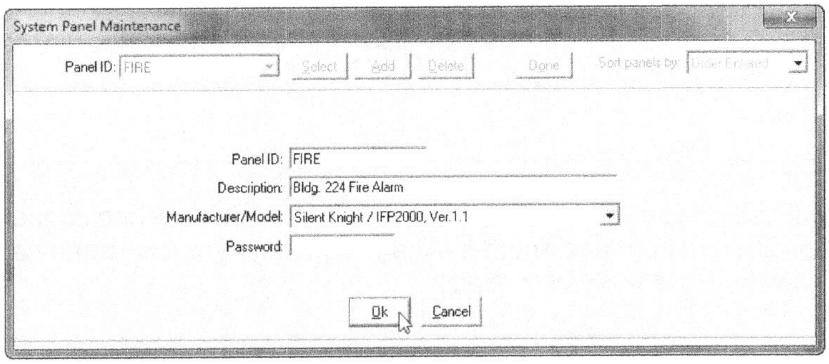

Click in the Panel ID field, and change the text to “NODE 1.”

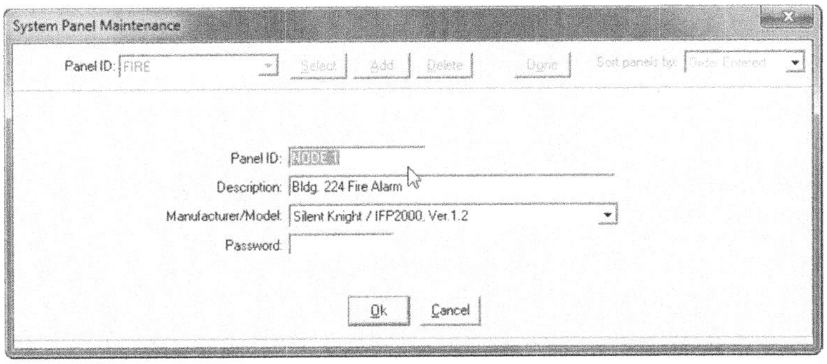

This works regardless of if the two panels are connected together or not. Each is an independent node, or data gathering point. You may be more familiar with network names, such as “Node 1.” The next field, Description, allows you to enter a longer, expanded label in addition to each ID. The information you enter will be displayed on the System Watch screen, so it should make sense to your end users. Be specific, and use a name that everyone on your staff will recognize: “Sample Company Headquarters,” for example, as opposed to a more generic “Panel A.” When you are through, click “OK.”

Helpful Hint: The Panel ID does not have to match the messages that the control panel sends. The Panel ID you enter on this screen will simply be displayed to System Watch users. If you have two networks of panels connected to one RescueLogic computer, for example, the first network might connect three panels: "Node 1," "Node 2," and "Node 3." You might want to differentiate the panels on the second network by adding a prefix number "Node 2-1," "Node 2-2," and "Node 2-3." Then, go back and ID the first network as "Node 1-1," "Node 1-2," and "Node 1-3."

Click on the drop-down arrow to see the manufacturer and model of the panel. The sample database uses Silent Knight as an example; if your site includes panels from other manufacturers, each type is added to the database, and will appear in the drop-down list.

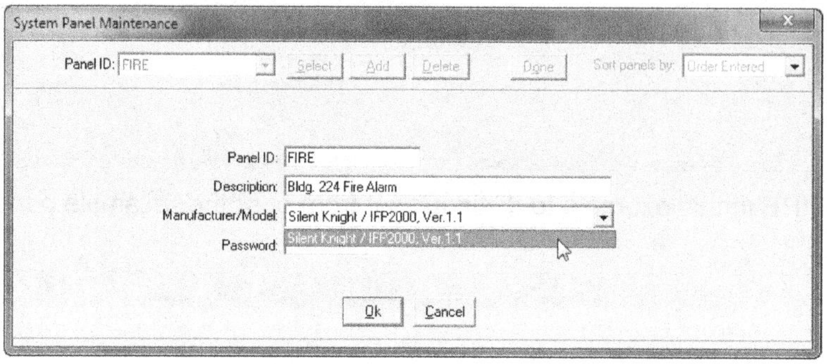

Helpful Hint: If this is the first time you've seen the System Panel list, don't be too concerned about the exact text. Just make each panel different from one another. At any time, and you can come back and change the labels after you've seen how they look in System Watch.

To add a new system panel to the pre-set list, click "Add."

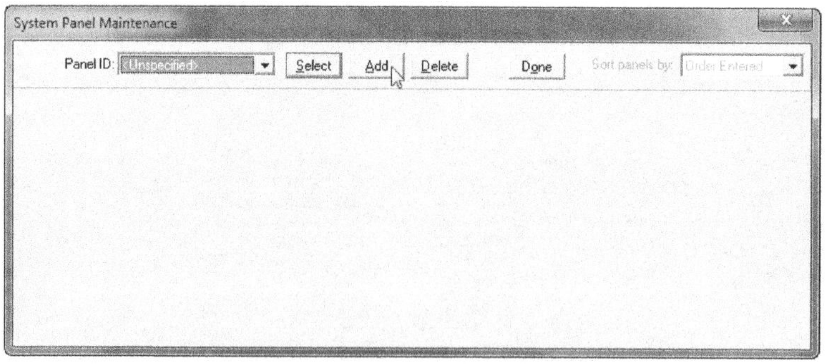

You will see the same fields to customize for your added panel. Simply replace the bracketed text with the names you used to overwrite the existing default panels. If you have more than one manufacturer/model, choose the correct one from from the drop-down list.

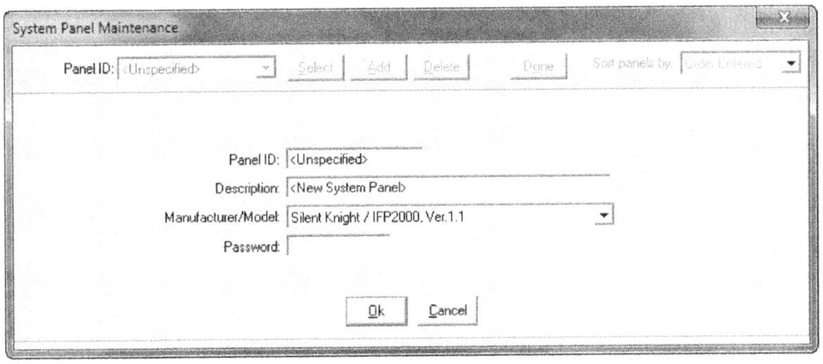

Give your new panel an ID, such as "Node 2," and a clear description that everyone on your staff will recognize. Select the correct manufacturer and model, and then click "OK." After the last new panel type has been added to the system, click "Done."

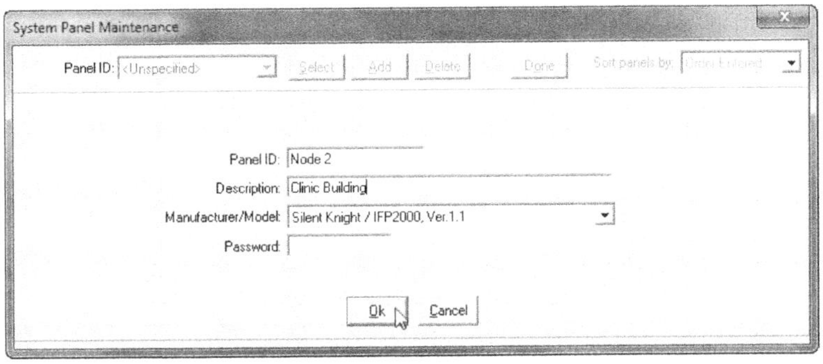

Helpful Hint: RescueLogic is programmed to work with a wide range of panels. RescueLogic also offers a Software Developers Kit that makes it possible to develop additional drivers to work with any panel. Email info@rescuelogic.com for details.

Delete Unused Panels

If you have only one system panel on your site, delete the extra one — either fire or security — from our sample database.

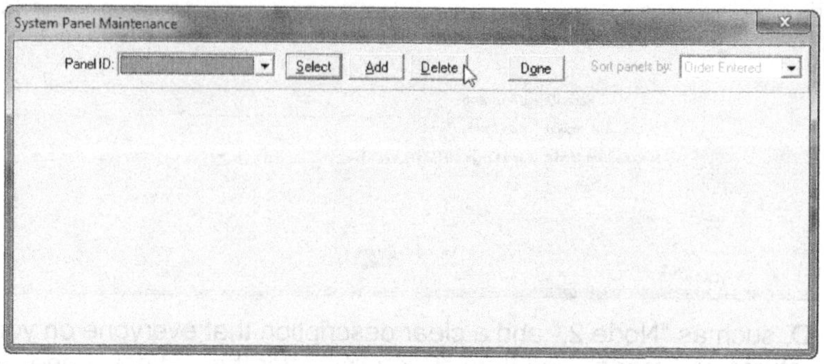

You will be asked to confirm the deletion. Click "Yes" to delete.

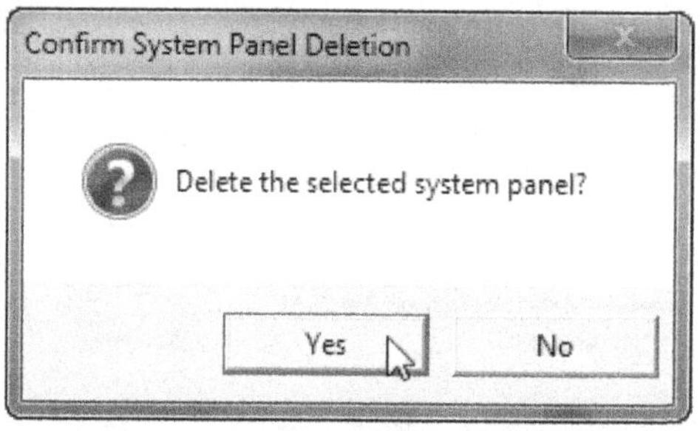

Helpful Hint: If you delete a system panel, you will wipe out RescueLogic's link with any devices that were associated with that panel. The devices themselves will remain in the database until you manually associate their addresses with a panel or delete them. However, you should only delete a panel if you also intend to delete the associated devices — as when you remove a sample panel from the default database, or if you are installing a new replacement panel with a new series of device addresses.

You can modify, add, or remove panels at any time. You don't need to set up your entire system all at once.

Panel Types

RescueLogic has been in use for about 25 years, and maintained compatibility with every alarm system that was ever connected to it. That means some systems use different methods of defining how a system is interpreted.

RescueLogic uses three methods of interfacing panels: Legacy Panels, Channel Applications, and Script Panel Types. First, we'll show you how to define Legacy Panel Types.

To define the panels on your site, open Configuration Manager, choose the Setup Menu, mouse over Panel Types, and then choose Legacy Panel Types.

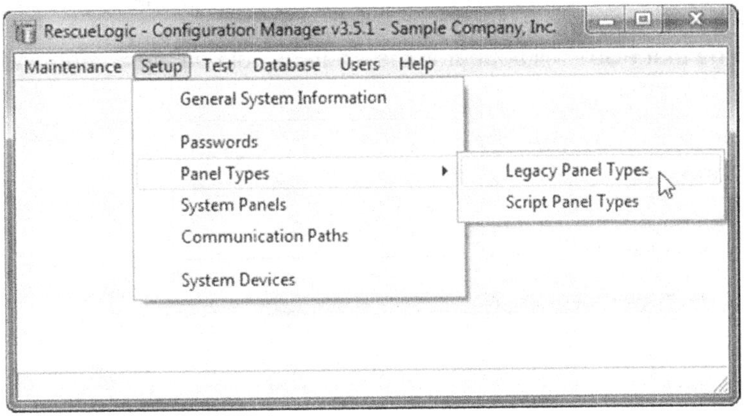

Use the drop-down menu to view a list of pre-set panel types. If your panel is not listed, click "Add." Enter a name and model number for your panel type. The name and model you type in are not fields that need to match anything specific; they are strictly for your own reference.

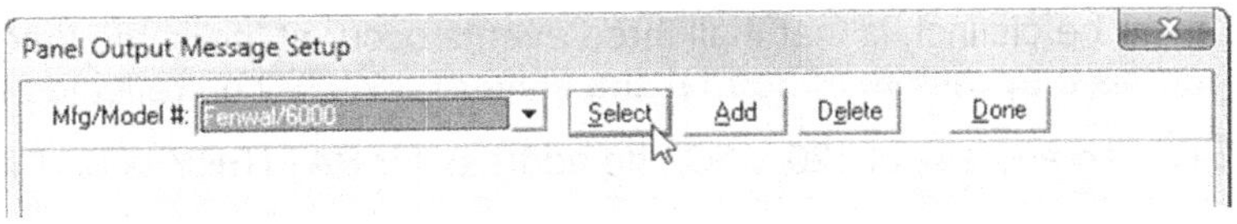

You will see a form to enter values that determine how messages from the particular type of control panel are to be interpreted. The purpose of these variables is to allow behavior of your system to vary from other systems, and also adapt to firmware changes of the control panel in the future.

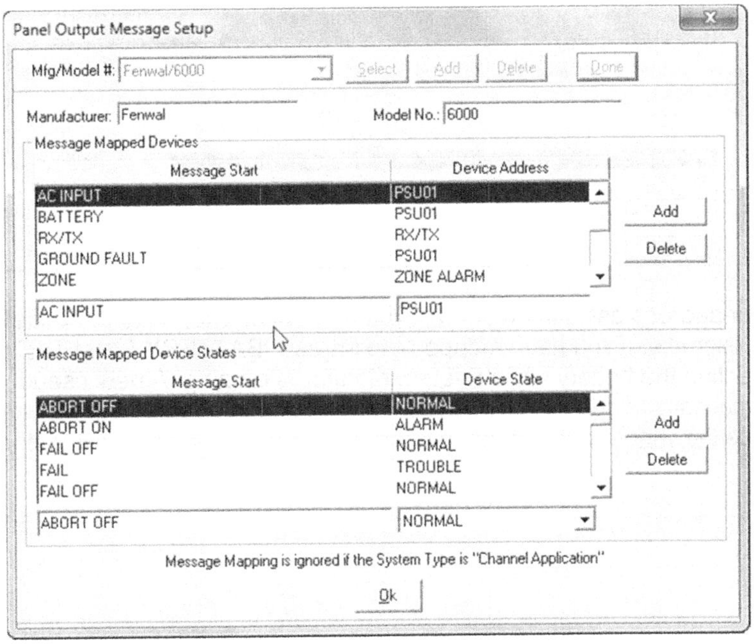

Pseudo Points

Some control panels have unique messages, such as low-battery warnings, that don't follow the normal device-address format. If you want to include them in your RescueLogic system, you will need to create an address, or *pseudo point*, that can be assigned to each message that you want to identify as a device. Then you will be able to locate those devices on a background map or floor plan.

The top half of the Panel Output Message form allows you to map messages to pseudo points. In this example, a message starting with AC INPUT is mapped to an address of PS01. Note that the next line item and also the third line item are also mapped to the same address, PS01. That is because, in this system, all three of those messages apply to the power supply, and the end user only wants one point to be created for any of those messages. The result will be that PS01 will appear in the Address field on the System Watch list, and underneath the icon on the floor plan.

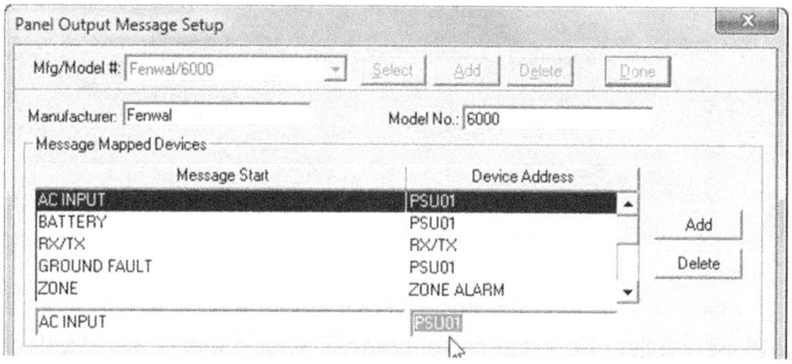

Alternately, you could assign three separate addresses to those three messages. In the next example, the same three messages are assigned to unique addresses, which will create three independent devices in the database. The advantage of having them be distinct, is that if all three events occur at the same time, three separate messages will appear. Then, as they restore to normal, the state of each will be reflected independently.

Here, you see AC INPUT has an address of 120 VAC, the address for BATTERY is BATTERY, and GROUND FAULT is GROUND.

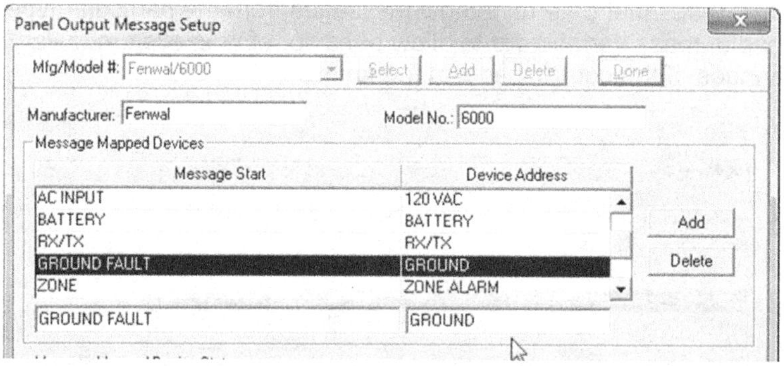

Helpful Hint: To test your address assignments, run System Monitor and make the panel report the message by activating the event. For example, if you have mapped the phrase "BATTERY FAILURE" to a new address called "BATTERY," try disconnecting the battery while System Monitor is running. A new pseudo device with the address "BATTERY" will be automatically added to the database, and it should appear in the System Watch list as a trouble. When you replace the wire, and the panel detects the batteries again, it will restore to normal, and its color will be green.

Modify an item in the list by clicking on it to see the values in the edit boxes below. Simply click on the <Message Start> and <Device Address> lines to highlight them, and type in your new text.

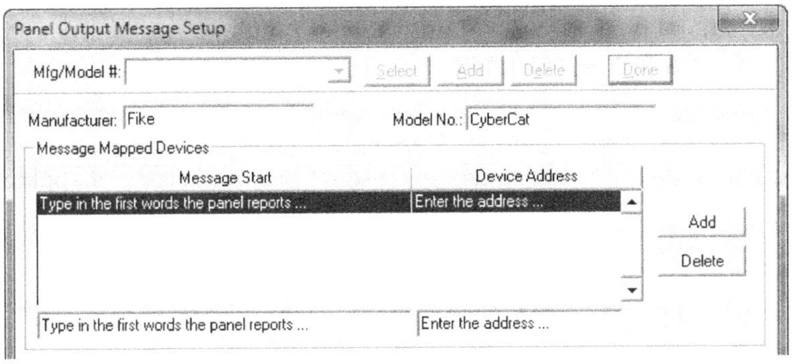

After the pseudo device is automatically created in the database, assign a device type, description, and any other information you would like to include in the System Devices list to further clarify the event. You may also want to drop an icon of that device onto your background floor plan – or have it blink on a photograph background picture of the panel on the wall.

Click "Add" to continue adding pseudo points.

Device State Mapping

The bottom half of the Legacy Panel Setup form lists terms as they will be reported from the panel, and assigns then to one of three states: ALARM, TROUBLE or NORMAL.

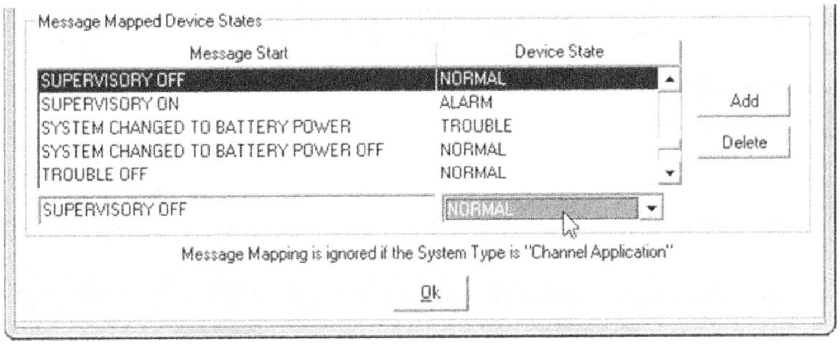

Each item on the left column list will match a message from the control panel. The corresponding choice on the right will determine how the event will behave in System Watch. To change the Device State between the three options, highlight the item in the list, drop down the Device State list to choose between ALARM, TROUBLE, or NORMAL.

You may wonder why there is only one choice for ALARM, and there is no way to distinguish between a FIRE ALARM and a SUPERVISORY ALARM. The type of alarm is determined by the Device Type category. One device type cannot be both a FIRE ALARM and a SUPERVISORY. Use the State/Image menu to modify and determine Logical State for each device type.

Click "Add" to continue adding message mapping for events.

Click "OK" on the bottom of the form when you are through.

Channel Applications

In addition to receiving information from COM ports, RescueLogic can receive information from other Windows programs — in other words, a custom channel application.

A channel application is a Windows program that runs separately from RescueLogic, but is pre-programmed to send messages to RescueLogic and display alarms. A channel number is a RescueLogic convention that allocates numbered pathways for data transfer between RescueLogic and channel applications.

You can use your own in-house programmer and the RescueLogic Software Developers Kit to create new applications.

Using Channel Applications

Channel Applications contain their own interpretation information, and do not use Panel Types information described in the Legacy Panel Types or Script Panel Types sections. To use a Channel Application, just determine which Channel number will be used to report the information. As many as 99 different channels – meaning 99 different Windows applications – can send alarm information to RescueLogic.

To configure your RescueLogic system to read a channel application, start by opening Configuration Manger. Go to the "Setup" drop-down menu and click on "Communication Paths."

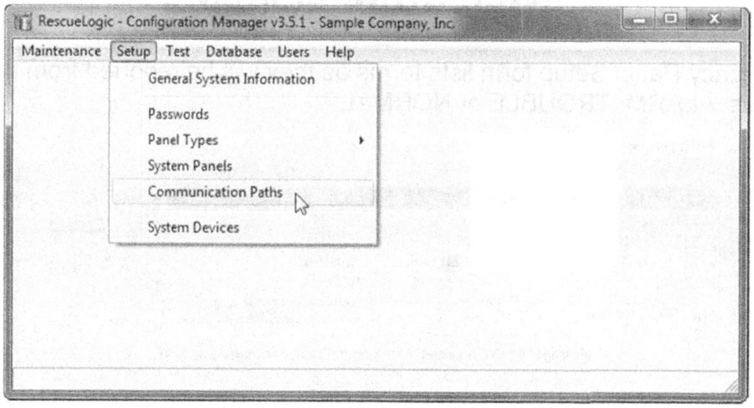

Click the "Add Path" button, or click the port that is already listed.

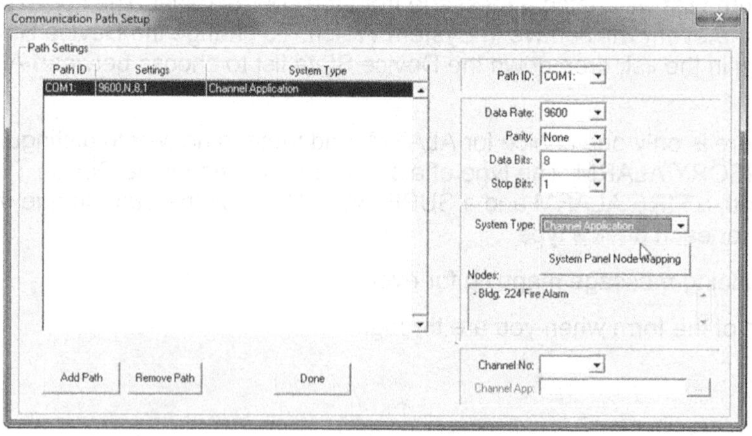

On the System Type drop-down list, choose “Channel Application.” Then use the “Channel No” drop-down list to assign a channel number. The number will match a corresponding channel for the other application.

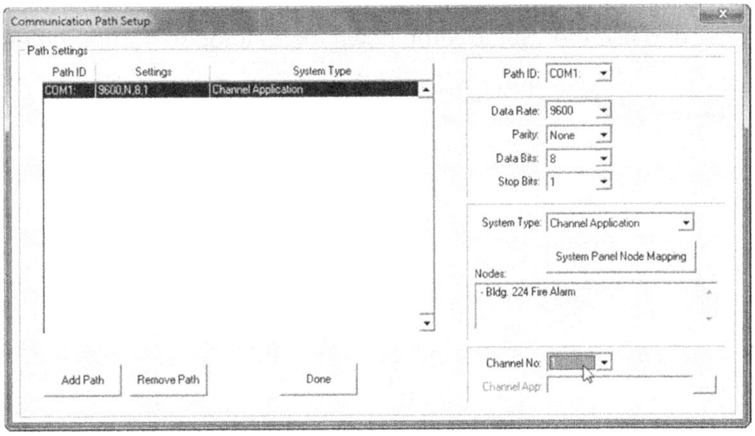

After you have selected your system type and channel number, you must assign each node that will be reported through the channel to a System Panel already defined in the RescueLogic database. Click “System Panel Node Mapping.”

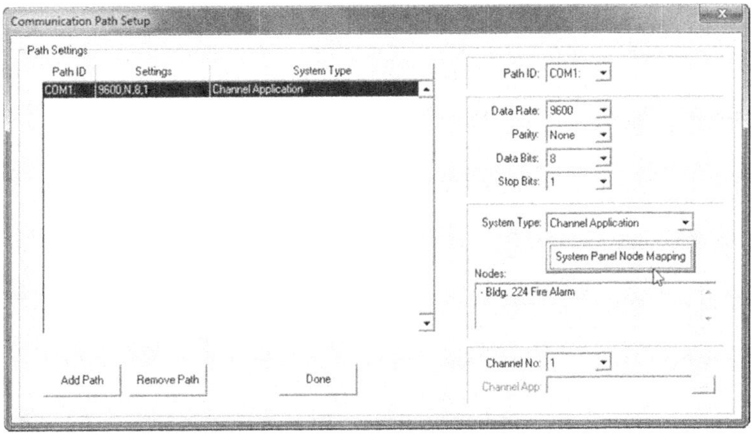

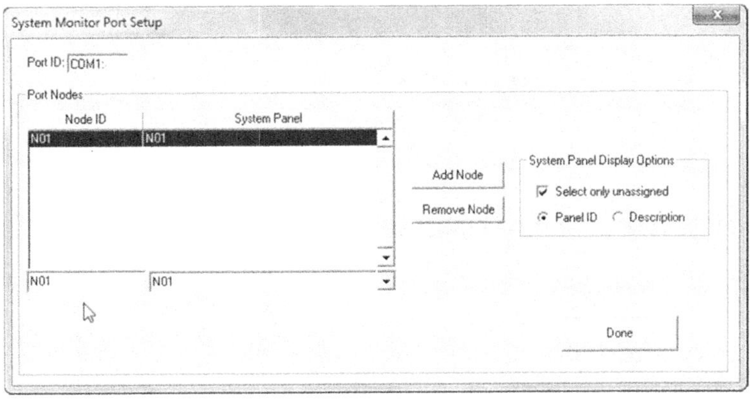

Add all Nodes as they will be reported from your Channel Application, and assign each to a System Panel.

Script Panel Types

Open Configuration Manager and use the "Setup" drop down menu to open "Script Panel Types."

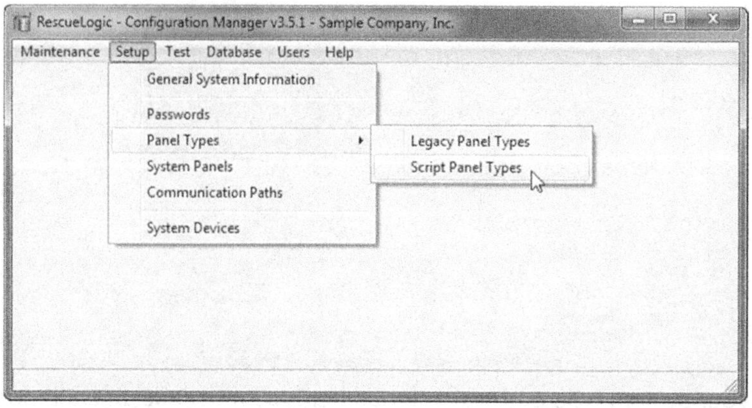

Choose the model of the panel you're editing, or click "Add" to create a new Panel Type.

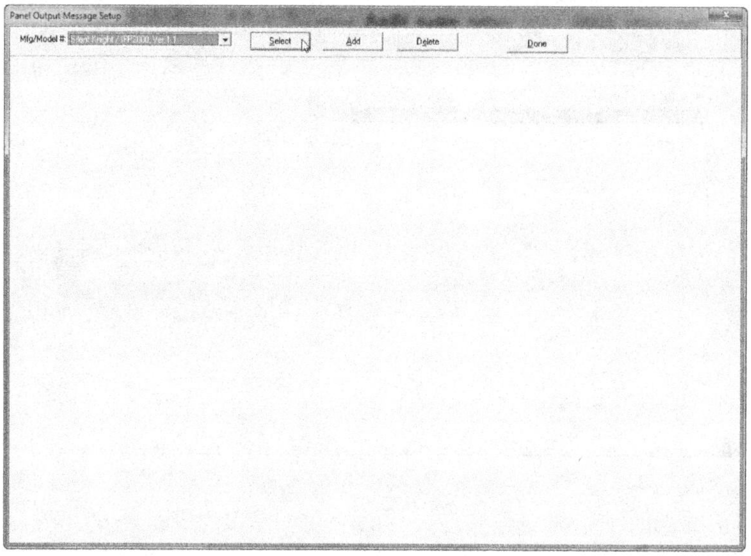

If you added a new Panel Type, enter the manufacturer, model, and version number.

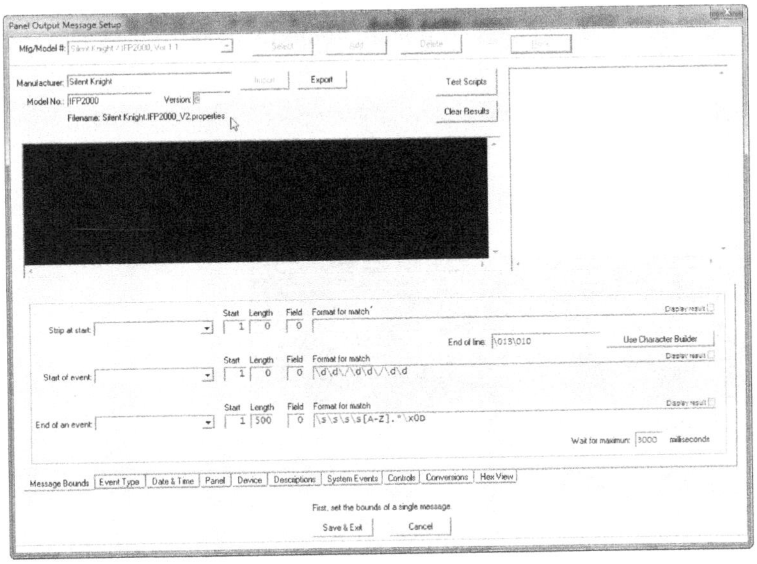

Now, look at the tabs on the bottom of the form. Each tab allows you to configure a different aspect of interpreting event messages from your alarm panel. The technique of extracting information will be familiar to many computer programmers. Basically, since the format of messages sent by your fire alarm panel is very consistent, you can define patterns to look for, and extract specific data, like Device Types and Addresses. Commonly used by computer programmers, you can buy books on regular expression pattern matching, or Regex.

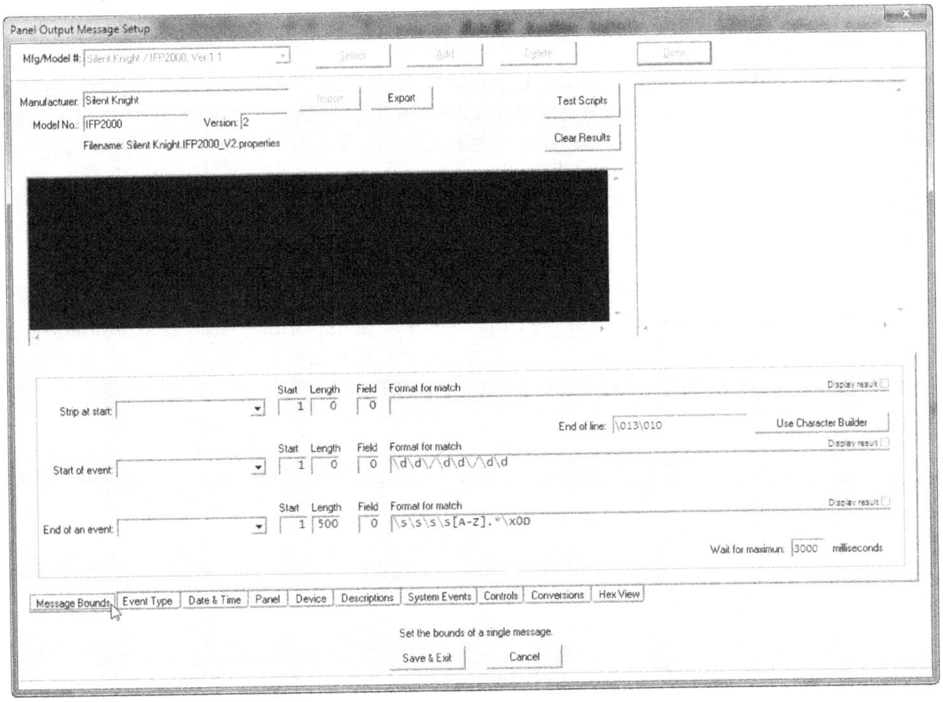

The black box is an area to paste text that was received from alarm panel events, and the white text box shows you the results of your script rules extracting messages from the panel text. Click Test Scripts to see the results of how the patterns are extracted from the sample text pasted in the black box. Click Clear Results to clear the white box between tests.

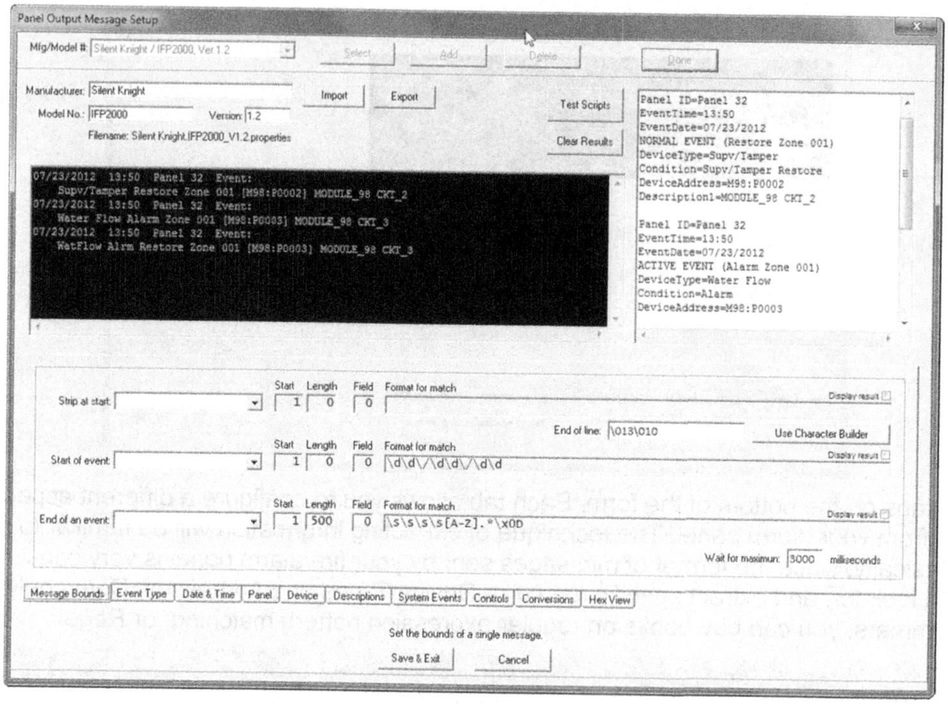

Each Script rule will use the pattern you define to extract specific data. The Format to Match field containes the pattern text. The Start and Length fields may be used to confine the extraction to a specific range within a message. When set to 0, the Length value will search the entire message. The Field value is for complex Scripts. It tells the processor which group of parentheses has the value to be used.

The sample above has an embedded variable name that refers to a list of possible text values. Each Script rule may contain a corresponding list. In this example the list is for the Device Types. In practice, the variable name is replaced with the list of possible text matches in the drop-down on the left.

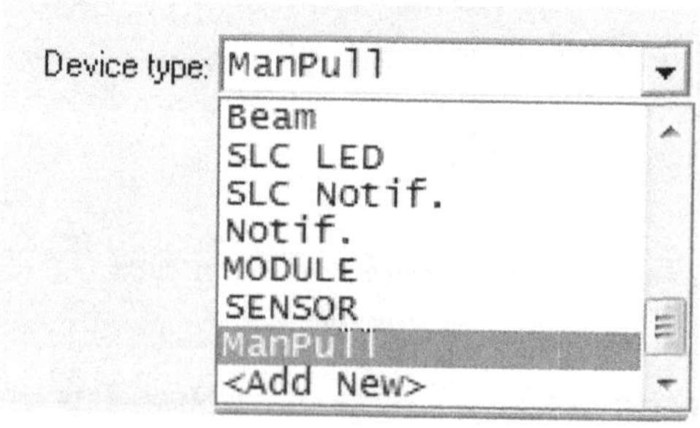

You can check the box below the list to see its Script format, where each item is enclosed in parentheses.

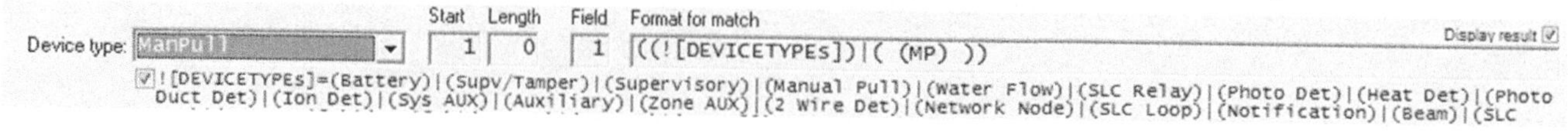

The first tab, Message Bounds, defines the beginning and end of each message. It also allows you to strip specified pattern from the beginning, and set a maximum time to wait for the end of an event.

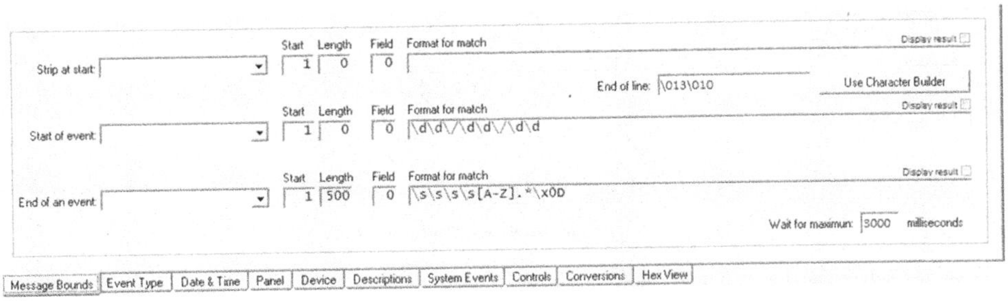

The Event Type tab allows you to define messages that are changes from Alarm, Trouble, and Normal state.

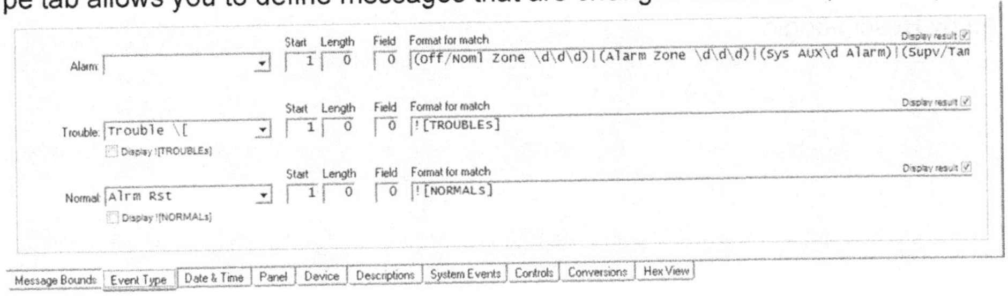

The Date & Time tab defines the format of date and time.

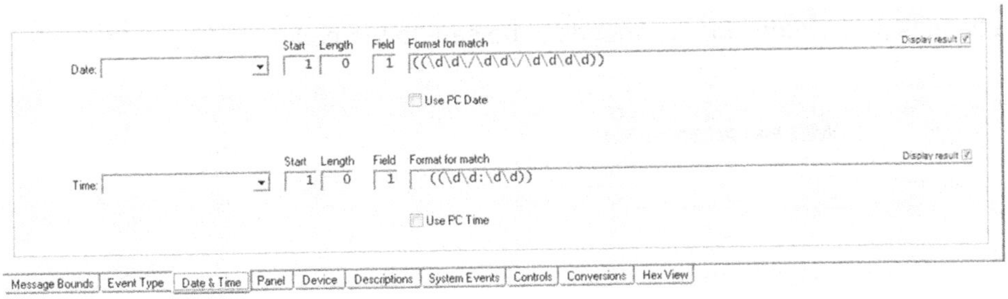

The Panel tab defines Node IDs, panel reset messages, and system events.

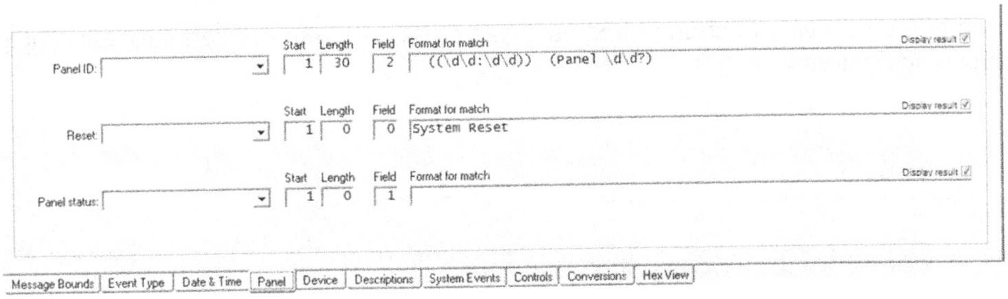

The Device tab allows extraction of Device Type, Address, and Condition text.

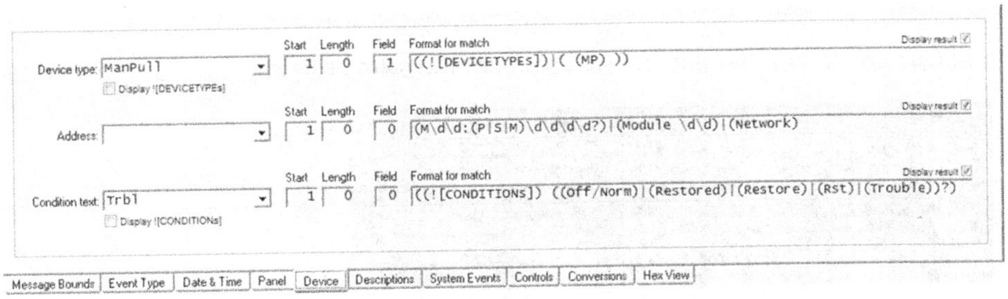

The Description tab allows you to extract Description text from events. If both are found, they are concatenated together to create a single Description for System Watch to display.

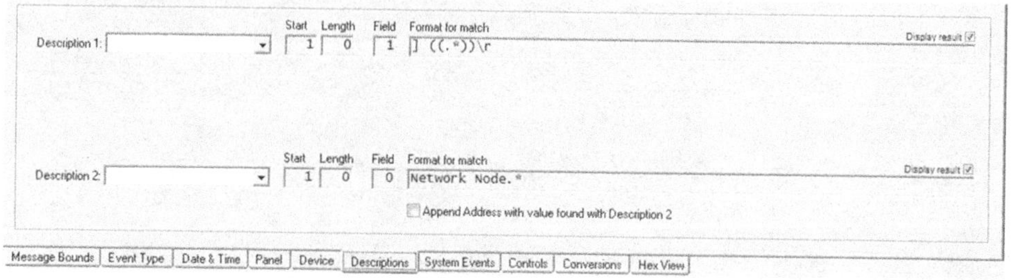

The System Events tab provides the parameters for a Heartbeat, and lets you define messages that are to be completely ignored by RescueLogic.

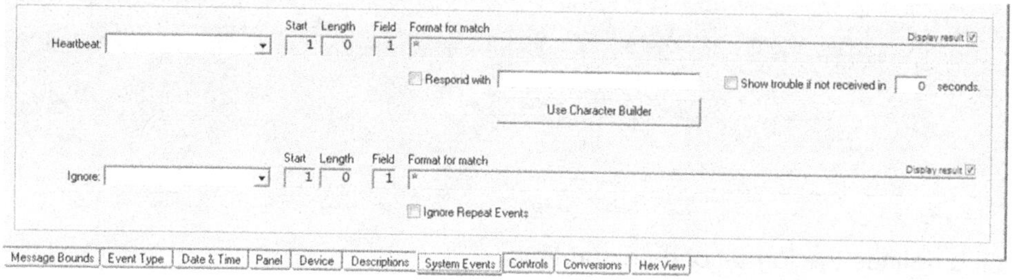

The Controls tab defines pushbuttons for commands to be sent to the panel.

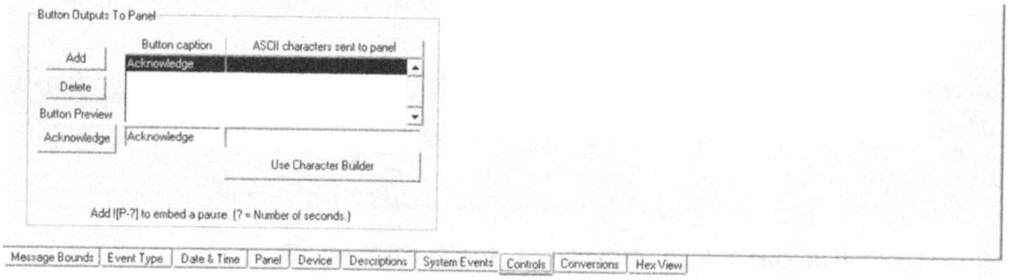

The Conversion tab provides a way to change text as it was extracted, and convert it to something more meaningful for display in System Watch.

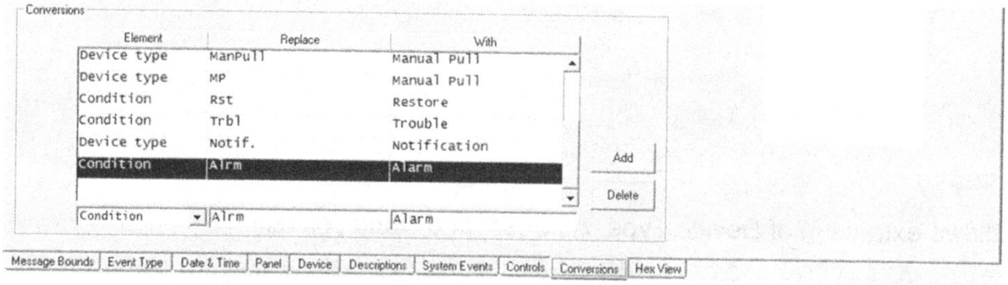

The Hex View tab allows you to see the actual hex values of the sample text pasted in the black window.

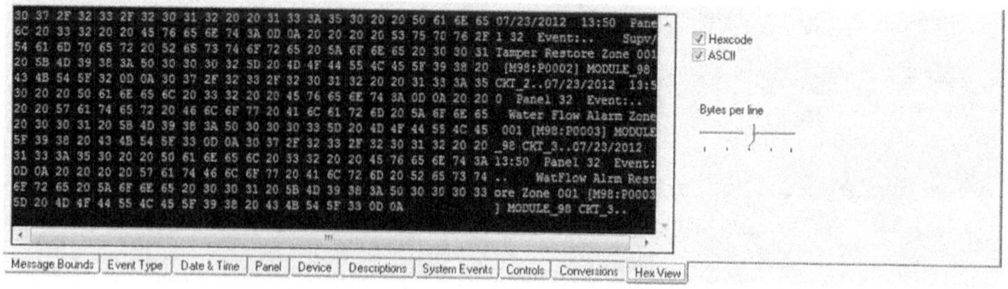

Communication Paths

A communication path is a route for information transfer between a computer and an alarm system. RescueLogic usually relies on two types of communication paths: COM ports and TCP/IP.

A COM port is a plug-in connection. Older technology uses COM ports and RS232 protocol to send information via a modem, a mouse, or a printer. By modern standards, RS232 specifications are slow. They're also limited to 50 feet of standard cable length. (Other protocols, such as RS485, RS422, and fiber optics, can speed up communication and extend the distance between COM port devices.)

Your alarm system probably has an RS232 port on its control panel that you can use to collect data as events occur. In some cases, usually UL-listed systems, information can also go from the computer to the RS232 port.

A TCP/IP connection uses an IP network. It plugs into the same Ethernet connection that's used for other information transfer, such as Internet access and file sharing between networked computers.

Your fire alarm panel may have an Ethernet port that can plug into an IP network. If your panel has an RS232 or RS485 data port, you can connect it to an IP network with a small device called a serial server.

Many RescueLogic systems use just one communication path — either a COM port or a TCP/IP connection. Those who want to connect several panels and computers, however, combine the two types of connections in order to connect remote COM ports over a local area network.

Configure Your Communication Paths

It's relatively simple to configure communication paths for your RescueLogic system. Start by opening Configuration Manager. Go to the "Setup" drop-down menu and click on "Communication Paths."

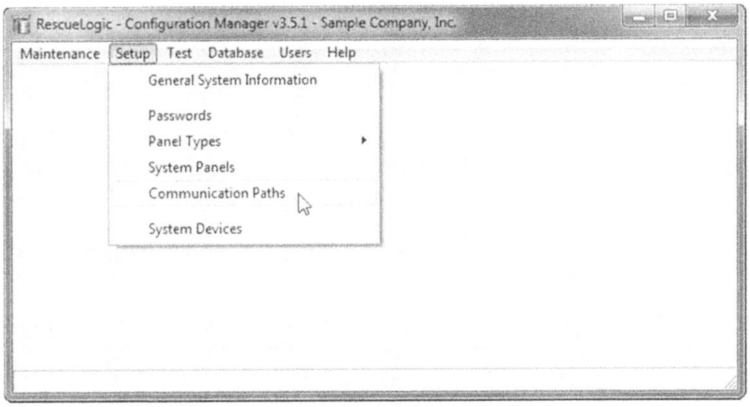

The Communication Path Setup screen will open. You'll notice that RescueLogic comes with a default COM port that's already set up.

Click on "COM1." The fields on the right will display the port's parameters: data rate, data bits, parity, and stop bits. You can edit them to match the COM ports you will use.

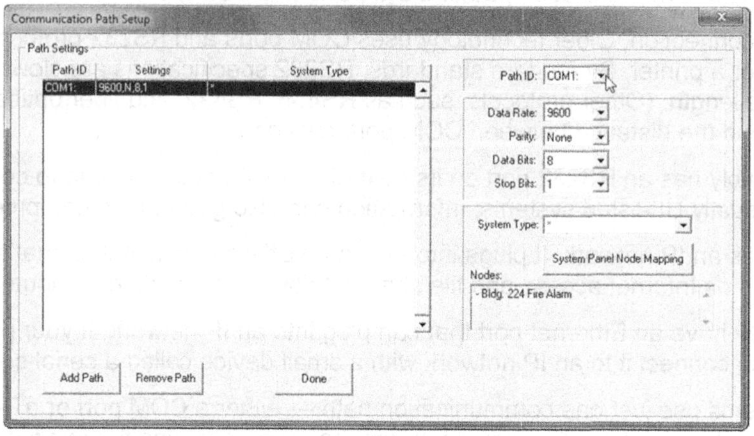

You can use the drop-down Port ID list to select any COM port from 1 to 99.

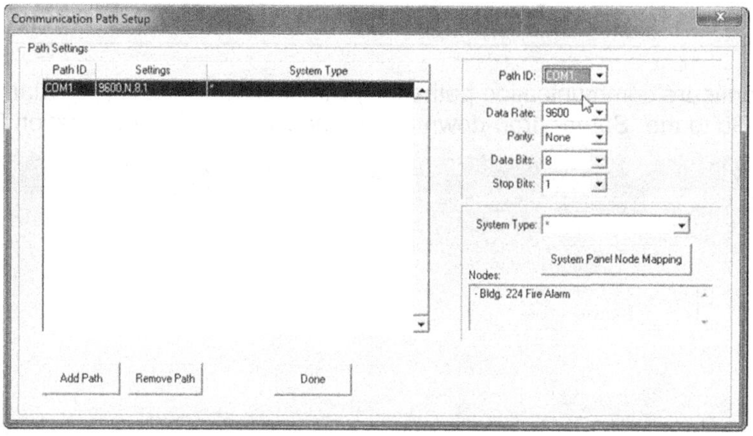

Set the Baud Rate, Parity, Data Bits, and Stop Bits to match the settings of your control panel.

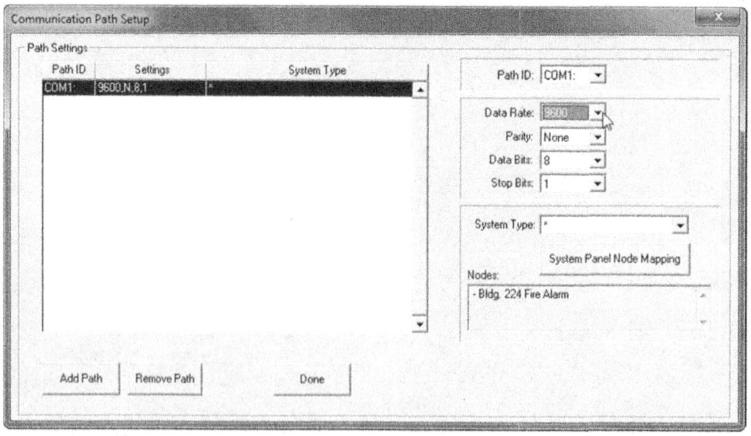

Your system might use TCP/IP connections instead of directly connected RS232 COM ports. In that case, the Baud Rate, Data Bits, and Stop Bits will be set at the remote serial device. If you have a newer panel, it might not use those settings at all. It would simply have an IP Address, and a data Port number. In IP network terms, the IP Address and Port are called a *socket*.

To set the pathway as a direct IP connection, change the Path ID selection to TCP/IP.

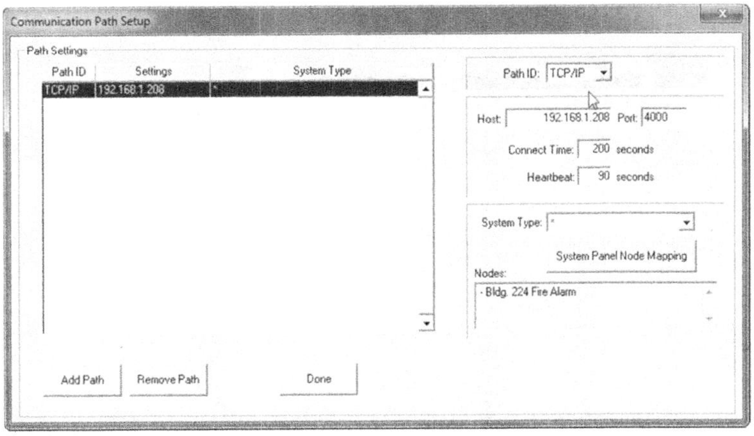

Next, type in the IP Address as the Host, and the data port number as the Port.

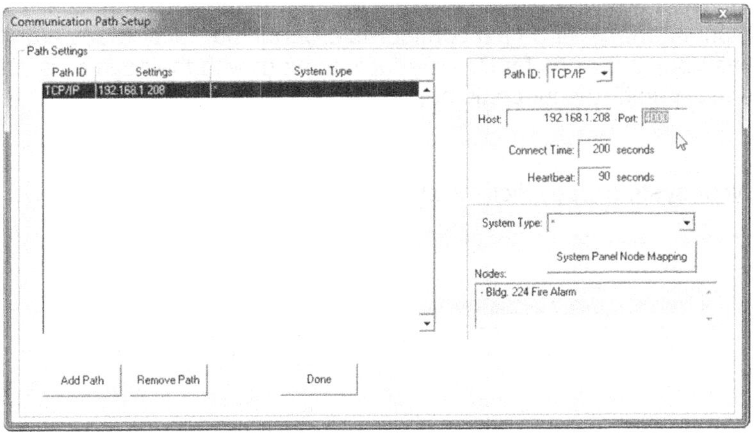

Connect Time is the allowable duration the IP socket may remain disconnected before it will report a problem. NFPA codes require the system to report a problem within 200 seconds. Therefore, the maximum allowable setting for Connect Time is 200. The default Connect Time is 90 seconds.

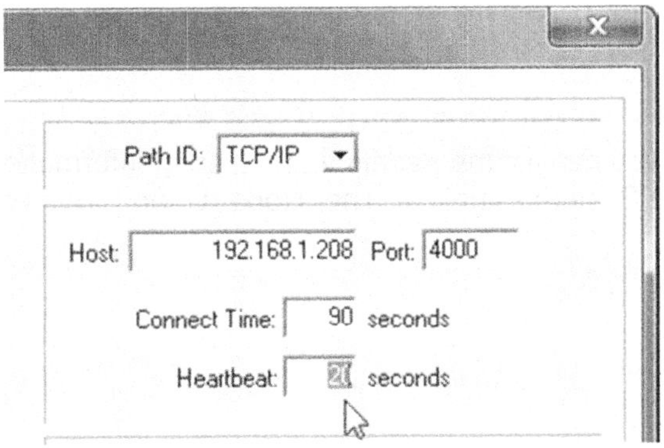

The Heartbeat value is the frequency of sending a string of text to the IP socket as a way to test its connection integrity. This is for systems that do not already have two-way communication. If no data is generated, the IP socket is not tested. For such systems, a heartbeat signal may be generated by RescueLogic as a periodic test of the path. Set the Heartbeat to '0' if your alarm panel is already communicating in both directions through the pathway. The default Heartbeat is 20 seconds.

Use the drop-down "System Type" list to select the system you will connect to your communication path. Select the last item in the list (*) if your system uses the new Script interface method.

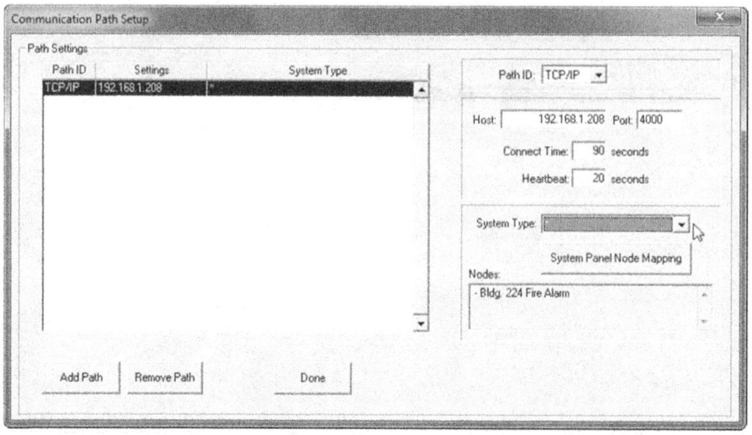

Helpful Hint: Your system might be one of those listed in the "System Type" drop-down list. If your system is not listed, you may use a custom interface, or a field configurable Script interface. Many alarm panel manufacturers have already developed interface solutions for RescueLogic to work with their systems. Call us toll-free at (866) 665-2100 for details, or e-mail info@RescueLogic.net.

Once you have selected your system type, click "System Panel Node Mapping."

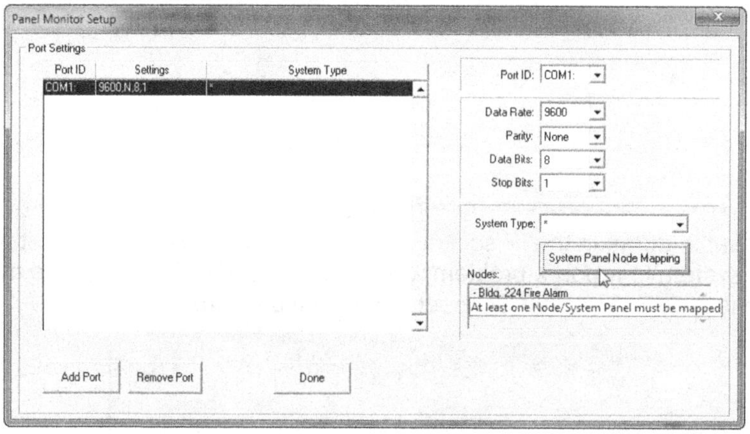

A new setup screen will open, so you can list the panels that will send information through the path. Start by highlighting the default node in the System Panel list. The "Node ID" and "System Panel" name will automatically appear in the fields on the bottom.

Highlight an item in the list. If the window is blank, click "Add Node."

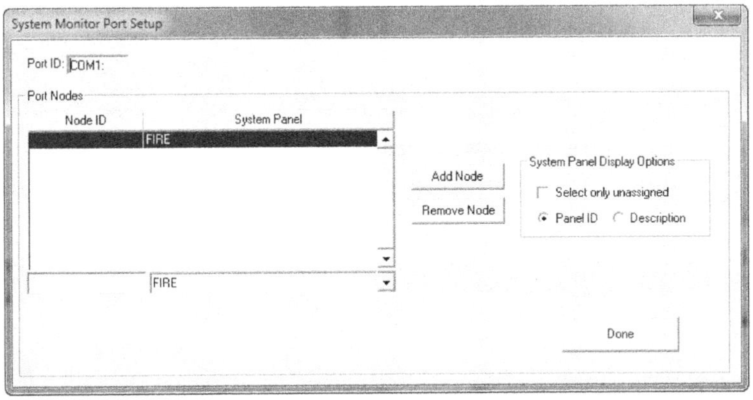

The "Node ID" must match the format that already has been established by your system manufacturer. System Panels defined earlier will appear in the "System Panel" drop-down list.

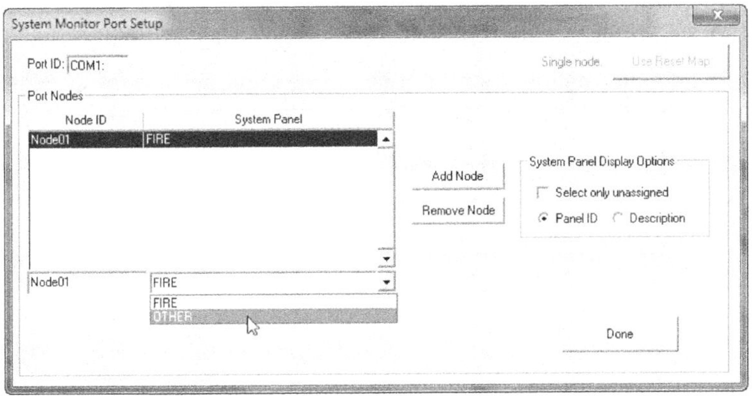

Click the "down" arrow on the System Panel field to see the list of panels you defined earlier using the "Setup System Panels" menu. Select the system panel that will send data to the new port. Repeat as needed for all panels that will report through this path. When you are finished, click "Done."

The "System Panel" column on this form allows you to see panels listed by either Panel ID or Description as you entered them in your RescueLogic database. You may choose to list panels by either Panel ID or Description. Additionally, if you have a long list of panels, you may want to check "Select only unassigned" to narrow the list as you apply the correct panel to the Node ID you've entered.

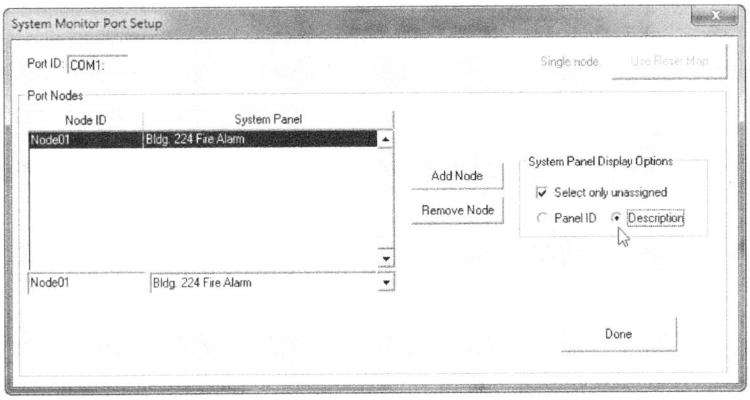

This image shows the same system panels listed by description.

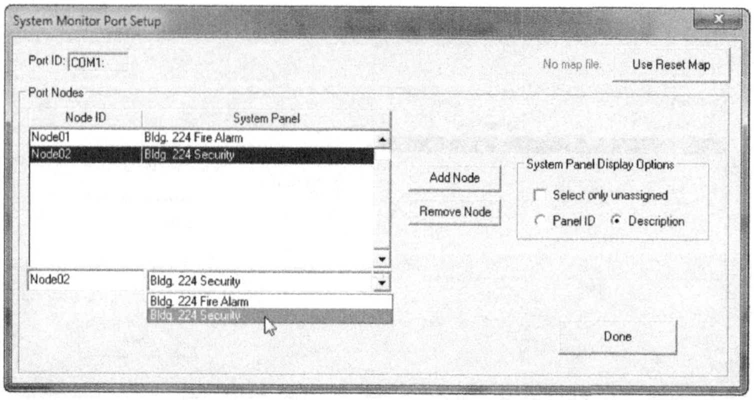

Helpful Hints: If your System Type is not capable of multiple nodes, and allows only one panel, the "Add Node" button may not be usable after you have assigned one system panel. However, the one node and system panel must be assigned to the COM port using this form.

If the new port receives data and information from more than one source or panel, click "Add Node." You will see "<New>" added to the list. Change the text to an appropriate entry, such as "Node02."

Enter ID exactly as it will be reported by each panel as a Node ID. The network message will tell RescueLogic which panel is reporting.

Reset Map

Some multi-node alarm systems allow a reset action on one panel to reset other nodes as well. The system may not report that other panels have been reset, and all devices are cleared. In order for RescueLogic to correctly represent those devices, you'll need to add a Reset Map.

Click the button on the upper right labeled Reset Map.

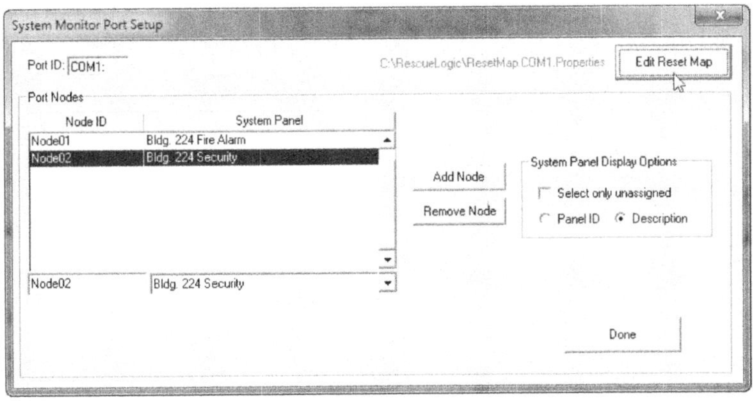

A new screen will appear that allows you to create statements about any nodes that reset other nodes (but do not report the event.) In this example, the statement means that a reset message about Node01 also performed a reset Node02.

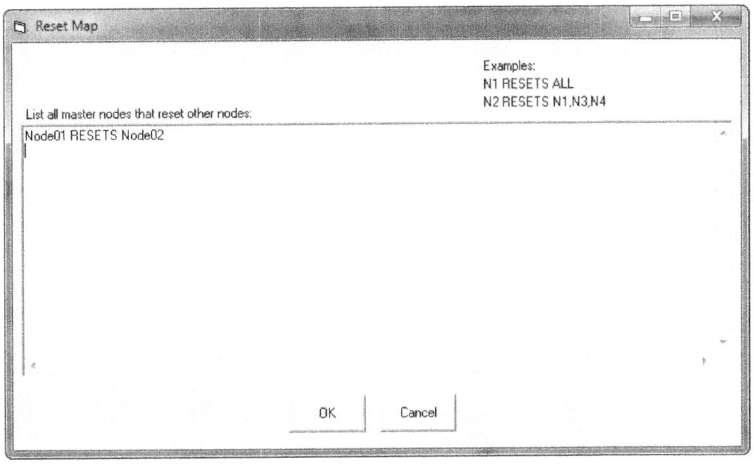

Click "OK" to go back to the Panel Monitor Setup screen. Double-check your port assignments and panel types, make corrections as needed, and then click "Done" to return to the Configuration Manager main screen.

Chapter 13: Connecting Ports and Panels

Up until this point, you have been configuring RescueLogic software for the big moment when you actually connect your alarm panels to the COM ports on your RescueLogic computer. We have worked with hundreds of RescueLogic installations, and we are happy to give you our advice about the hardware and peripherals you will use to link ports and panels. This chapter will show you how to get connected.

COM Ports

COM ports, also known as serial ports, are one of the most basic ways to get data into and out of a computer. COM ports are the "plug ins" that, in earlier times, let you attach devices, like modems and printers, to your computer. When you set up your RescueLogic system, you will use COM ports to attach your system panels to your RescueLogic computer. COM ports are usually nine-pin ports that look like this:

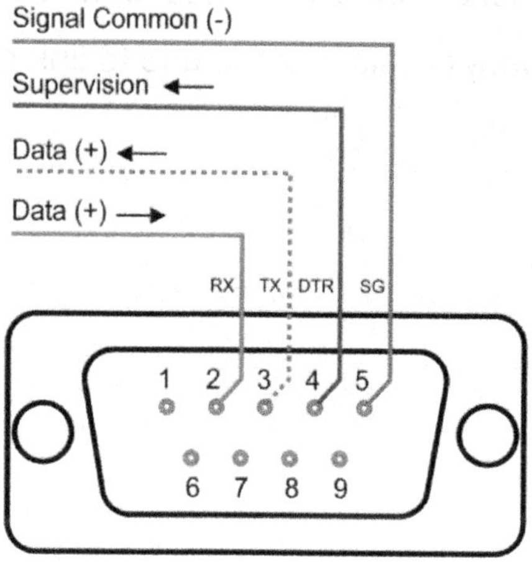

CADgraphics PC
EIA232 Port
COM1 or COM2

Most desktop computers still come with one COM port. If you need more ports to handle the panels on your site — or to connect to your printer or other peripherals — you can add them quickly and easily:

If you need to add one or two COM ports to your computer, you can plug an adaptor cable into any available USB port.

By combining TCP/IP networks with COM ports, you can add thousands of panels to your RescueLogic system.

Helpful Hint: For brand-name recommendations of currently available products and accessories, email info@rescuelogic.com.

COM Port to COM Port Connections

This diagram illustrates a COM port to COM port connection in its simplest form. Technically speaking, you only need two wires to connect your RescueLogic COM port to an alarm panel's COM port: a common wire and a transmit wire running from a panel's transmit pin to the RescueLogic receive pin. In theory, you can also connect the RescueLogic transmit pin to the alarm panel's receive pin. If your RescueLogic system is UL listed, you could transmit information from RescueLogic to the alarm panel, to control the alarms. In practice, you might actually want to double check that RescueLogic does not transmit information to the alarm panel, to ensure that your RescueLogic station is used strictly for monitoring purposes.

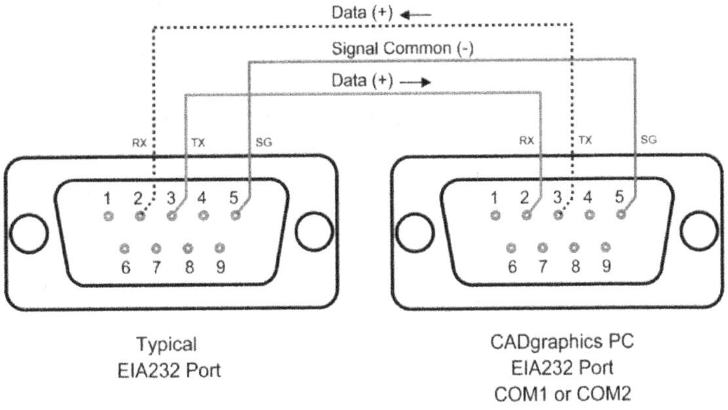

Here is a sample diagram that shows the COM port connector on a fire alarm panel, wired to the COM port on a computer.

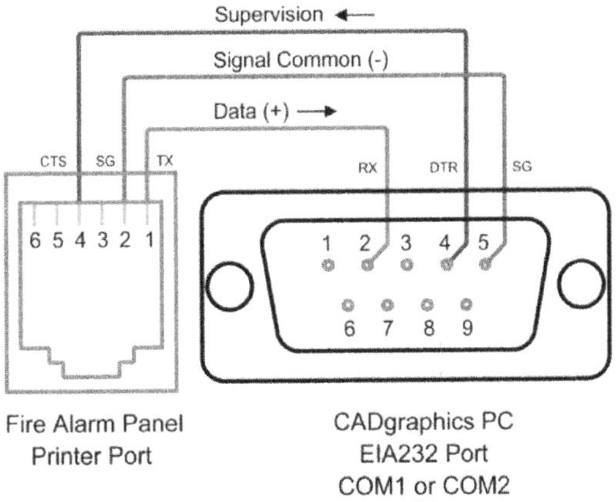

Helpful Hint: If you need to connect your RescueLogic computer to a panel that is more than 50 feet away, you can use converters that will carry the signal over twisted pair copper wire, fiber optic cable, or a wireless signal. The best method is a seriod-to-IP converter. Having an IP address makes it possible for RescueLogic to supervise the IP address and report when it is powered down or disconnected.

Connect Ports and Panels

You can use practically any combination of cabling, network switches, and wireless networking devices to connect all of the devices and panels on your site to your RescueLogic monitoring station.

You may use commonly available RS232 cable to connect the COM ports on your computer to the COM ports on your alarm panel. (The RS232 standard is one of the oldest data transfer standards still applicable to computers today. It was renamed the "EIA232 Standard" in the early 1990's.)

RS232 cable is designed to run a maximum of 50 feet. In its most basic form, it's twisted pair copper wire, consisting of a common wire, a transmit wire, and a receive wire. The three wires work together to complete an electrical circuit. The common wire is continuously connected. The transmit wire pulses to transmit a code. And the receive wire receives any information that comes in from the transmit wire of another device.

A Typical Installation

Here is a prototypical installation that includes five alarm panels. One alarm panel is directly connected to a COM port. A second alarm panel is connected to the main computer with RS485 converters, to extend the connection range. A third alarm panel uses RS232/EIA232 cable connect to a TCP/IP converter, to exchange data over the building's local area network. A two-node network of alarm panels also connects to the LAN via TCP/IP protocol.

The system also employs RescueLogic hyperlinks to connect a closed-circuit video camera and HVAC building controls.

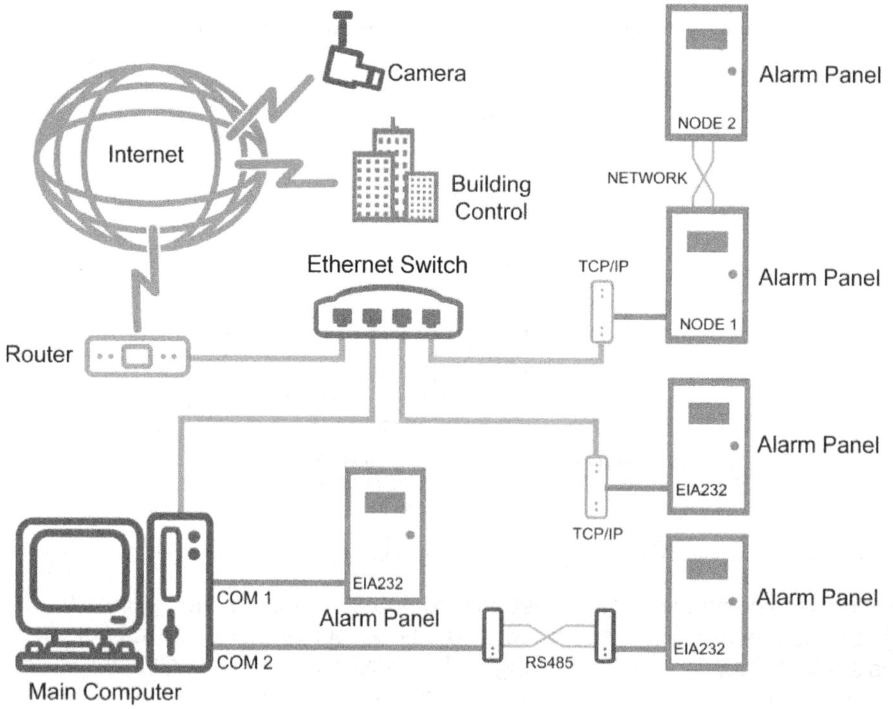

Chapter 14: System Monitor

The System Monitor program handles communication between your alarm panels and the RescueLogic database file. It functions as an interpreter: when panels send data to the RescueLogic computer through COM ports, the System Monitor program sorts that information, updates the database, and translates it into usable information that the System Watch program can display in the form of color-coded lists, maps, floor plans, and action messages. This chapter will show you how to get your System Monitor program up and running.

Customize System Monitor

The RescueLogic System Monitor program connects your fire alarm panels to the RescueLogic database file, and a text window displays data as it comes in from a control panel. If you are using more than one port on your computer, each will have its own window in the System Monitor program.

To start customizing System Monitor, go to your "Start" menu, slide the "RescueLogic" program group open, and click on "System Monitor."

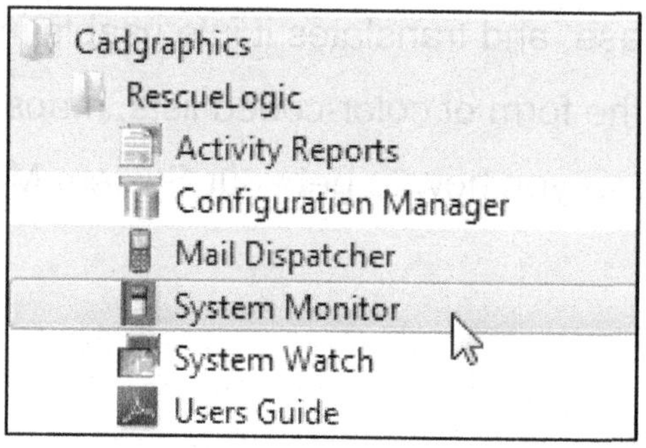

Invisible Operation

System Monitor is designed to run almost invisibly in the background, so you can concentrate on System Watch. While running in Hidden mode, these two windows may appear on the bottom right of your computer screen to provide control of the System Monitor program.

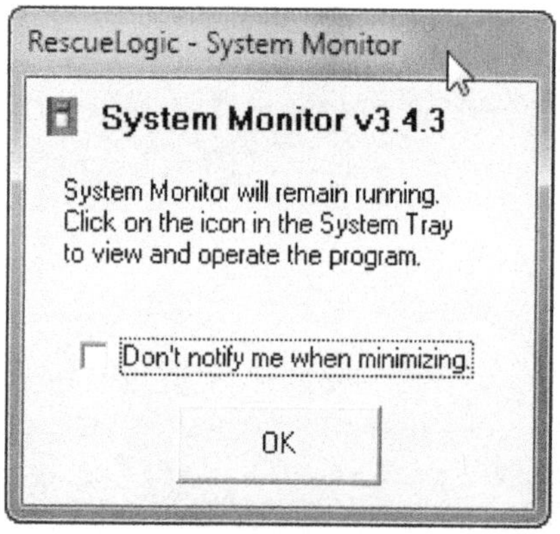

Whenever System Monitor is running in normal mode, you will see its red System Monitor icon in the program tray in the bottom of your screen. Click on the icon to open the System Monitor icon to bring it in front of other windows.

System Monitor Settings

To change the settings of the System Monitor program, choose "Setup" and "Parameters."

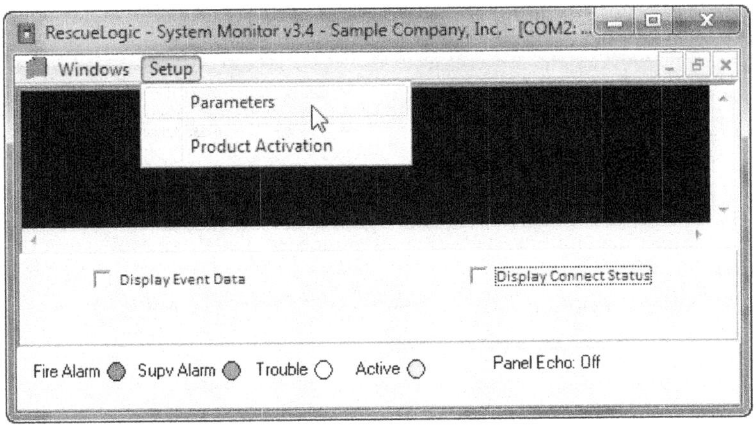

Enter your level-three password. (The default password is the number **3**.)

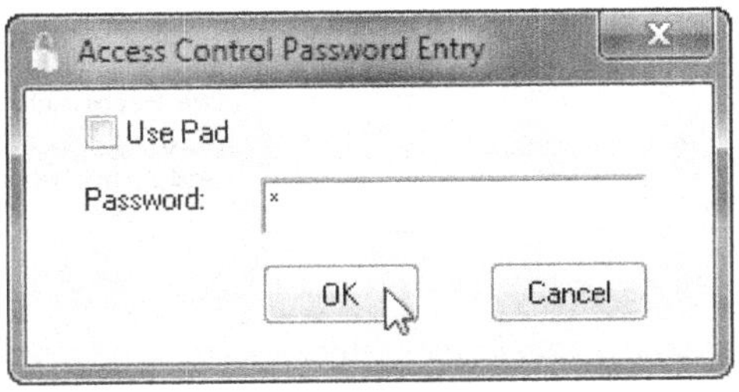

Acknowledge the warning that port monitoring will be suspended.

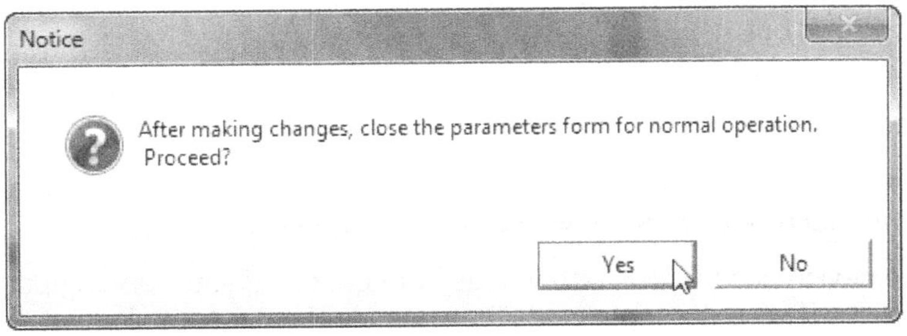

System Monitor Parameters

A “System Monitor Setup” screen will appear, and you can set the System Monitor parameters.

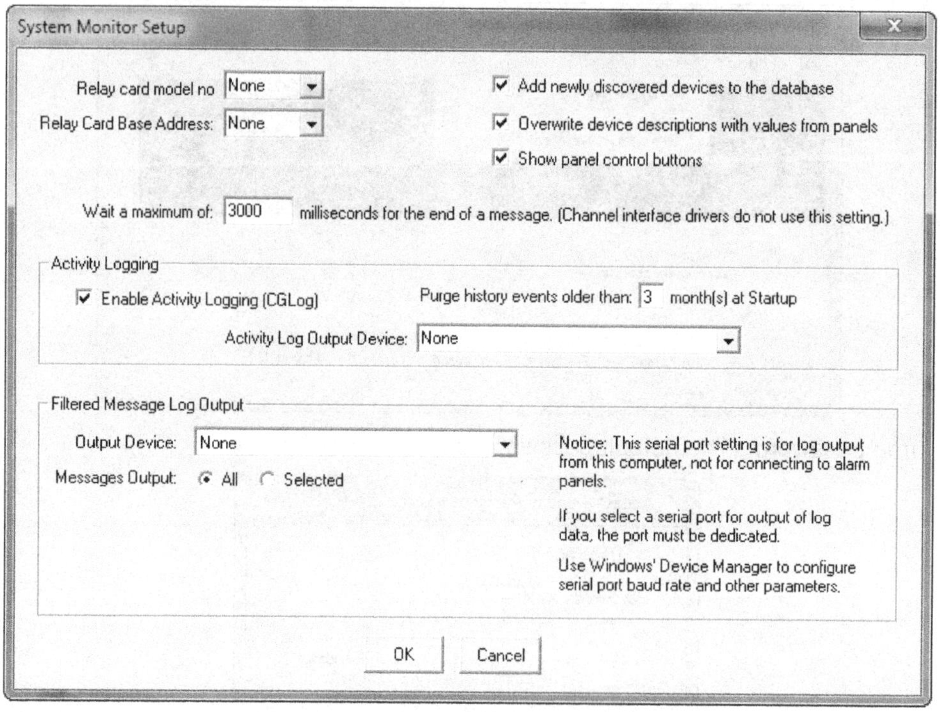

- The “Wait a maximum of:” setting is the amount of time RescueLogic will wait from the start to the end of an incoming message. Most systems do not use this setting. In UL 864 listed systems the “Message Wait Interval” may be grayed out.
- The “Relay Card Base Address” must match the hardware setting if you are using an ACL-7125 relay board on an existing system.
- Check “Add newly discovered devices to the database” if you want incoming data to create new devices in the database when a new address is reported from the panel.
- Check “Overwrite device descriptions with values from panels” if you want to update your RescueLogic database with revised device descriptions as they come in from a control panel. You may have deleted a device, for example, and then sometime later used the same address number for another device — in which case you would have updated your description. On the other hand, if you use RescueLogic to provide longer, more expanded descriptions than your alarm panel reports, you should not overwrite device descriptions. In either case, you can override the “overwrite” function. See page 70 for the screen you would use to overwrite descriptions, or not, based on device types.
- Check “Show panel control buttons” to display buttons such as “acknowledge,” “silence” and “reset” for the panel or network of panels connected to System Monitor.

Activity Logging

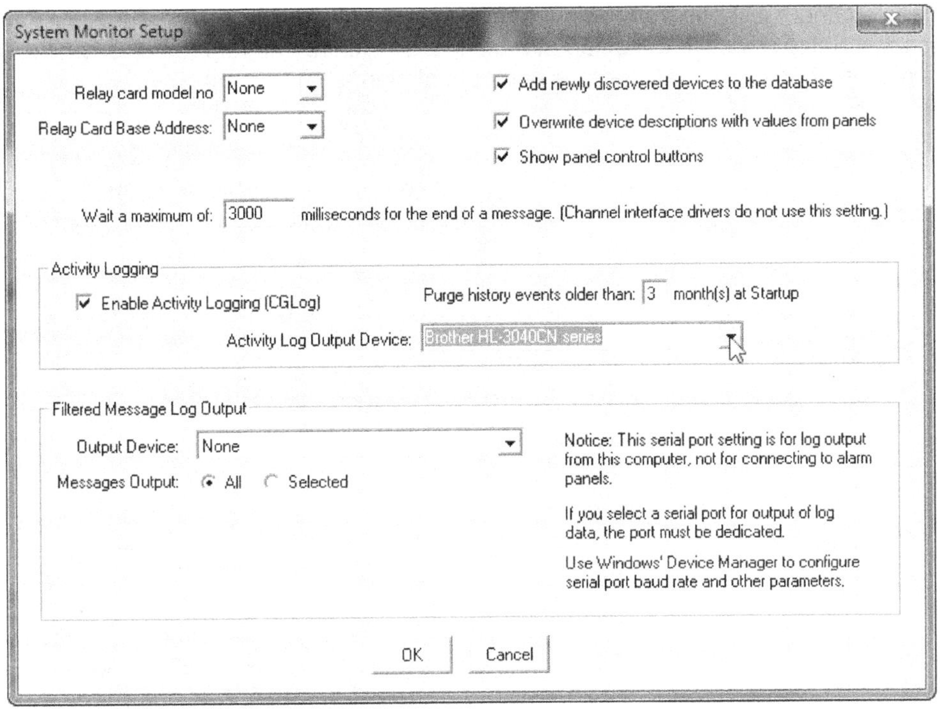

- Check "Enable Activity Logging" if you will ever want to print reports of alarm and trouble events.
- Determine how long you want to keep records of events in your system, and set the "Purge" function accordingly.
- Use the "Activity Log Output Device" drop-down menu to assign a printer to automatically print the text for events as they are reported from the alarm panels.

Filtered Messages

A filtered message is a panel message that RescueLogic forwards to another device. First, RescueLogic interprets the message, determines the condition of a device, and filters the output. For example, you may have a remote printer in an office that should only receive printouts of alarms and resets.

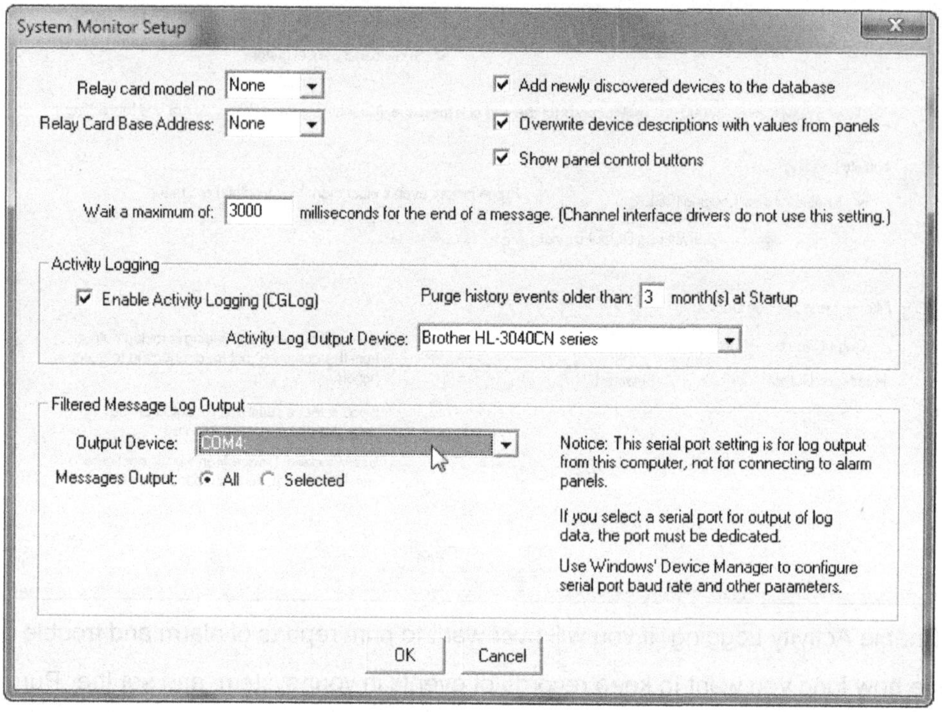

- Use the "Output Device" drop-down menu to assign a COM port to transmit, or printer to print the filtered data message as it comes in from control panels.
- Messages Output: Choose "All" if you want to print all events, or "Selected" to print just some of events.

When you are done setting up System Monitor, click "OK."

Reset Your System to Normal after an Alarm

Some panels report trouble and alarm status, but they don't report the ultimate return to normal. Security devices, for example, may continually transmit while in alarm, and then simply stop reporting when the alarm is cleared. The Quick Restore function allows selected items to be removed from active status on the System Watch list when they have been investigated and resolved. To establish the Quick Restore function on your system, start by opening Configuration Manager. Go to the "Maintenance" drop-down list and click on "Quick Restore Device List."

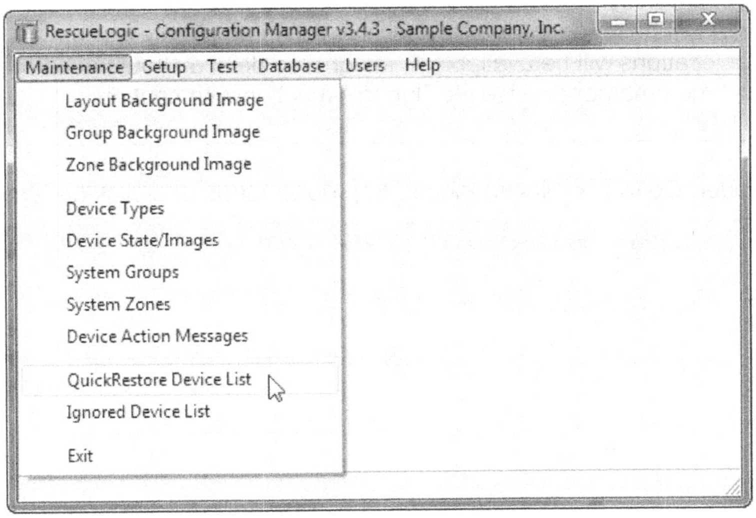

A warning will appear. Remember, any item in the QuickRestore list will be removed from active status on the RescueLogic list whenever someone clicks the "Remove Cleared" button in System Watch.

Click "OK."

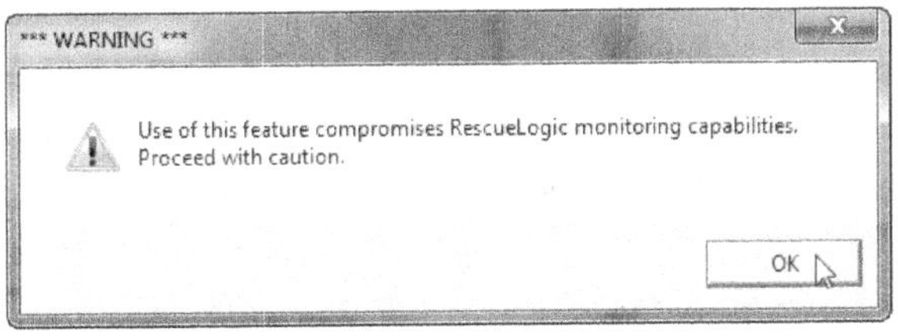

All of the devices in your system will be listed in the bottom half of the screen. Highlight any one of them and click "Add" to move it to the "Quick Restore Device List" at the top of the screen. A quick double-click will also move an item to the Quick Restore list.

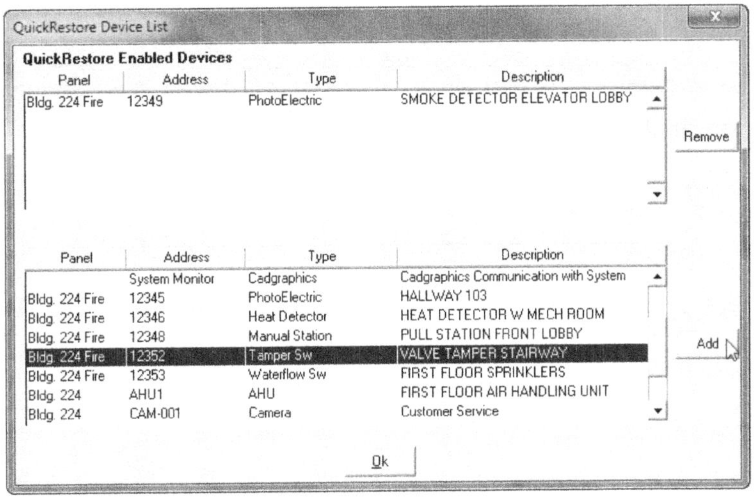

Ignore Devices

Some systems have numerous devices programmed in a complex chain that causes the control panel to report about 20 devices in trouble or alarm every time a single smoke detector goes into alarm. The number of alerts can make it hard to find the one device that is actually in alarm. To filter out auxiliary events, you may want to "ignore" some device addresses. (In UL 864-listed systems, you may not be able to use this function.)

> **Helpful Hint:** Remember, any item in the Ignore Device list will be completely ignored by RescueLogic. No color-coded lines, floor plans, or locations will be available. If an ignored device should go into trouble or alarm, RescueLogic will not report the emergency. Use the "Ignore" function with caution.

Open Configuration Manager. Go to the "Maintenance" drop-down menu and click on "Ignored Device List."

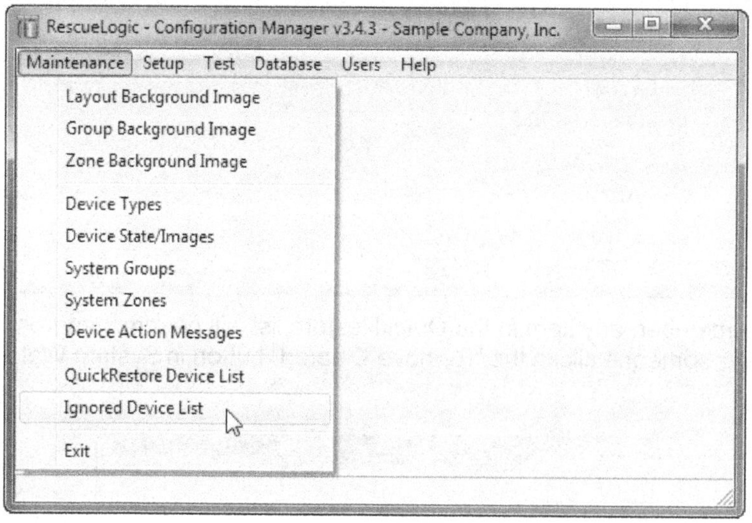

A warning will appear. Remember, RescueLogic will completely ignore any item in the list. Click "OK."

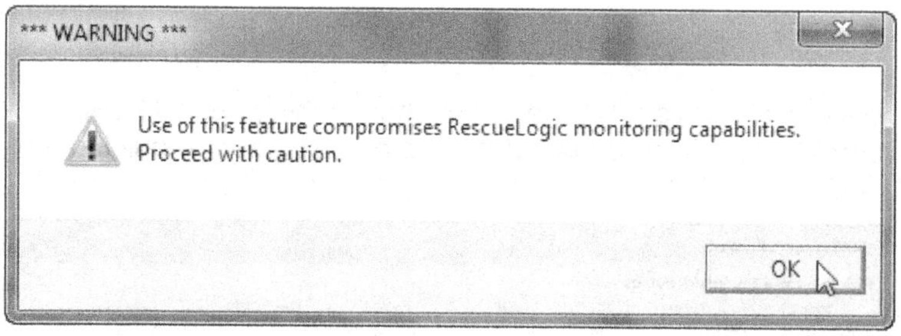

All of the devices in your system will be listed on the bottom half of the window. Highlight any one of them and click "Add" to move it to the "Ignore Devices" list at the top of the screen. (A quick double-click will also move an item to the "Ignored Devices" list.)

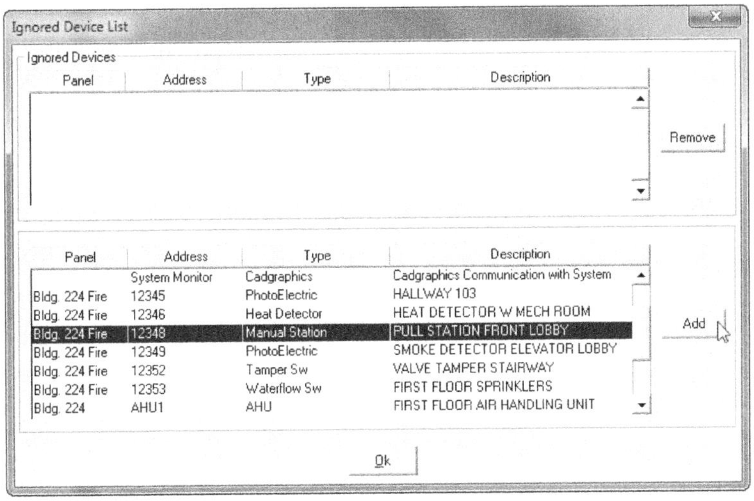

Chapter 15: Database Maintenance

You have put a lot of effort into setting up and customizing your RescueLogic system. Now is a good time to save your work by updating your database. This chapter will show you how to back up your data, compact and purge old log files, and maintain your database in smooth running order.

Back Up Your Database

Once you have finished setting up your RescueLogic system, it is a good idea to back up your database, just in case your computer's hard drive fails. You should routinely back up your hard drive — and you should also back up your database anytime you make significant changes to your system. You can start the backup process by opening Configuration Manager. Go to the "Database" drop-down menu and select "Backup."

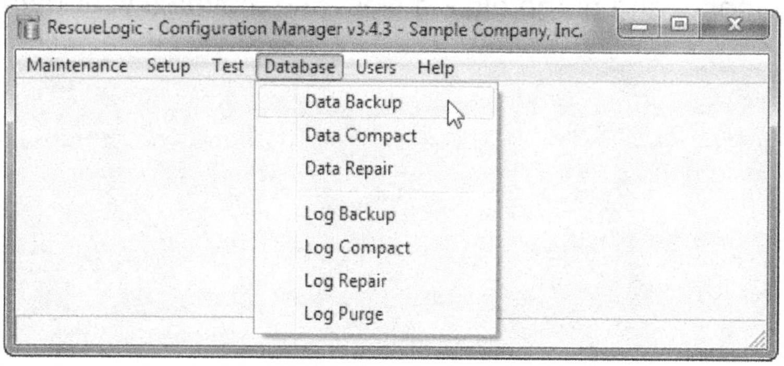

All of the data unique to your system — the Cadgraphics.mdb file — will be copied into a new file named Cadgraphics.001 in the Program Files\RescueLogic folder. RescueLogic will automatically save the last five versions of your RescueLogic.mdb file. The names will be numbered from 001 through 005. When you do a backup, all five files are cascaded to replace the earlier version. The file named Cadgraphics.005 is always the earliest backup.

Compact Your Database

Microsoft reserves some open space in your database, which grows over time. When you import and change images, that extra space can include a large amount of empty space. Before you transmit database files via e-mail or copy them onto disk or CD, you should compact them. Compacting files will not change their readability. It will simply delete unused space. To compact files, go to the "Database" drop-down menu and select "Compact."

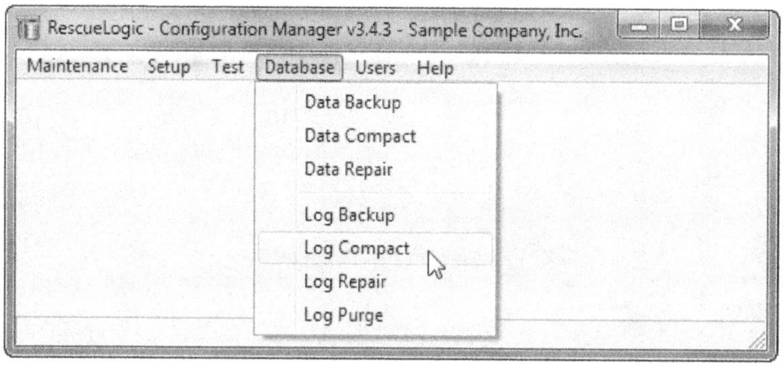

Back Up Your Log File

It may be your policy to back up your log file. When you choose "Log Backup" from the "Database" drop-down menu, the current CGLog.mdb file will be copied to a file named CGLog.001 in the RescueLogic folder on your hard drive. RescueLogic saves up to five backup files in a cascaded fashion; CGLog.005 will be the oldest.

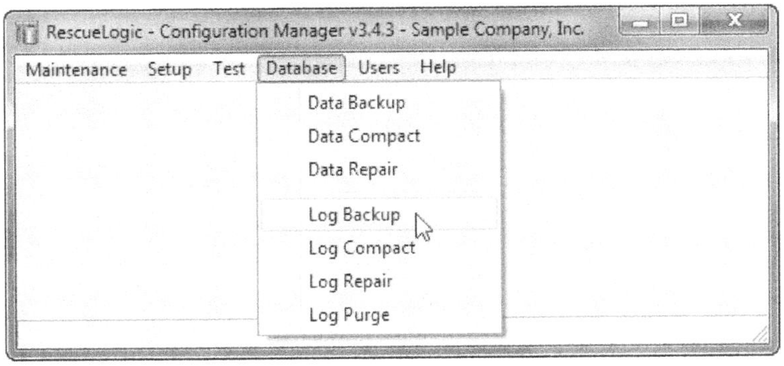

Compact Your Log File

If your RescueLogic system processes a lot of activity, your historical log file might grow large. You can use the "Log Compact" function to reduce the file size.

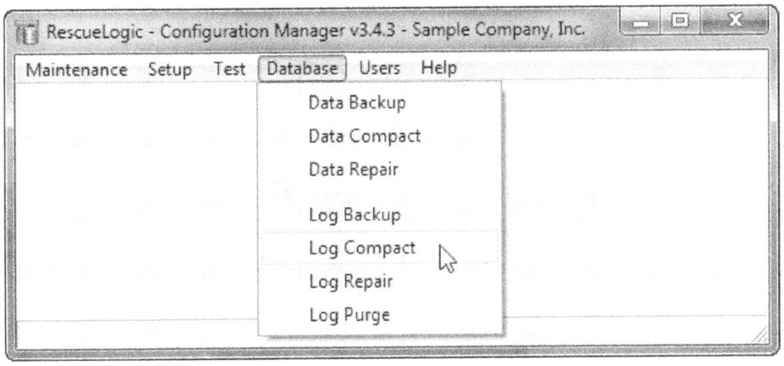

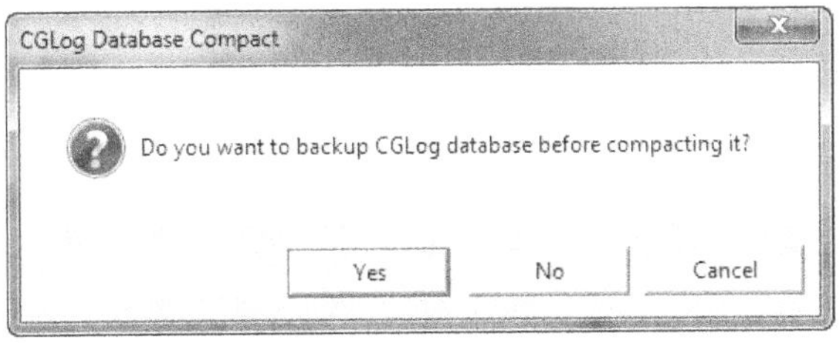

Repair Your Database Log File

If RescueLogic is trying to write to the database at the same moment that the computer is turned off, the database file might be corrupted. If you see a message that the CGLog.mdb file is corrupt, open the "Database" drop-down menu and click "Log Repair."

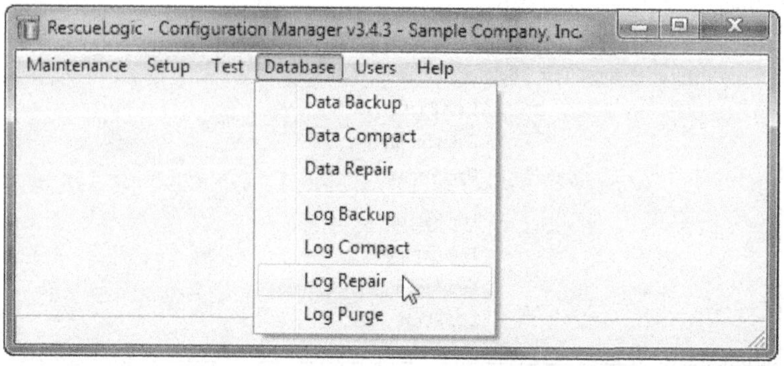

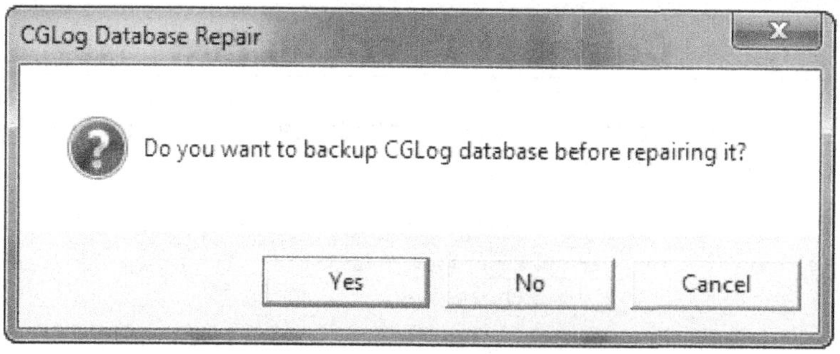

Purge Old Log Files

If your system has a lot of activity, the database file might become so large that it slows down the system. Click on "Log Purge."

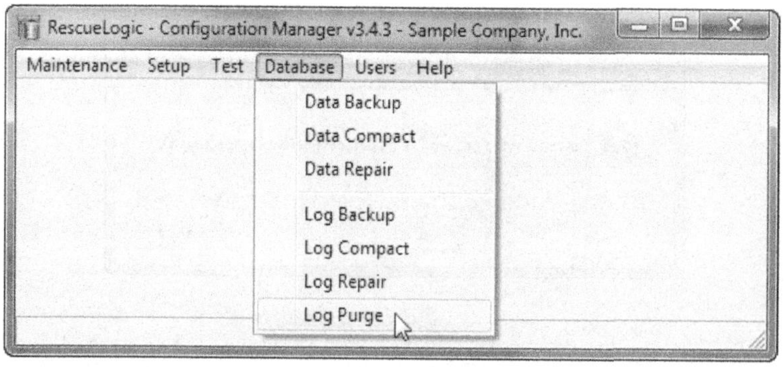

You may be asked to backup your database before you purge it.

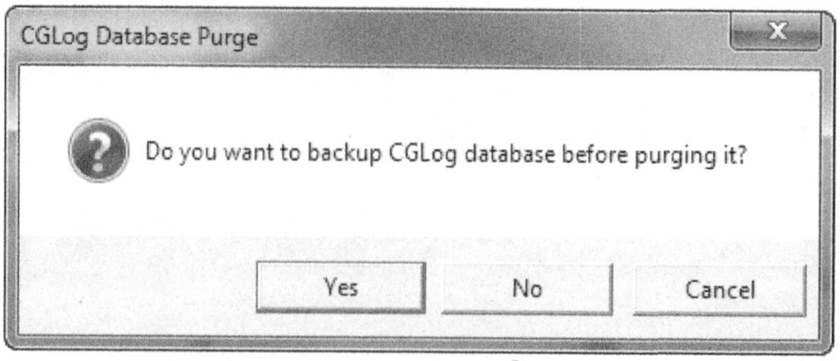

You can remove events prior to any date you select. Enter the date, and then click "OK" to purge.

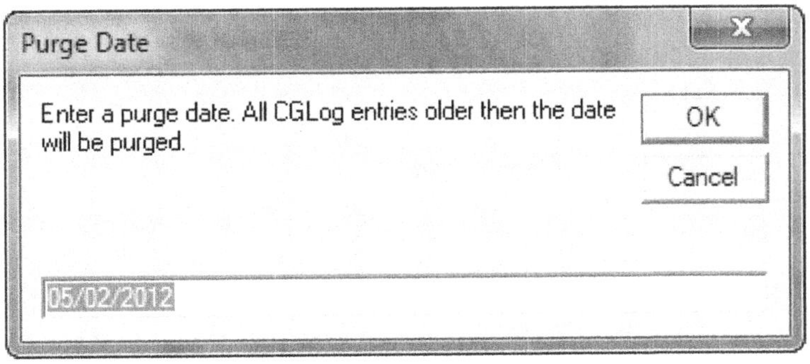

See Changes to Your Database

You can see any changes you make to your database. Start by opening Configuration Manager. Go to the "Test" drop-down menu and click on "System Watch."

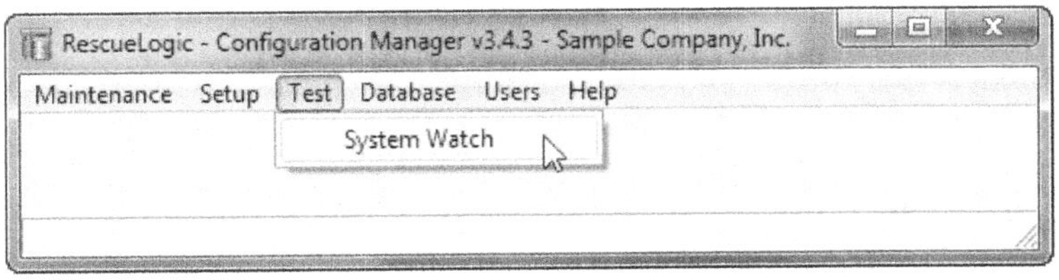

Helpful Hint: When you test, System Watch might not be online with control panels. To test the control panels themselves, exit Configuration Manager and start both the System Monitor and the System Watch program. See the System Monitor and System Watch sections of this guide for more information.

The "Test" function in Configuration Manager has a 10-minute timeout to help ensure the test version of System Watch isn't left on screen instead of the actual System Watch program.

Chapter 16: System Watch

The System Watch program responds to incoming data from every fire alarm and security device on your site, and immediately alerts your staff to alarms and malfunctions. Simple color-coding indicates at a glance whether each device is in normal standby mode, malfunctioning, or in alarm. The System Watch program also allows users to pinpoint alarm locations on floor plans and review emergency instructions for each device.

System Watch

You can customize your System Watch screen to emphasize information that is important to you. If your system is UL listed and allows you to control the fire alarm system, rather than simply monitor it, you might not be able to change all of the System Watch settings. Unavailable options will be grayed out to prevent unauthorized use.

To begin, click the "Start" button in the lower left-hand corner of your screen. Go to "Programs," slide the RescueLogic folder open, and click on "System Watch."

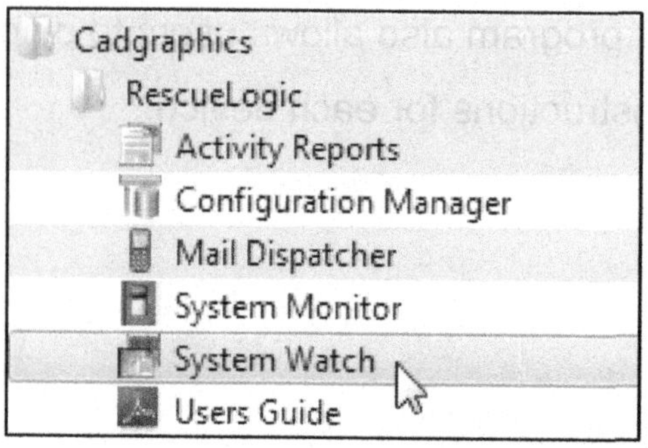

Helpful Hint: System Watch won't work if your System Monitor program isn't running, too, because System Watch receives current data from System Monitor. Make sure you open System Monitor in addition to System Watch.

The System Watch List

The System Watch list shows every alarm and device in your RescueLogic system. One "current" alarm is always the focus of attention. Alarms are sorted by priority and time.

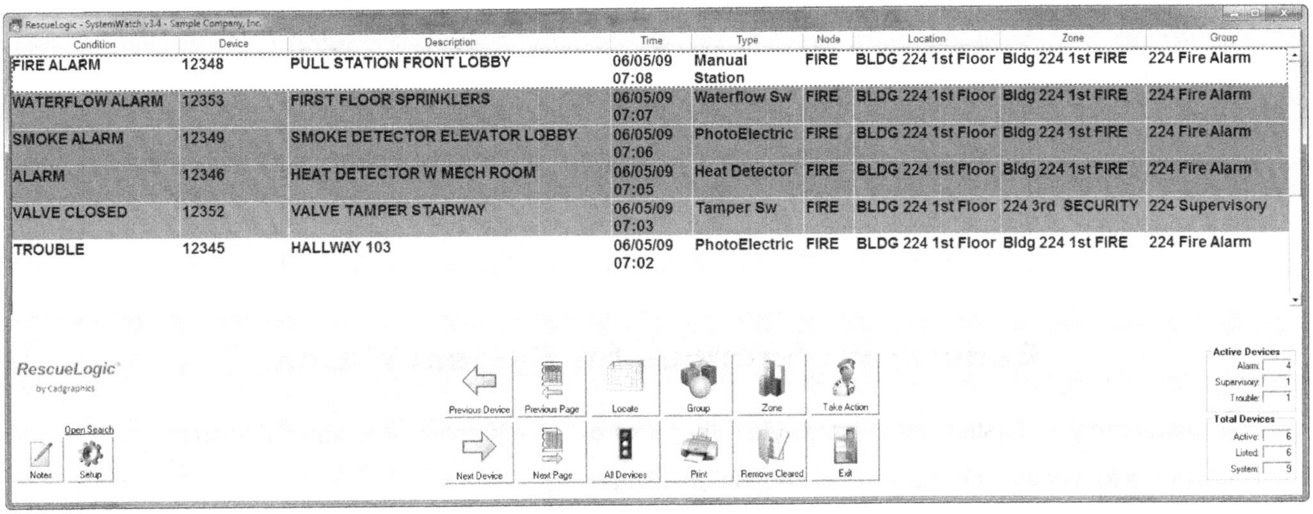

Color Coding

The System Watch screens are color coded, so you can see the status of every alarm and device at a glance. You can choose colors to fit your needs, but most users follow a fairly intuitive color scheme:

- Red: High-Priority Alarm
- Yellow: Trouble or Fault
- Green: Normal
- Violet: Tamper Switches, Firefighter's Phones
- Blue: Security, Abort, Nurse Call

Push-Button Navigation

The System Watch interface also includes navigational buttons at the bottom of the screen. The buttons are intuitive, with clear, easy-to-understand icons. There are no drop-down menus in System Watch, because they could hide on-screen information that could be crucial in an emergency.

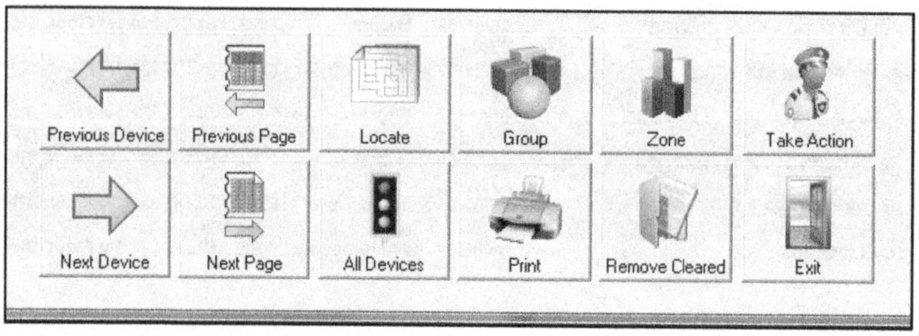

General Preferences for System Watch

You can customize your System Watch screen to reflect your own preferences. You can, for example:

- Use the font of your choice for "Take Action" messages.
- Allow System Watch to minimize on screen. (It will not minimize by default.)
- Print graphics, no matter what type of printer you have.
- Display new devices that have not yet reported trouble or alarm.
- Choose whether to update the date and time when a device is restored, or to leave it set to the time of the alarm.
- Choose to sort your list by time or by alarm priority with fire alarms at the top of the screen, supervisory alarms below, and troubles beneath. UL 864 Listed systems will be preset to sort by alarm priority.
- Automatically locate devices on maps and floor plans.
- Display a "screen saver" image when all devices are in normal mode.
- Show the "Acknowledge" button in System Watch.
- Show the "Silence" button in System Watch.
- Show the "Reset" button in System Watch.
- Require a password to Acknowledge, Silence, or Reset alarms.
- Allow hyperlinks to replace "Take Action" messages when a user clicks on a device in alarm or trouble. (The "Take Action" button always displays the Take Action message screen.)

To get started, click the "Setup" button in the lower left-hand corner of the System Watch list window.

System Watch Settings

Once you click on the System Watch "Setup" button, the "System Watch Setup" window will open.

You might need to enter a password. The default password is the numeral "3."

The first tab, "Settings," outlines a number of options for the System Watch screen, regarding general settings, graphics settings, and colors.

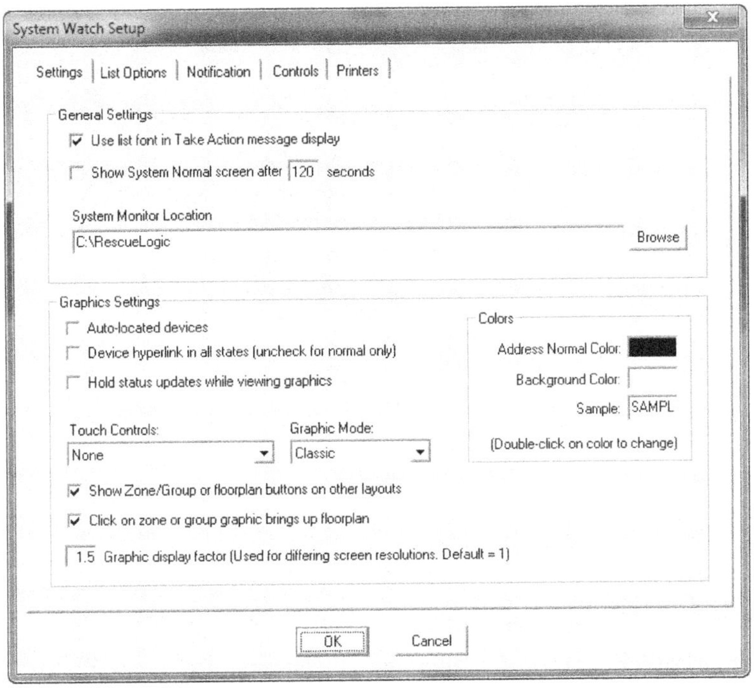

Look at the "General Settings" options. We recommend that beginners use the same font for their device lists as for their "Take Action" emergency messages — so check the first box.

Also check "Allow System Watch to Minimize." It is a handy feature to use when you're setting up your system.

Finally, look at the "Colors" section. Double-click on either the "Address Normal Color" or the "Background Color" to try new combinations. Black and white work well for most users.

When you are through with the "Settings" tab, click on the "List Options" tab.

System Watch List Options

Now that you can see the "List Options" screen, set your list options as shown, including a check mark for "Save Column Widths on Exit."

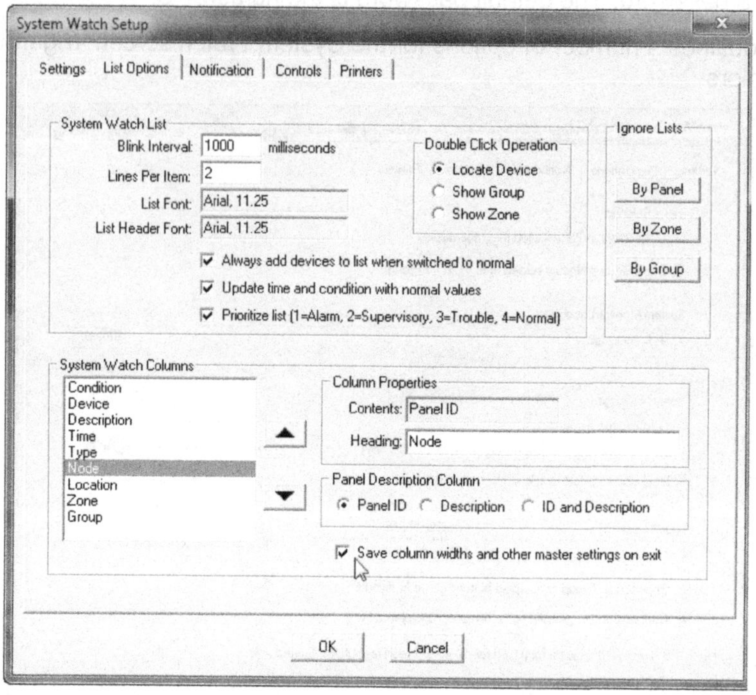

The "Blink Interval" setting determines how fast the "current" device will flash on screen.

"Lines Per Item" controls the height of each line of text used to list a device. If you choose to use multiple lines of text, the lines will wrap automatically.

If you want to change the list font, you'll see this familiar interface:

System Watch Columns

When you are in the “List Options” tab window, you can change the order and the headings of your System Watch columns. Simply highlight any line in the “System Watch Columns” field.

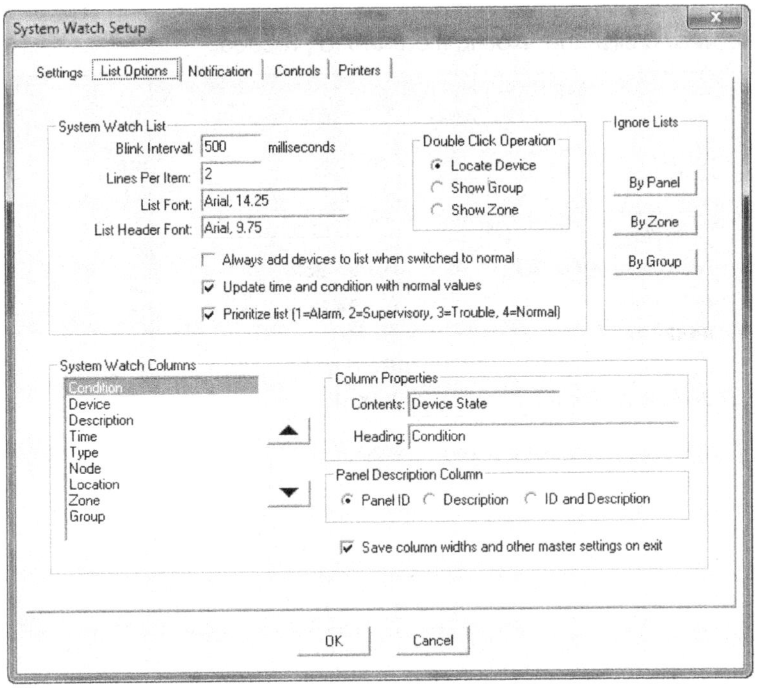

Use the up-and-down “System Watch Columns” arrows to change the order of the columns.

Change the column heading in the “Heading” field under “Column Properties.”

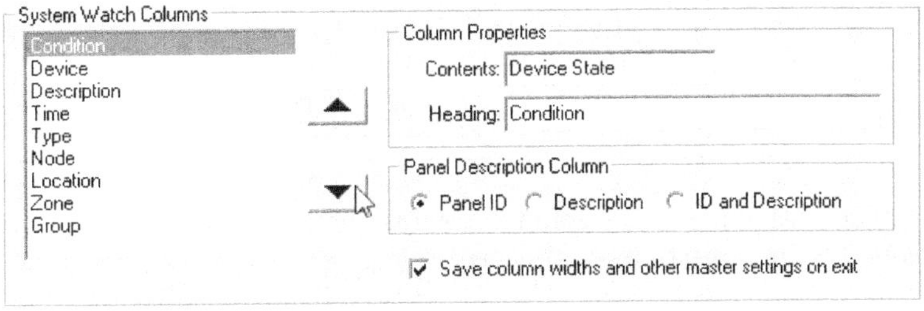

The “Panel Description Column” may contain the panel ID, the panel description, or both. These are the values that were added in the “System Panels” part of the database.

If you want to change the default column width for System Watch lists, make sure the check box at the bottom of the form is filled in. (Please note, though, that you will actually change column widths permanently from within Configuration Manager’s test mode.)

System Watch Fonts

To change the font for your System Watch list, double-click in the "List Font" and "List Header Font" fields. You may use any standard Windows font you like. Choose new fonts for both your list items and your headers, and then click "OK" to close the "Font" window and return to the "List Options" screen. Then go back to the top of the System Watch Setup window and click the "Notification" tab to proceed.

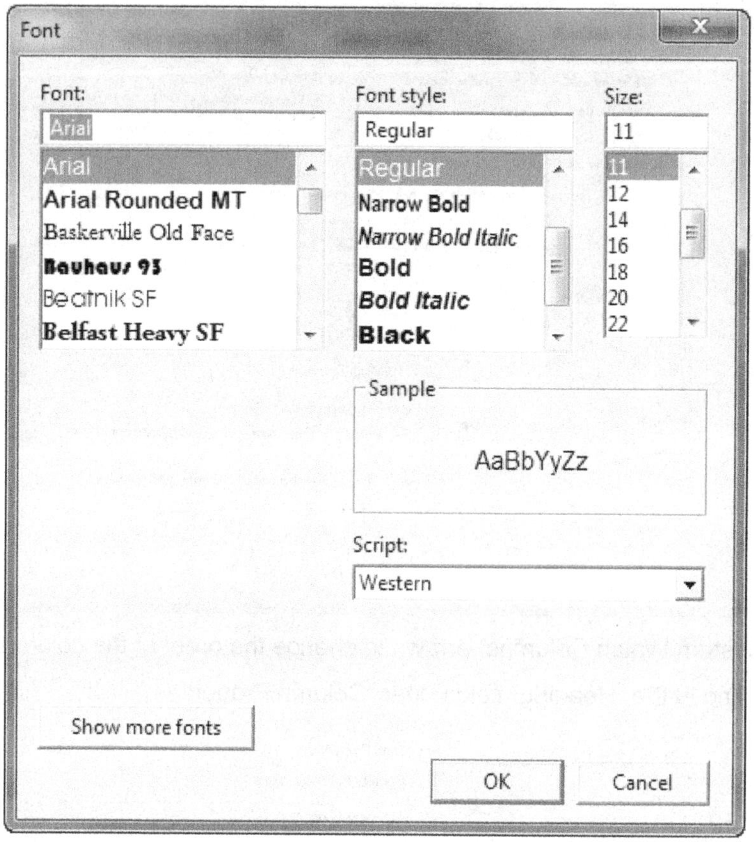

Helpful Hint: You might notice that you are not able to use this Window to choose font colors. That's because color settings are determined by the state of each device.

Ignore by Panel

If you use a single RescueLogic station to monitor alarms from a number of buildings, you can set some stations to completely ignore devices from other buildings. The Administrator password is required to set lists of ignored items. A station may be set to ignore Panel, Zones, and Groups of devices.

To configure a station to ignore a panel and all its devices, click the "By Panel" button, and enter the Administrator password.

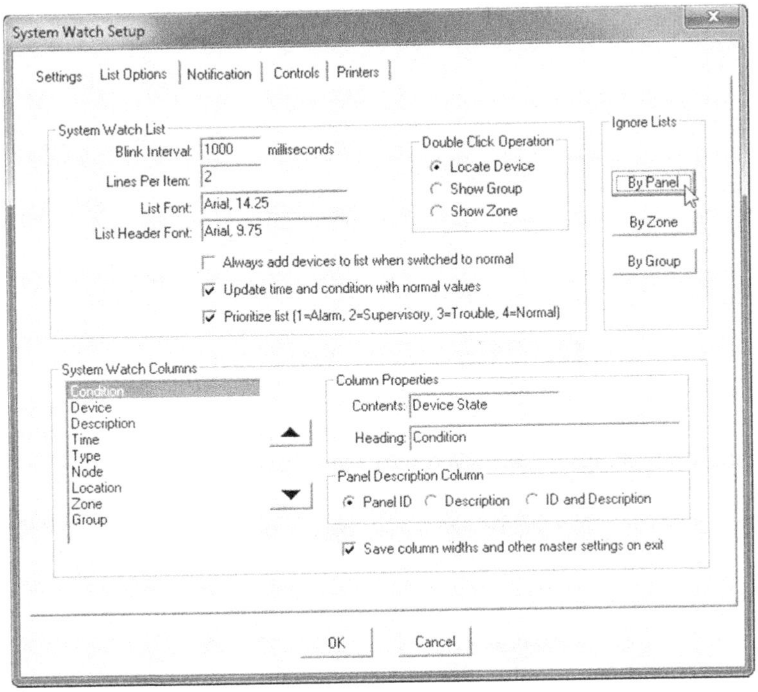

The next screen shows a list of System Panels in a column on the right, and a blank list of Ignored System Panels on the left.

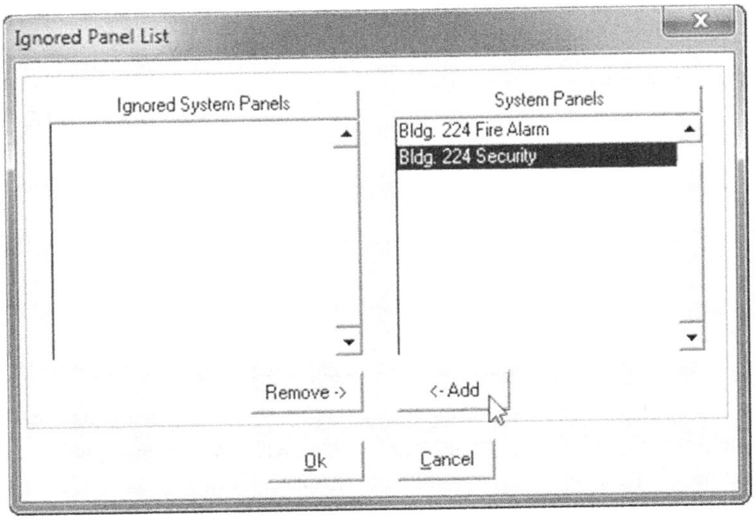

Highlight a System Panel, and click the Add button to see it move to the left-hand column, indicating that it will be ignored. Click "OK" when you are finished selecting panels to be ignored.

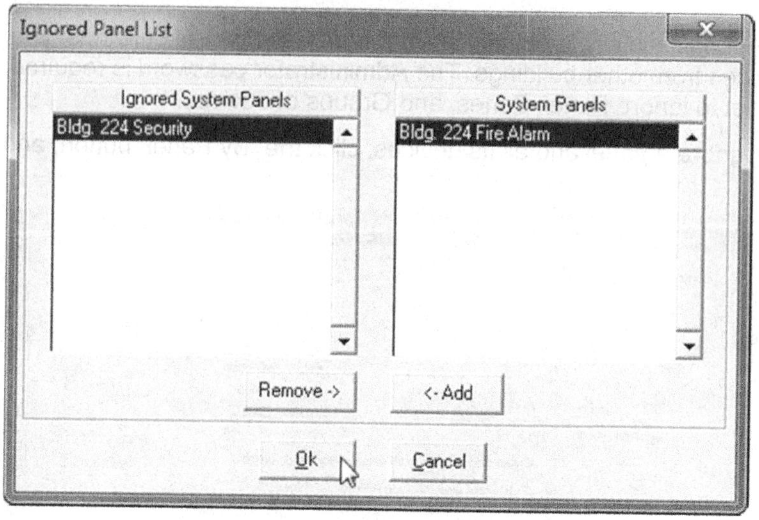

Notification Options

Click the "Notification" tab to set notification preferences. For this example, click the "Standard Beep" option and check the "Continuous Alert," and "Bring System Watch to Top" boxes.

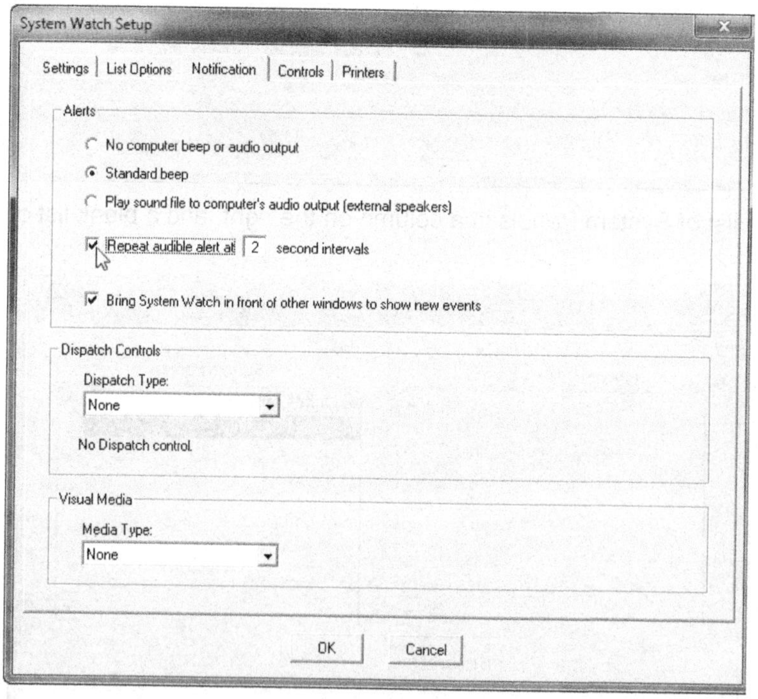

Use the Notification Alert section to choose whether your system will play an audible alert during trouble and alarms. UL 864 listed systems will be preset for continuous, audible alert.

To hear an audible alert, select a standard beep or WAV sound files.

To force RescueLogic' System Watch screen to come to the forefront on a new alarm or trouble (interrupting other Windows programs) check the option "Bring System Watch to Top."

Click "OK" to close the System Watch Setup window and see the changes you've made to your System Watch list.

Control Options

You will use the “Controls” tab section to allow selected levels of control for each System Watch station.

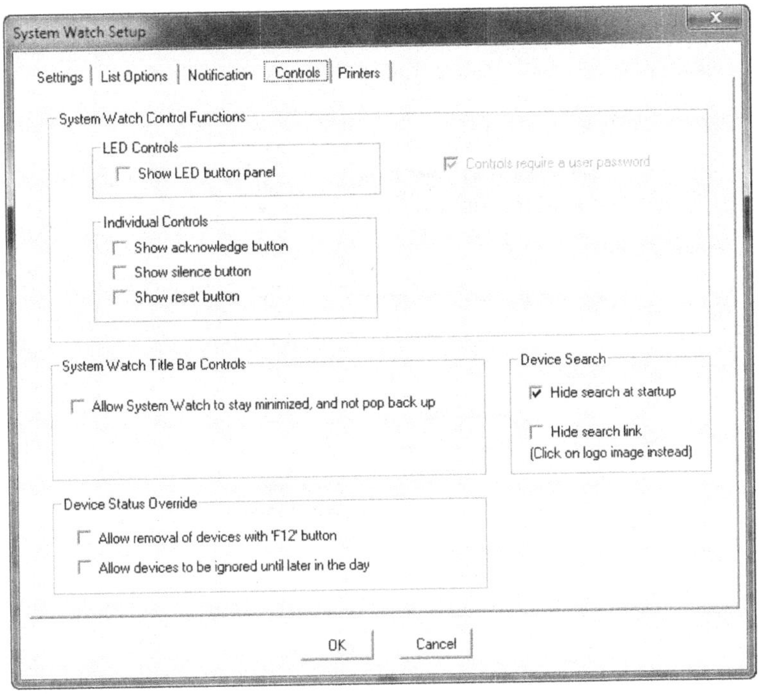

If you are an expert user, you may want to check “Allow System Watch to stay minimized.” You’ll probably want to minimize the screen while you set up your system. When you’re through setting it up, however, uncheck the box to ensure that your RescueLogic computer will display full-screen as a monitoring station.

The “System Watch Control Functions” relate to UL-listed systems. Leave them unchecked.

The Device Search control allows you to hide the search window, which will leave more screen space for the main System Watch screen. An optional Search link can be shown as a reminder of that search function. In any case, the Device Search window will appear if the user clicks on the system logo.

Printer Options

You will use the "Printers" tab section to set your printing preferences.

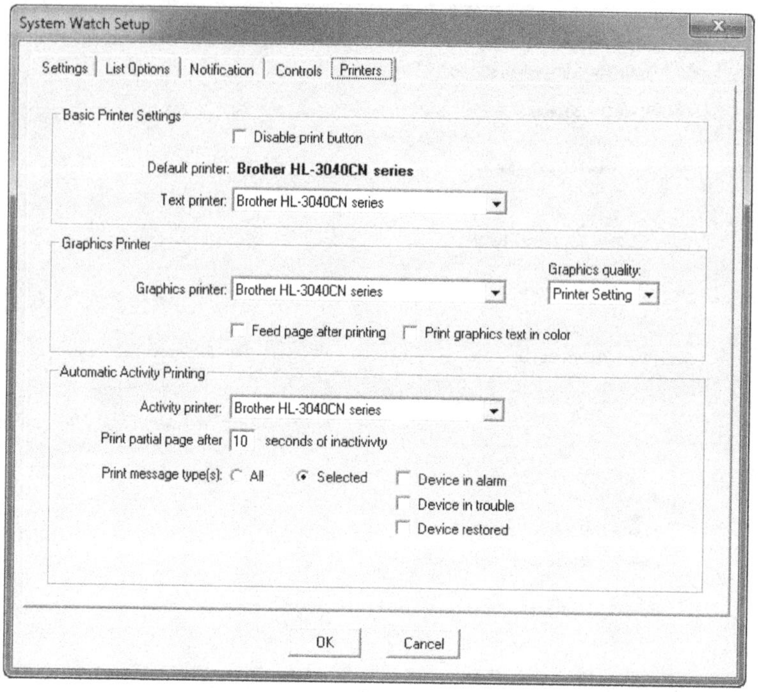

If your RescueLogic computer isn't connected to a printer, you may want to check "Disable print button" as a reminder that nothing will print by pressing the button.

The Basic Printer Settings allow you to choose the printer that will receive text-based printouts such as the device list and reports.

The Graphics Printer option selects the printer that will print floor plans, zones, and group graphics screens. (It may be the same printer as the text printer.)

Automatic Activity Printing determines which printer will print event logs, which can often be lengthy.

When you have set up your printing preferences, click "OK" to close the System Watch Setup window and see the changes you have made to your System Watch list.

Active Devices

When you are looking at the System Watch list, you can toggle between two modes: "Active" and "All."

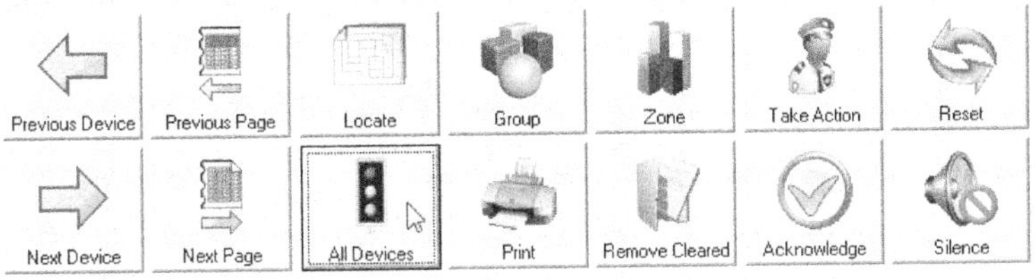

The active list shows the devices that requires attention, either because they are malfunctioning or in alarm. Click the "Active" button to see the devices that need attention. By default, they will appear with the newest items reporting alarm or trouble at the top of the list.

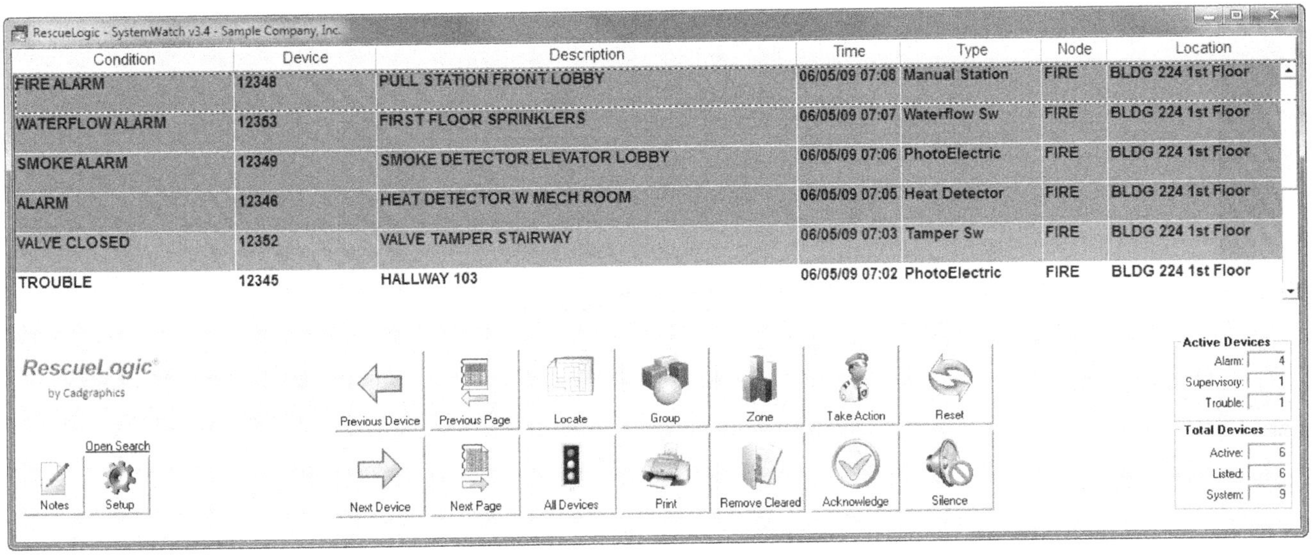

All Devices

When all devices are in normal condition, the active list will be empty. (The screen will either be gray or show a "System Normal" screensaver image.) To see a list of every device in a system, click "All Devices." Those that are in normal mode will be listed in green. You can click the "All Devices" and "Active Devices" button to toggle back and forth between the two screens.

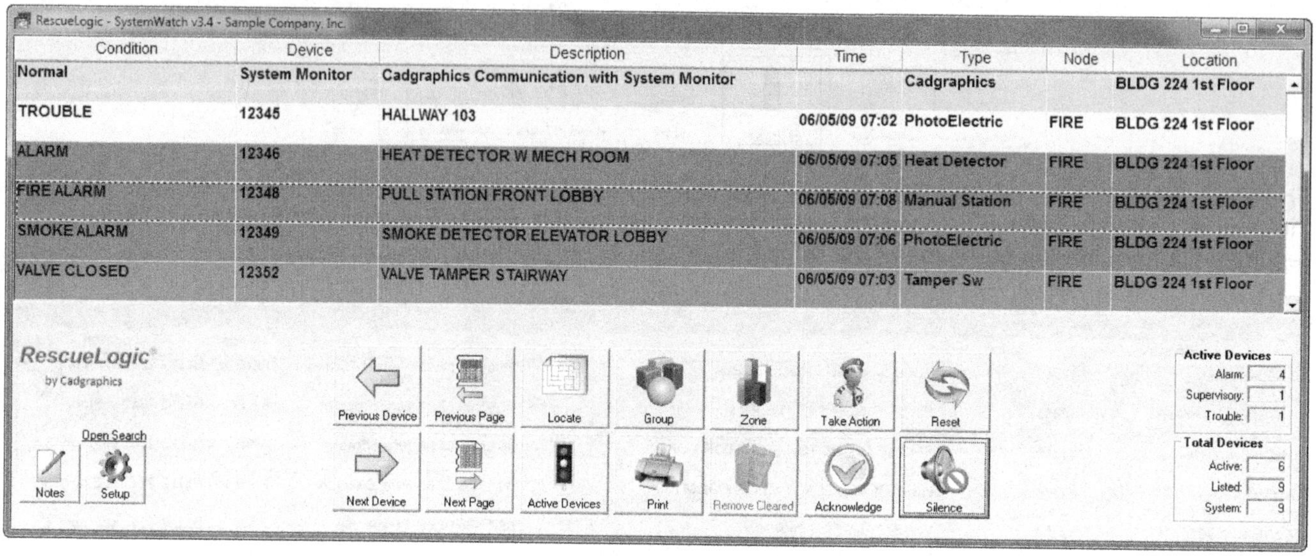

Locate Devices

When you click on any device in a list and click the "Locate" button, you will be able to see it on a map or floor plan of your site. You can click on any device in any System Watch list to locate it on a background map or floor plan.

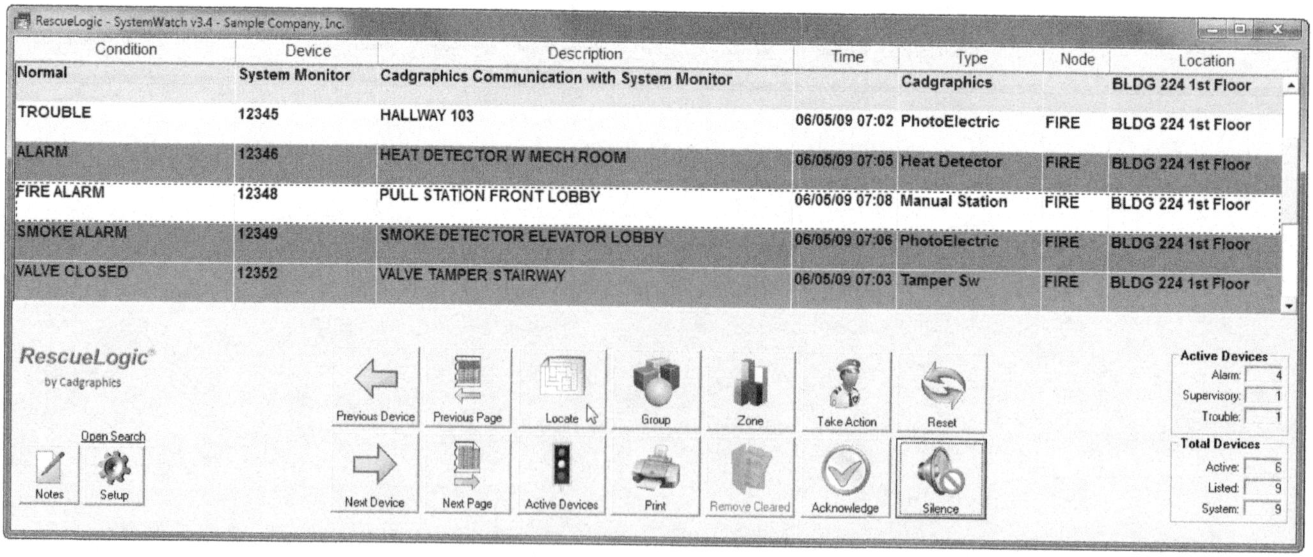

Locate Maps and Floor Plans

When you click "Locate," you will automatically switch from the System Watch list view to the System Watch graphics window. The graphics window shows the floor plans of your site and all active devices. A blinking box now surrounds the device that was highlighted in the list.

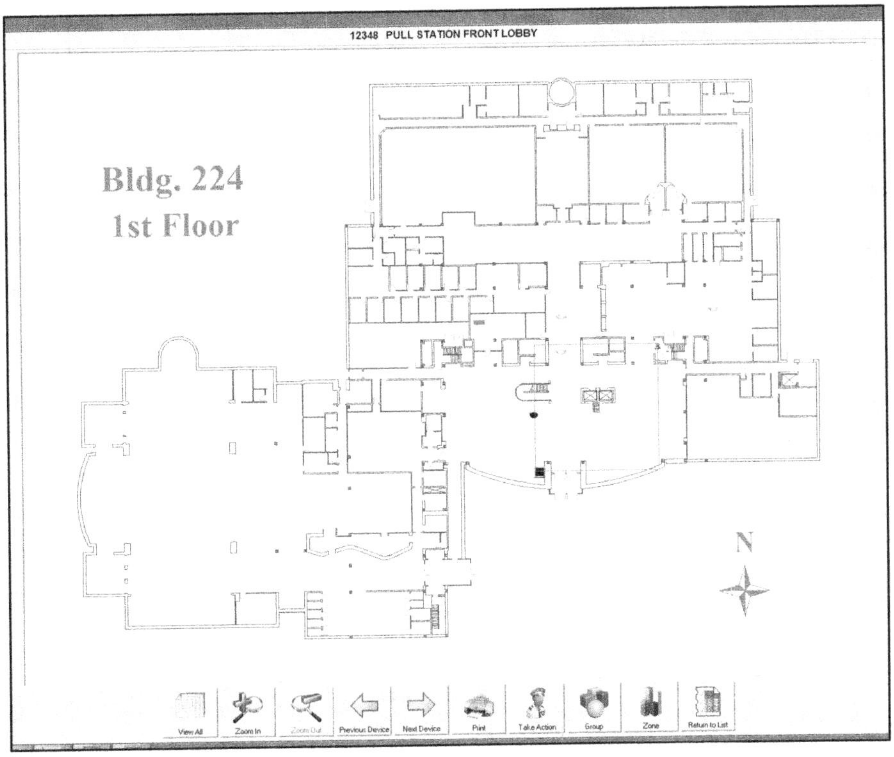

Zoom In and Zoom Out

You can click the "Zoom In" button for a closer look, or "Zoom Out" to see more of the floor plan. You can also click "View All" at any time to see the full floor plan. Once you have zoomed in as much as possible, the "Zoom In" button will be grayed out.

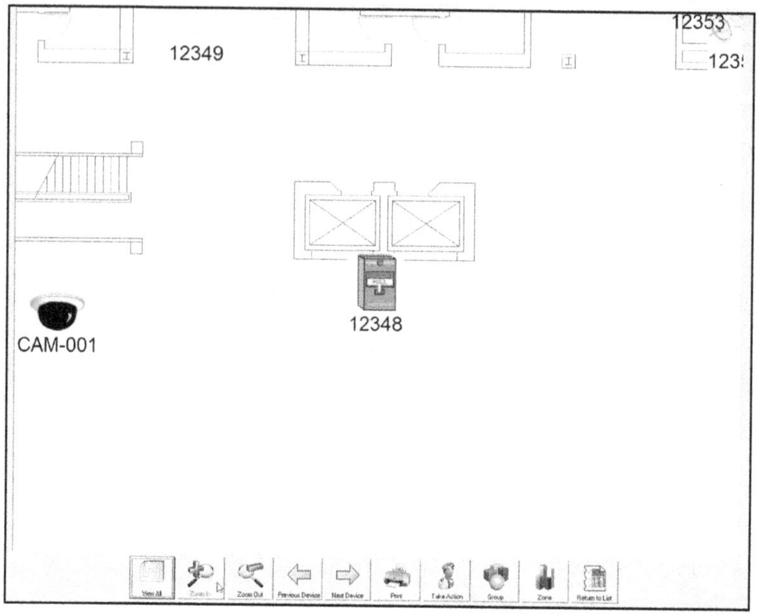

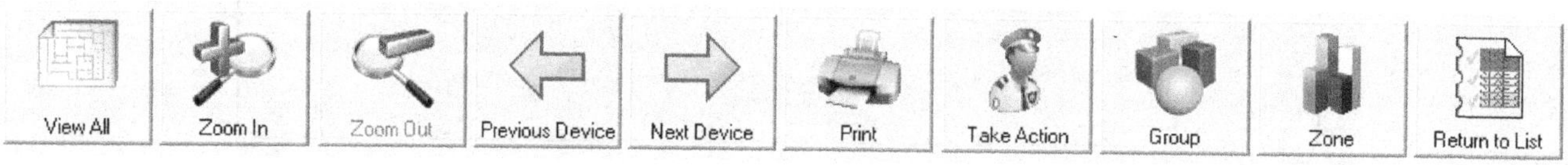

View All

Click "View All" to display the full floor plan again.

Previous Device and Next Device

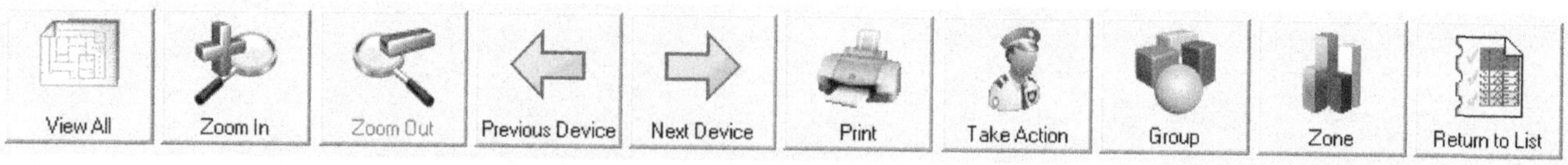

Use the "Previous Device" and "Next Device" buttons to review the current state of each alarm in the System Watch list. You can also click each device in the list, or use the arrow bar.

The "Previous Device" and "Next Device" buttons are also used on the "Layout Background" screen to highlight each alarm with a blinking box. The "Current Device" is displayed at the top of the screen.

Once you have returned to the list, you can click "Previous Device" and "Next Device" to continue working your way through alarms and devices that need attention.

Print

The "Print" button will send the information on the current screen to your printer.

Take Action Messages

Whenever devices go into trouble or alarm, they will automatically appear on the RescueLogic monitor, either on the System Watch list or on a floor plan. Click the "Take Action" button or click on any active device for the customized "Take Action" message.

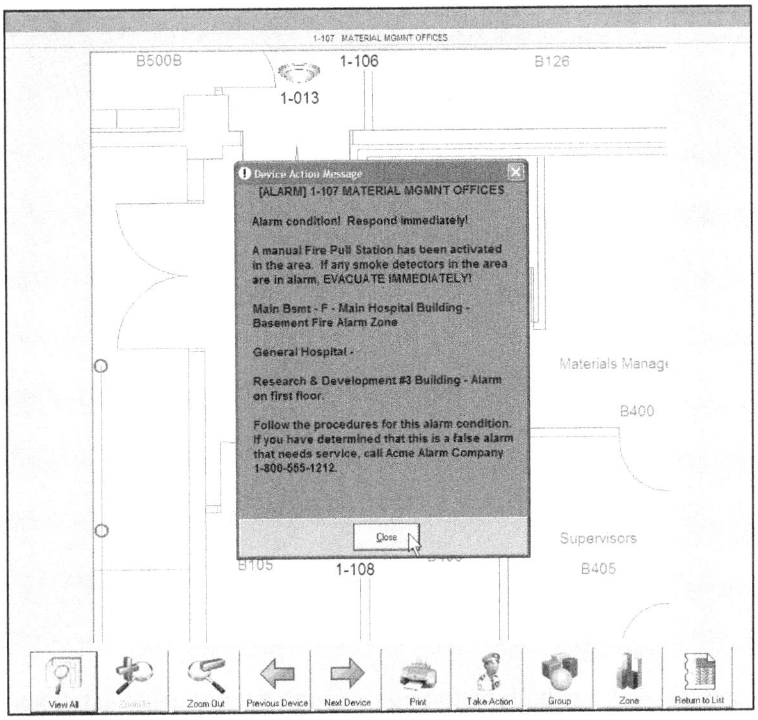

"Take Action" messages explain each alarm and give specific emergency instructions. When you are done reading the instructions, click the "Close" button at the bottom of the window.

Groups and Zones of Related Devices

Use the "Zone" button to view zones of related devices, usually within a specific area. The System Watch displays the zone name for each device.

Use the "Group" button to view groups of similar or related devices, usually by a category of device type. The System Watch displays the group name for each device.

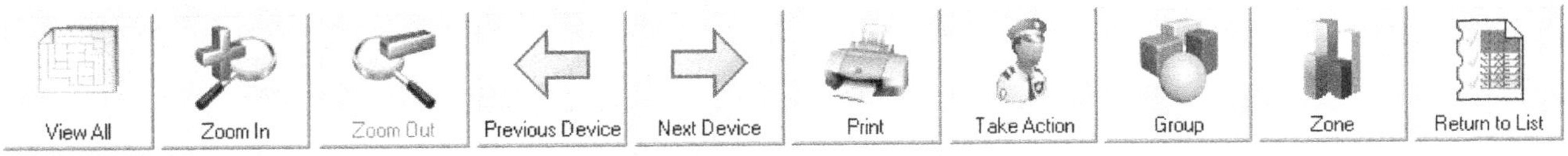

Return to List

After viewing the graphics, return to the System Watch list by clicking "Return to List."

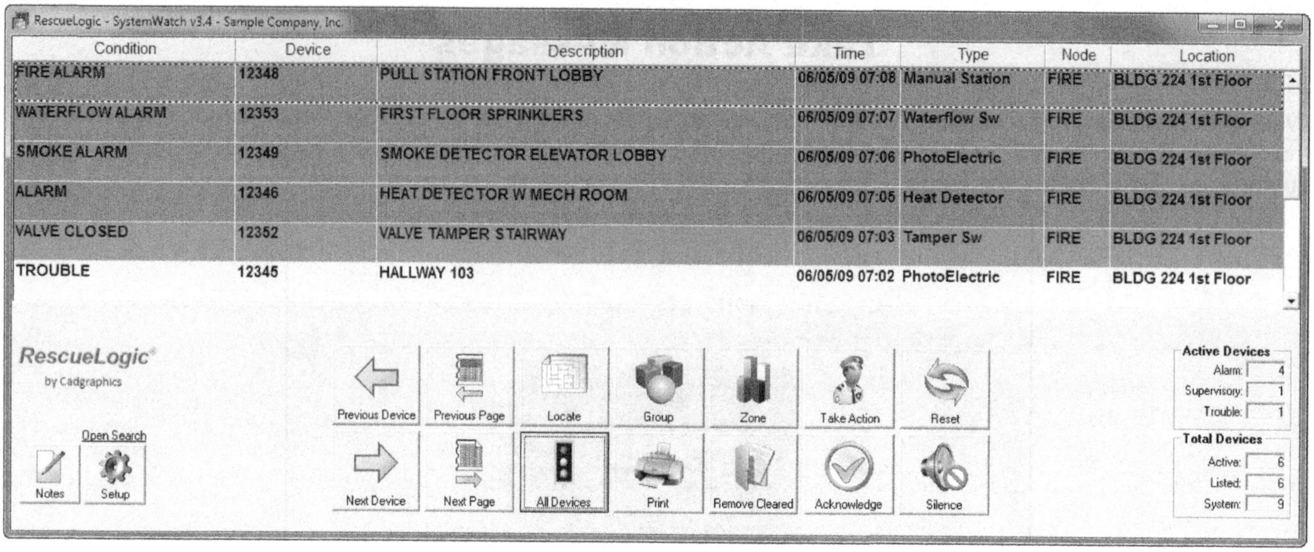

Previous Page and Next Page

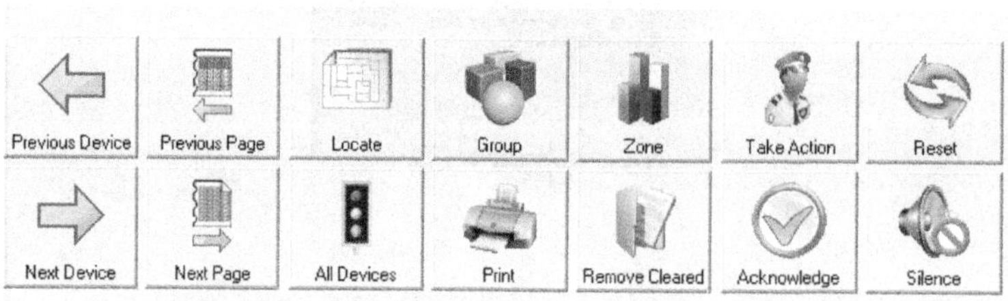

Use the "Previous Page" and "Next Page" buttons to page through the complete list. If you are viewing all devices, you will see every alarm and device in the system.

Remove Cleared Devices

When devices malfunction or go into alarm, they will stay on the System Watch active list — even after they are restored to normal — until you click the "Remove Cleared" button.

The fact that an alarm stays in the system until you click "Remove Cleared" gives you time to investigate a situation, even if an alarm automatically clears itself from the system. Cleared alarms change to green and the condition column changes to reflect the current status.

Optional System Watch Features

You can add even more features to your System Watch program: Reset, Acknowledge, and Silence. (These features might not be available unless your system is UL listed.)

To add the features, click "Setup."

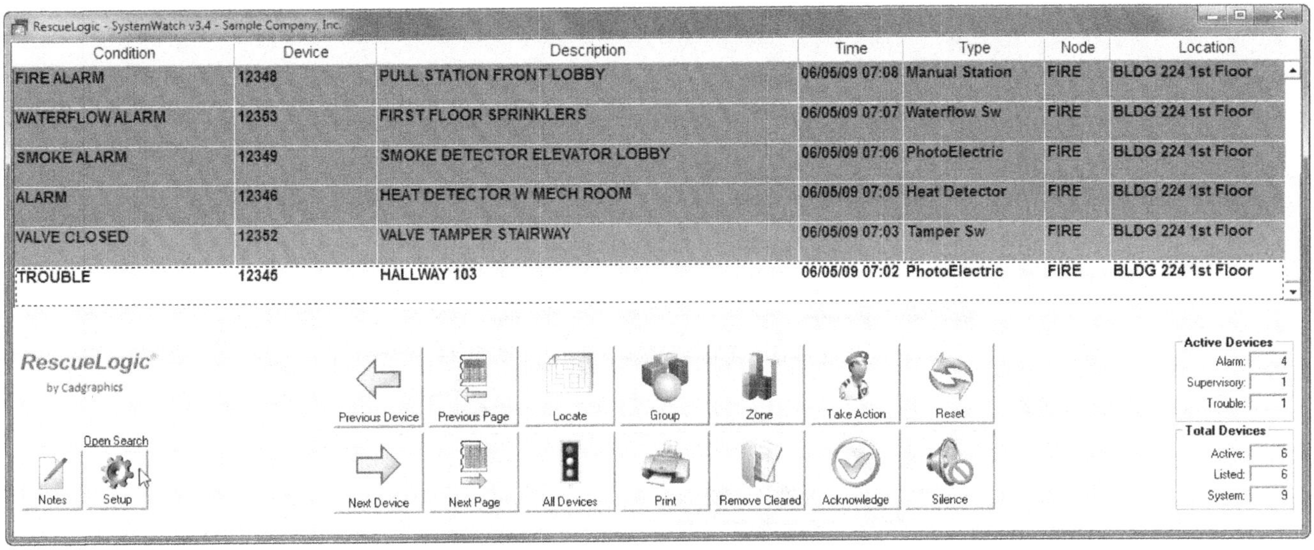

You may be prompted for a password. Enter your Level 2 or 3 Access password. (The default is 3.)

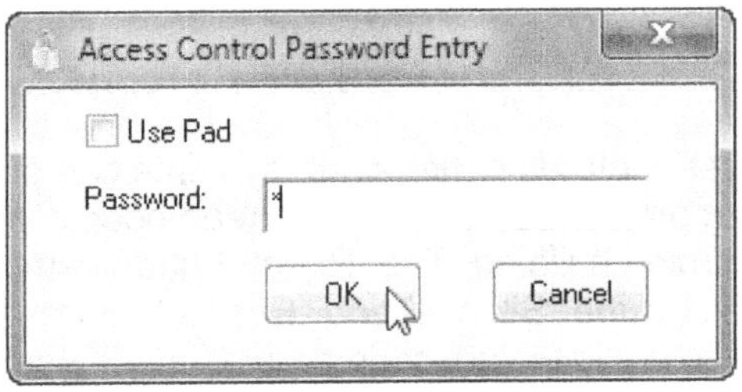

Extra Settings

To include the extra features, check "Show Silence Button in System Watch," "Show Reset Button in System Watch, and" "Show Acknowledge Button in System Watch."

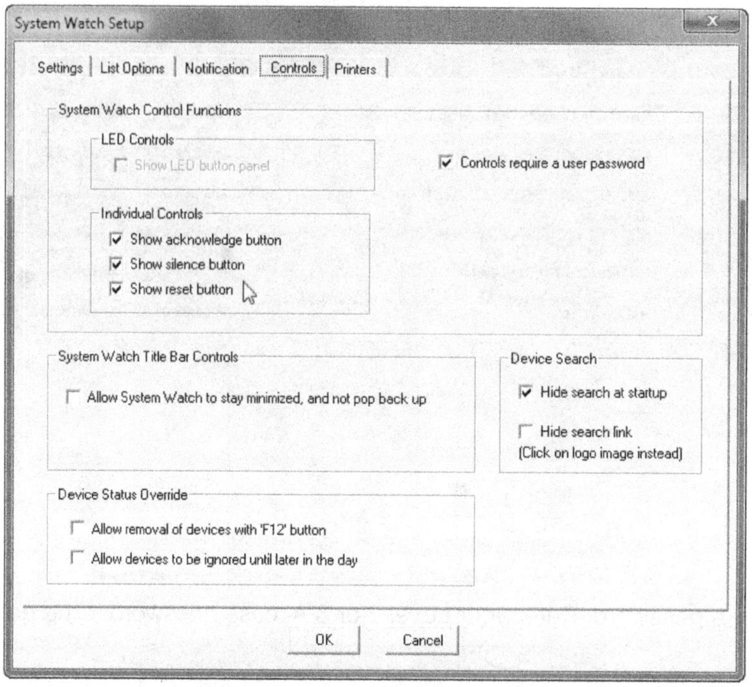

Helpful Hint: The "Silence" and "Reset" features of fire alarm systems can put people and property in danger. In particular, the "Silence" button will turn off alarms, which could keep people in the path of a fire or seem to indicate they should go back into a burning building. The "Reset" button can turn fans on, keep elevators in operation, and open fire doors. Obviously, the "Silence" and "Reset" features are not intended to be used from a remote monitoring station, and doing so could violate code regulations. If you are not physically in a building, and you have not checked the validity of an alarm in person, do not use the "Silence" and "Reset" buttons to quiet an alarm that is in progress.

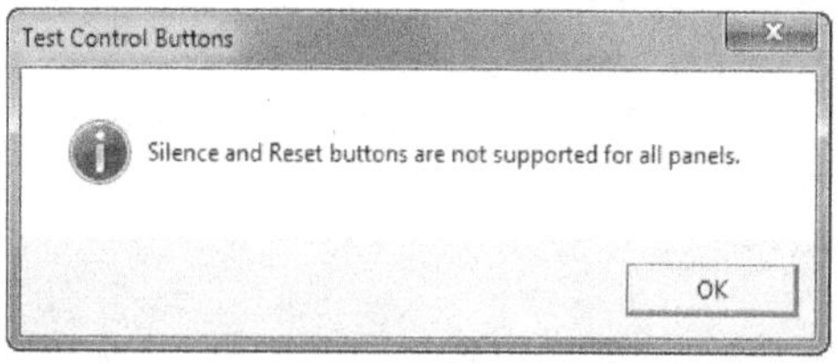

The added button appear to the right of the navigation buttons on the System Watch list.

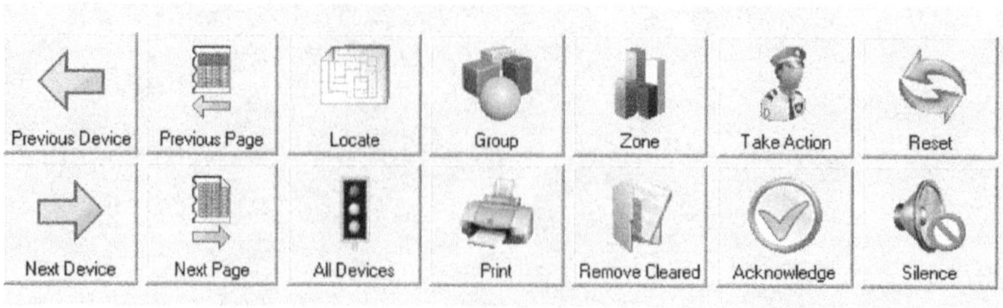

Acknowledge Alarms

The "Acknowledge" button allows you to acknowledge that you have received a message from a system. Typically, clicking the "Acknowledge" button will silence the internal beeper in a panel that is reporting trouble or alarm. If you have set RescueLogic to play a continuous audible alert, the "Acknowledge" button will silence your RescueLogic system, too. The "Acknowledge" button is optional.

Silence Alarm Sounds

The "Silence" button sends a signal to the fire alarm system. That signal lets you turn off alarm horns, so that you could stop a building evacuation. (The "Silence" button might also turn off strobe lights.) On some systems, clicking the "Silence" button a second time will reinstate an evacuation signal. The "Silence" button is optional.

Reset the System

After an alarm, the "Reset" button will send a signal to the fire alarm system and restore the system to its normal monitoring state. The "Reset" button is optional.

RescueLogic System Messages

In addition to the messages received from field panels and devices, RescueLogic may report messages that indicate its operation may be impaired. One such message lists "System Monitor" as its address. If you see this message, check to make sure that the System Monitor program is running.

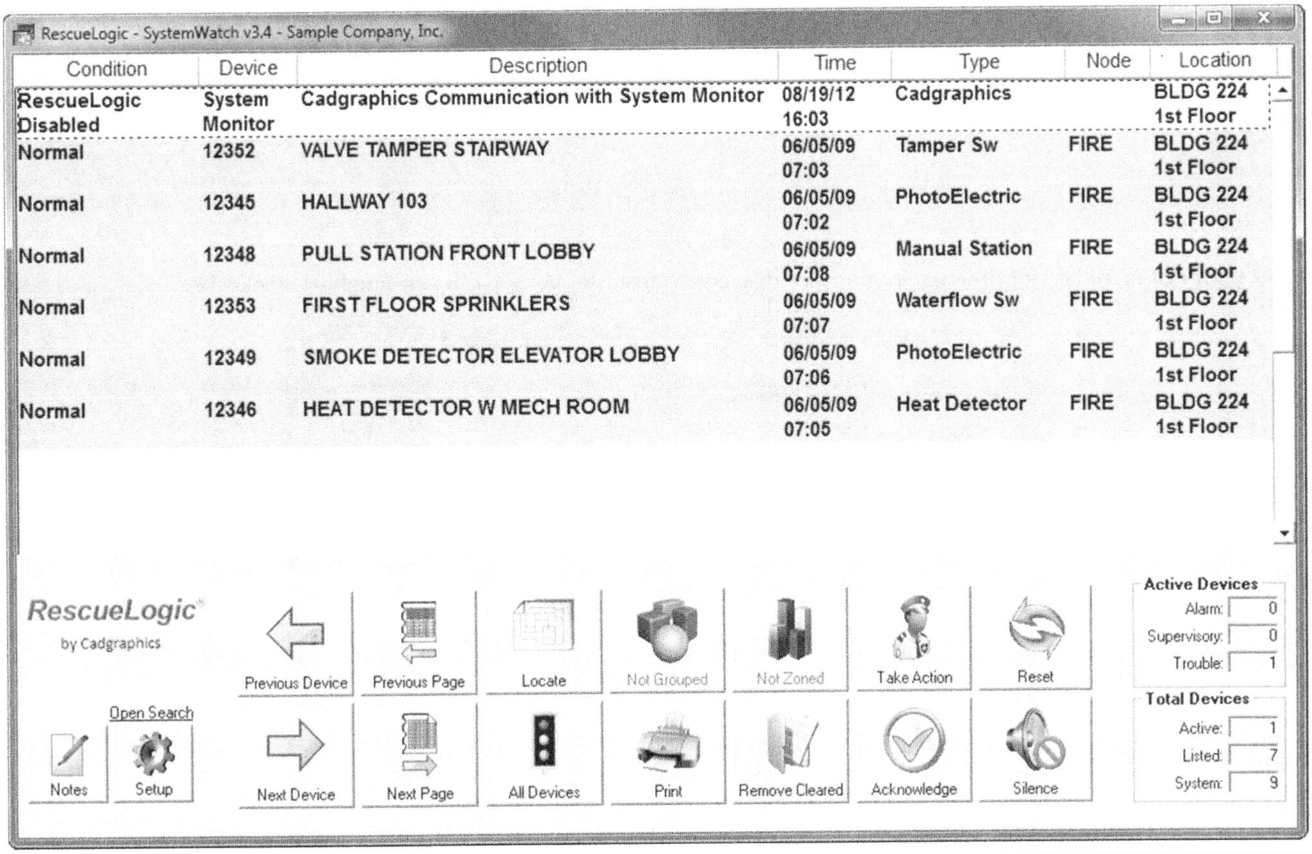

Helpful Hint: Both System Monitor and System Watch must be running for RescueLogic to function.

Add Notes and Comments

You might want to add notes to the "Take Action" messages, to inform other users about special situations or conditions. The process of adding notes is simple: Select the device for which you want to add a note by clicking on it in the list, and click "Notes."

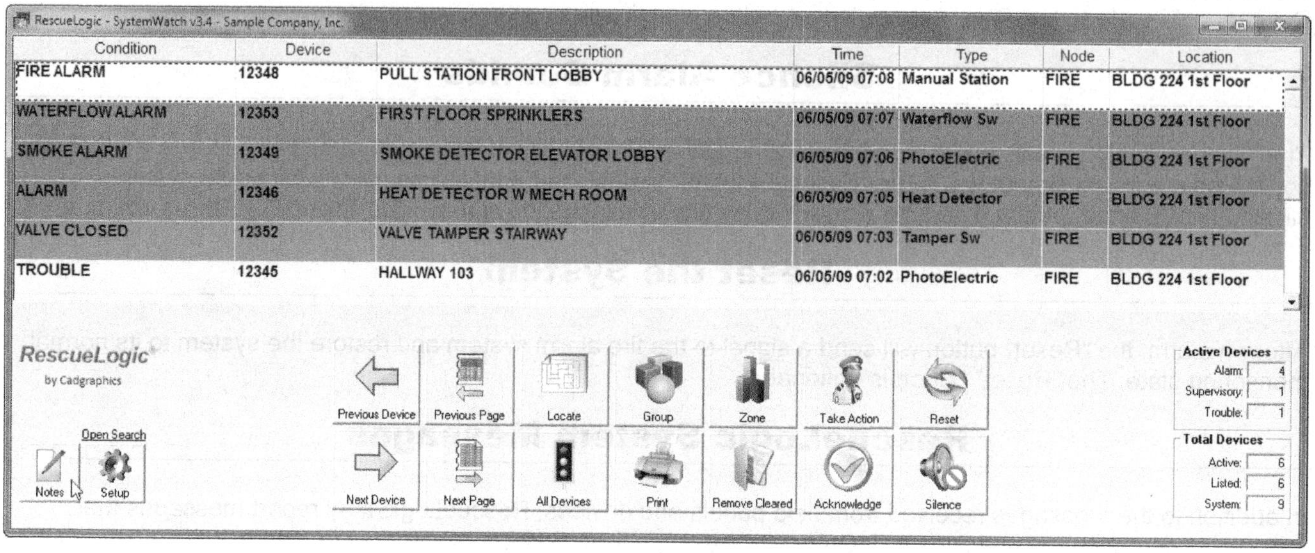

Enter your level-one password. The default is the numeral "3,"

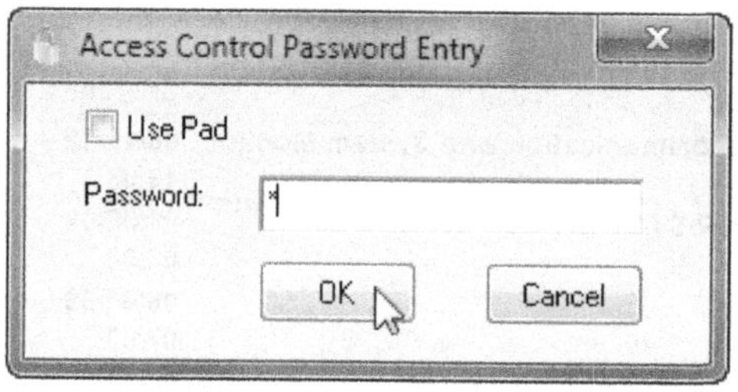

Type your notes, either for devices in alarm or devices in trouble. When you are finished, click "OK."

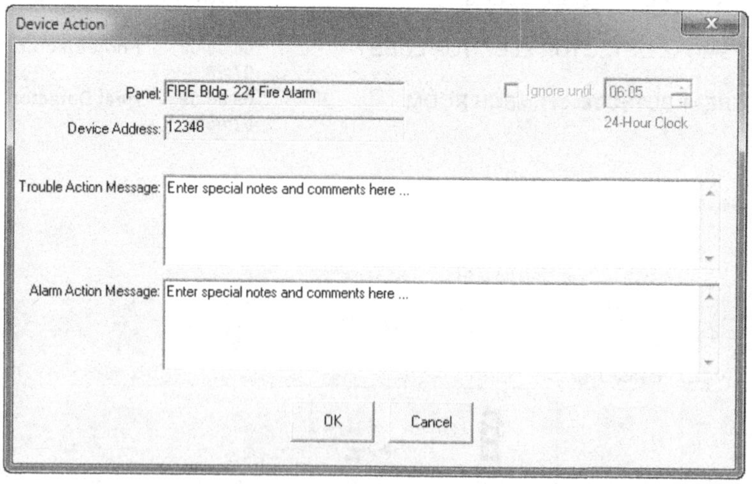

Click the "Take Action" button to see the new notes.

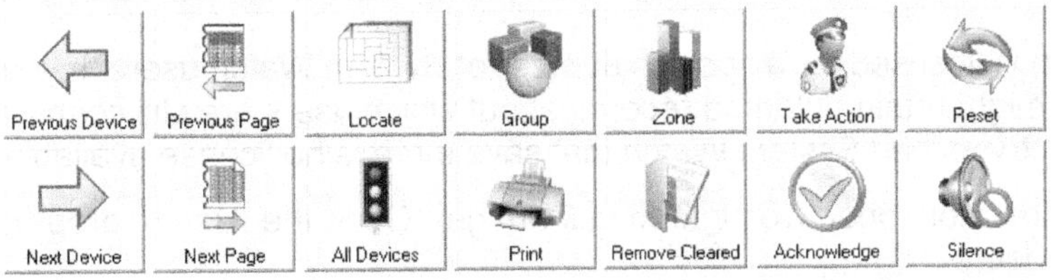

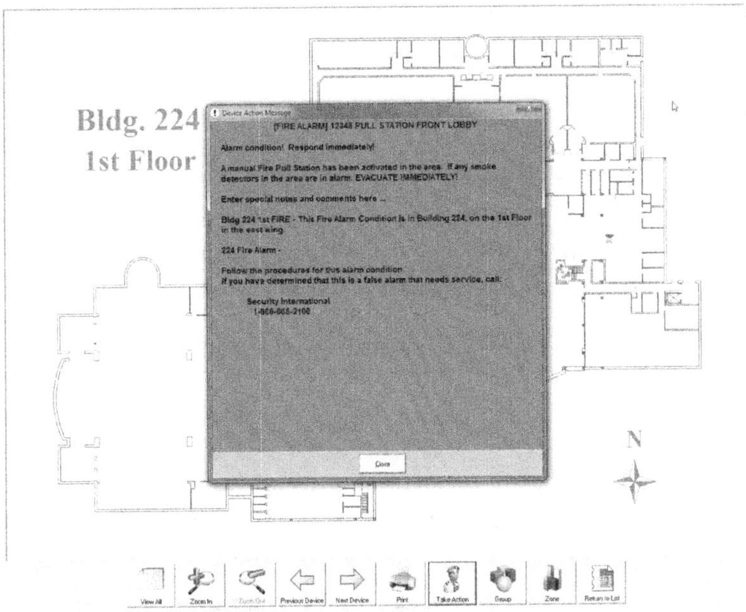

When you are through checking your notes, click "Close."

Clear All Users

Your RescueLogic system is licensed for a specific number of System Watch users. If you change a computer, the RescueLogic system might retain outdated records about which users are still connected. In that case, you'll see a message when you try to load System Watch that says there is no license available.

To clear the outdated information, open Configuration Manager. Go to the "Users" drop-down menu and select "Clear All System Watch Users."

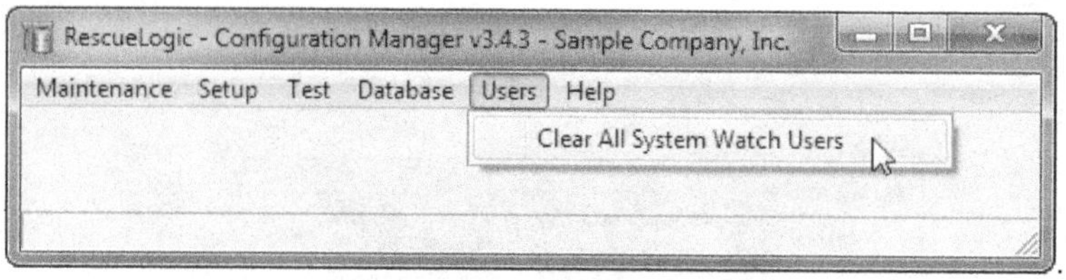

You will be asked to confirm the process. Click "Yes," and RescueLogic will clear all System Watch users.

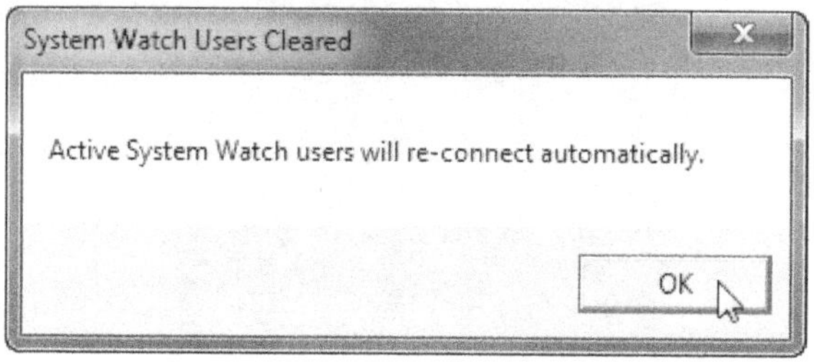

When you clear all users, the connection will be automatically re-established with any users who are there. The clearing process will help re-establish accurate communication between all RescueLogic computers.

Exit RescueLogic

Click the "Exit" button — or the "X" in the top right-hand window of your screen — to leave the System Watch program. You will need a level-three password to shut down RescueLogic. The default is the numeral "3."

Chapter 17: Reports and Records

RescueLogic automatically collects second-by-second, minute-by-minute data of alarms and events, exactly as they occur. With RescueLogic reports and records, you can reconstruct emergency events after the fact — both to verify that the proper steps were taken, and to improve future responses. You can print and distribute reports with a single click, and you can modify them to highlight any information you think is especially important.

The Activity Reports Program

Activity Reports is an optional program that will allow you to study the course of events as they happened in real time, because the complete sequence of devices that report trouble and alarm are recorded. You can create individual reports, using filters to isolate the data you desire. You can also sort reports in any order you like.

After you've installed the Activity Reports add-on, you may run it from the same menu as you other RescueLogic programs. To begin, click the "Start" button in the lower left-hand corner of your screen. Go to "Programs," slide the RescueLogic folder open, and click on "Activity Reports."

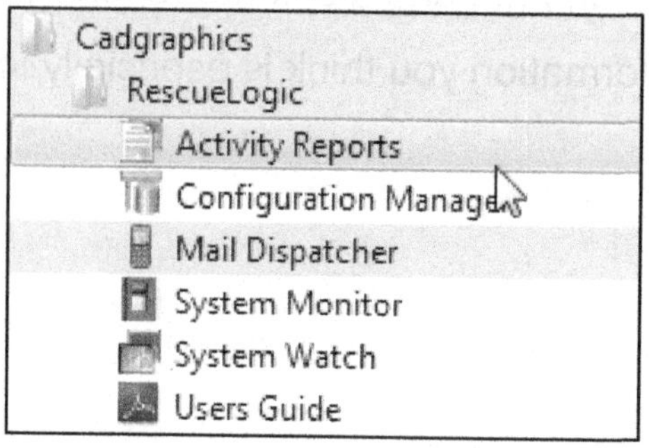

After you've installed the Activity Reports add-on, you can also open Reports from within Configuration Manager. Go to the "Setup" drop-down menu and select either "Configuration Reports" or "Activity Log Reports."

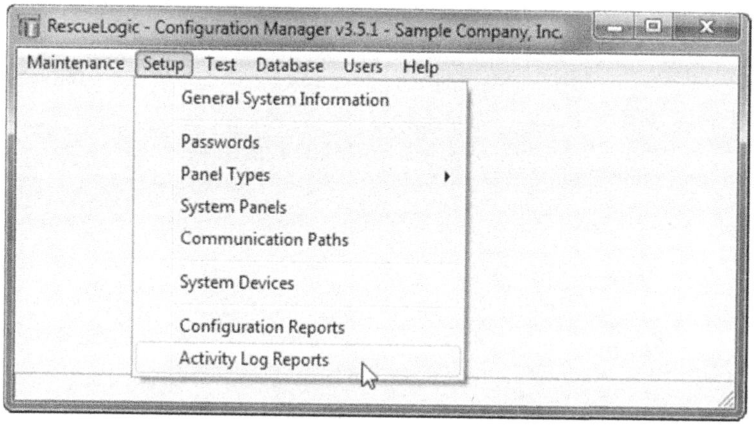

When Activity Reports opens, you'll see the default "Activity Reports" tab, with every filter set to "All," and the "Sort Report" option set to "Date/Time." If you click "Print," you will get a full report of the current status of every panel and device in your system.

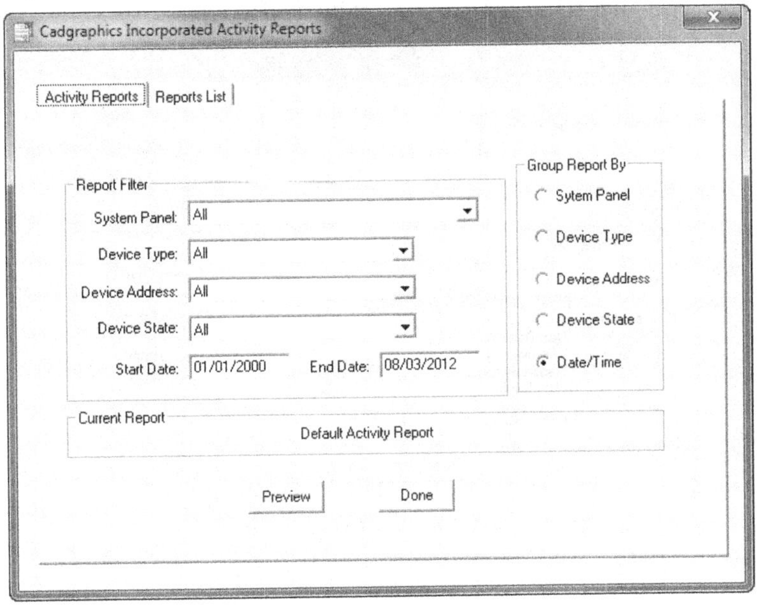

Filter by Panel

Use the drop-down "System Panel" menu to filter your report by panel.

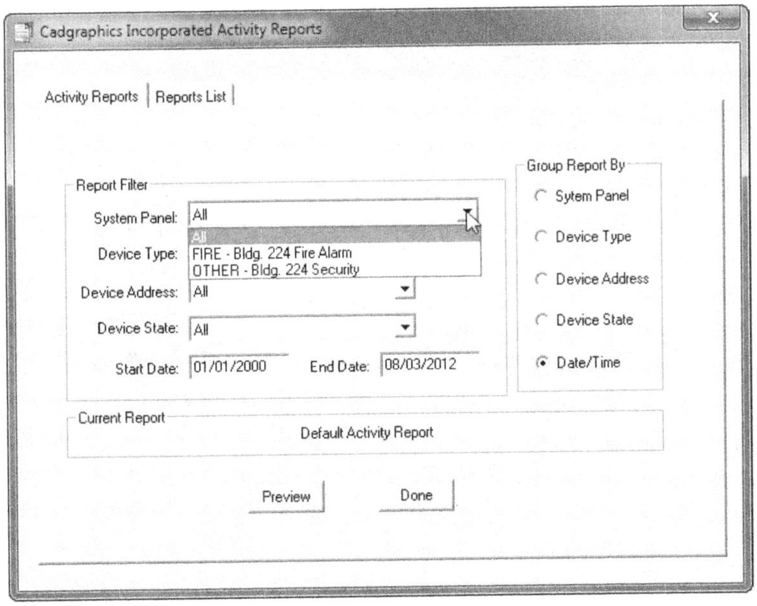

Filter by Device Type

Use the drop-down "Device Type" menu to filter your report by device type.

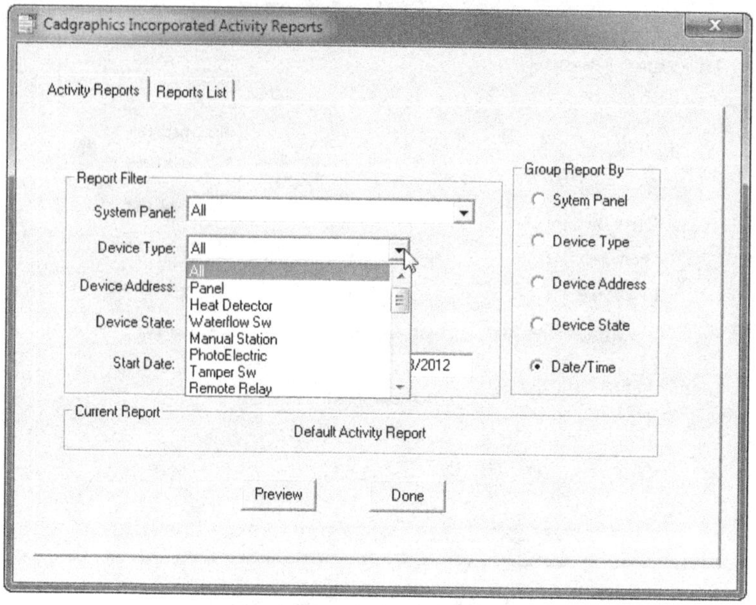

Filter by Device Address

Use the drop-down "Device Address" menu to filter your report by device address.

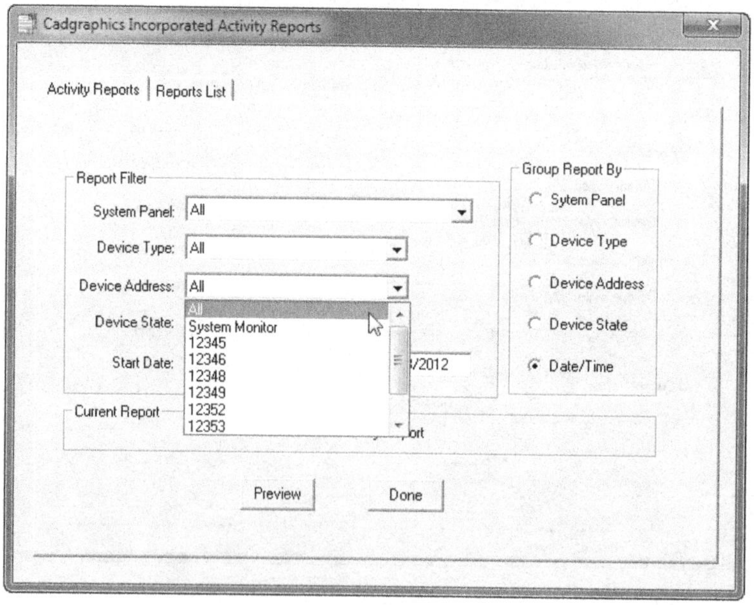

Filter by Device State

Use the drop-down "Device State" menu to filter your report by device state.

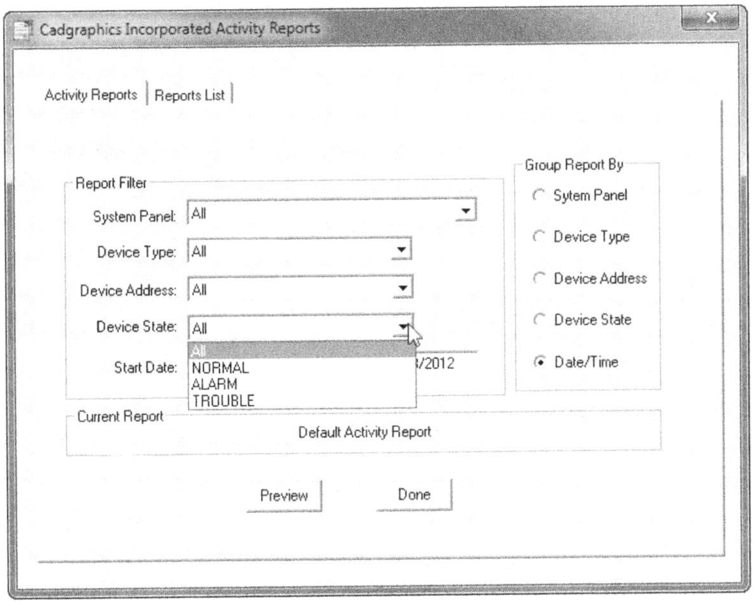

Filter by Date

Use the "Start Date" and "End Date" fields to filter your report by date.

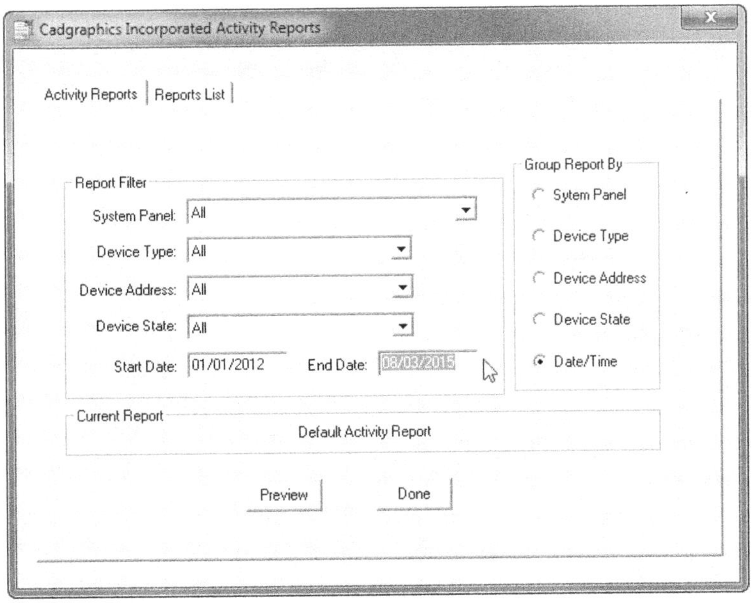

Sort Reports

Use the "Sort Report By" check boxes to filter your report by panel, device type, address, state, or date and time.

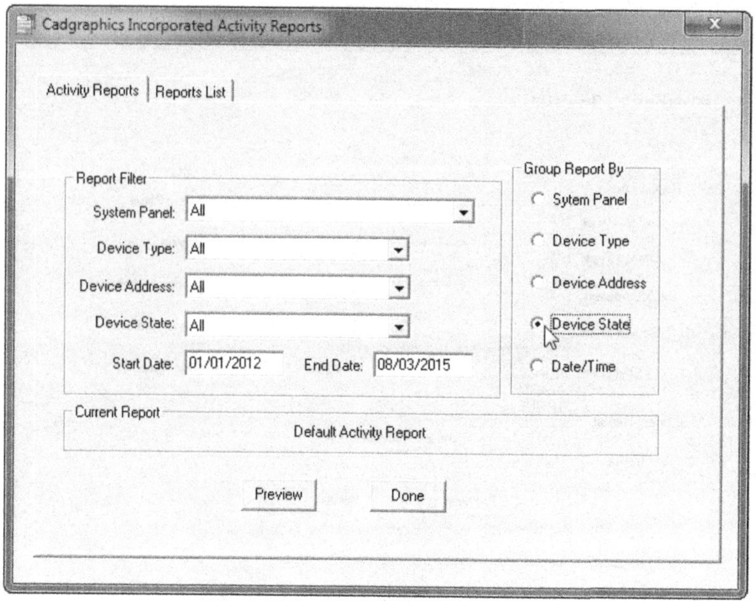

Report Formats

RescueLogic comes programmed with default activity and service reports. To access the report formats, open the "Reports List" tab screen and click "Add."

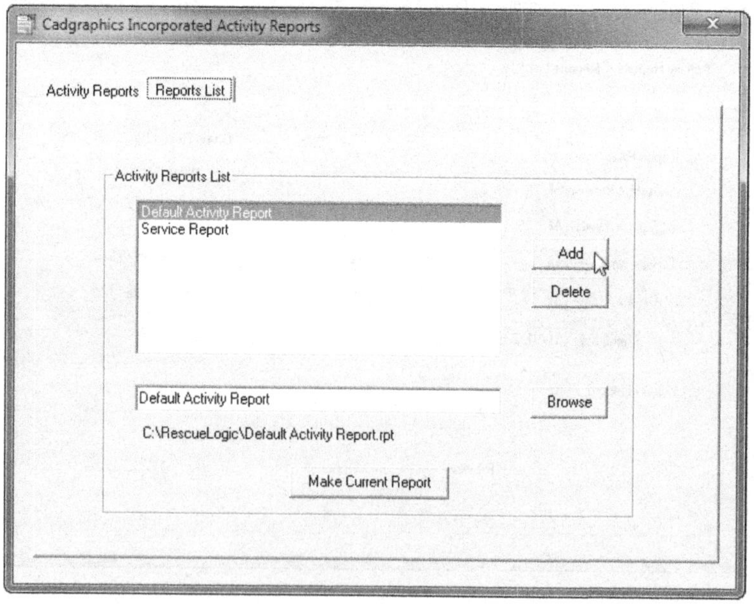

You will see a <New Report> line item added to the “Activity Reports List.” Highlight it and click “Browse” to find a new pre-set report format.

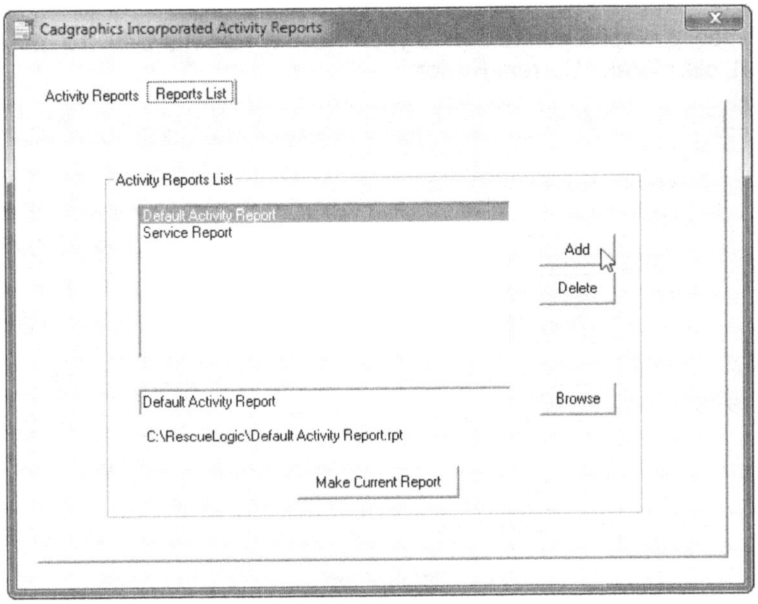

Select a Pre-Set Report Format

The pre-set report formats are in the RescueLogic program folder on your hard drive. (The file path is **C:\RescueLogic**.) Highlight the report format of your choice and click “Open.”

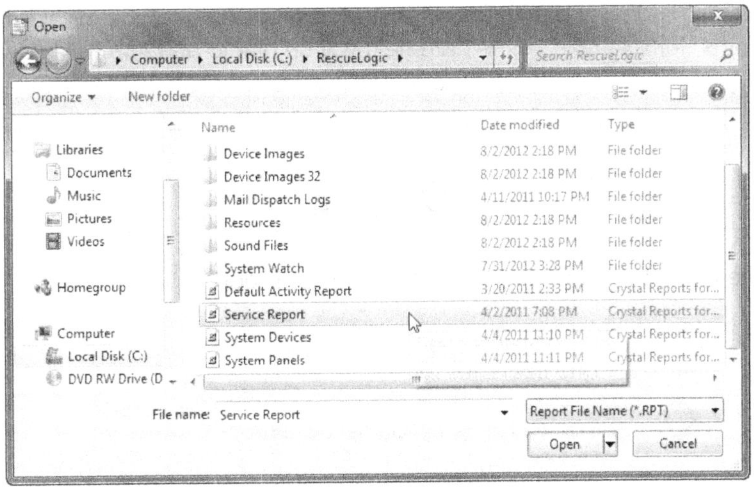

Change Your Current Report

RescueLogic will add the new pre-set report format to your "Activity Reports List." To make the new Activity Report your current report, click "Make Current Report."

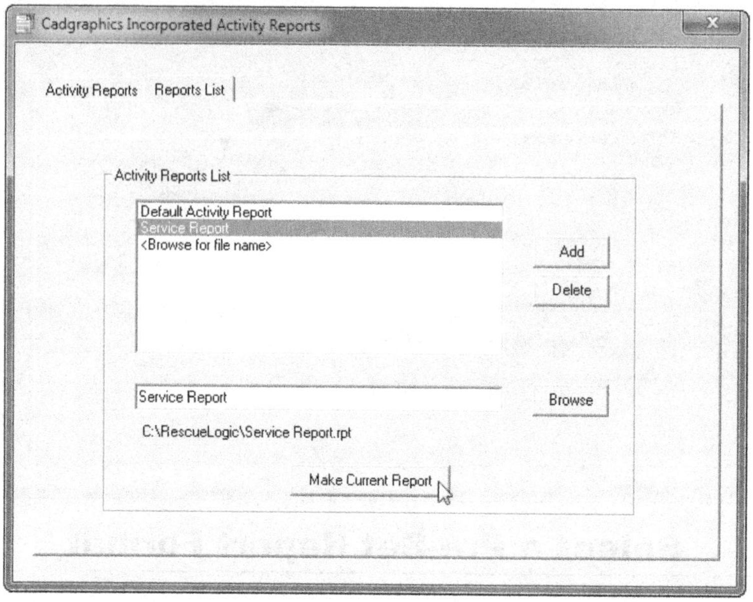

Helpful Hint: The "service report" format is especially handy, because it lists the most recent service date of every device in your system. If a device has not been tested or reported a trouble or alarm within a specified period — the last six months, for example — the date field will be blank, and you will know it's time to schedule service.

Update

You can choose to update the activity log before you compile the report.

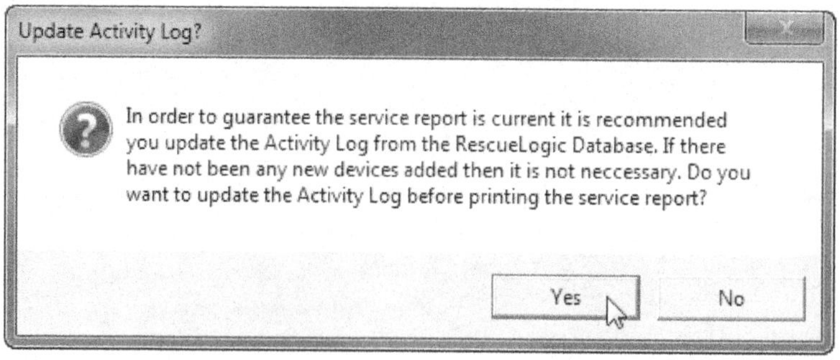

Print Preview

You will see an on-screen version of your report.

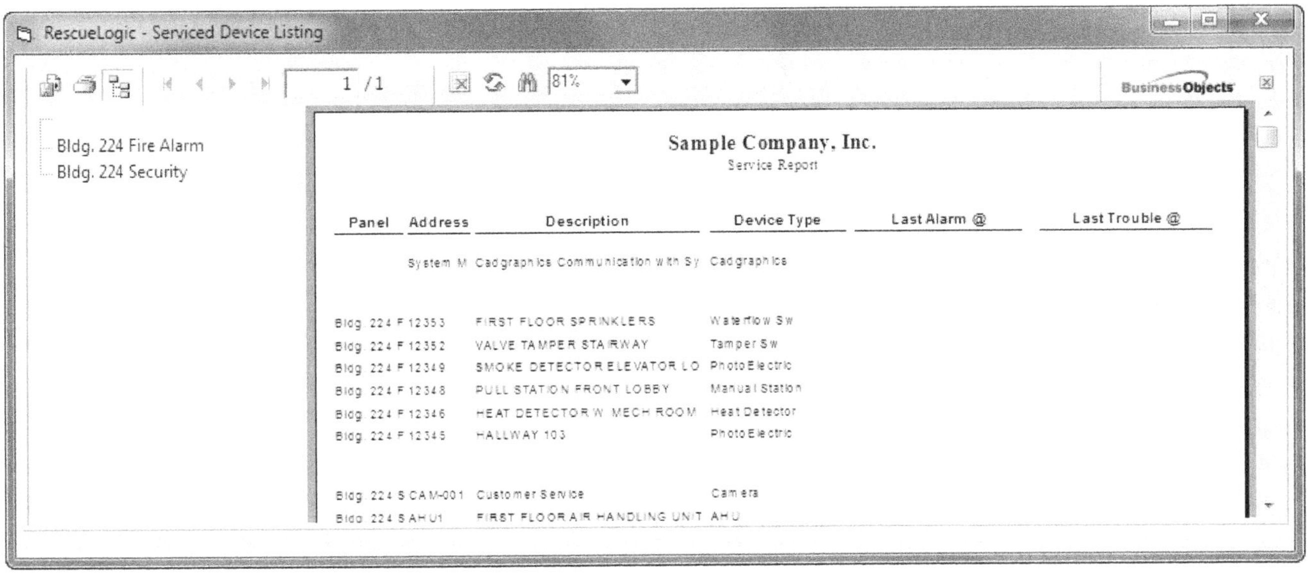

Print, Export, or E-Mail Your Report

Click the "print" icon to send your report to your system printer.

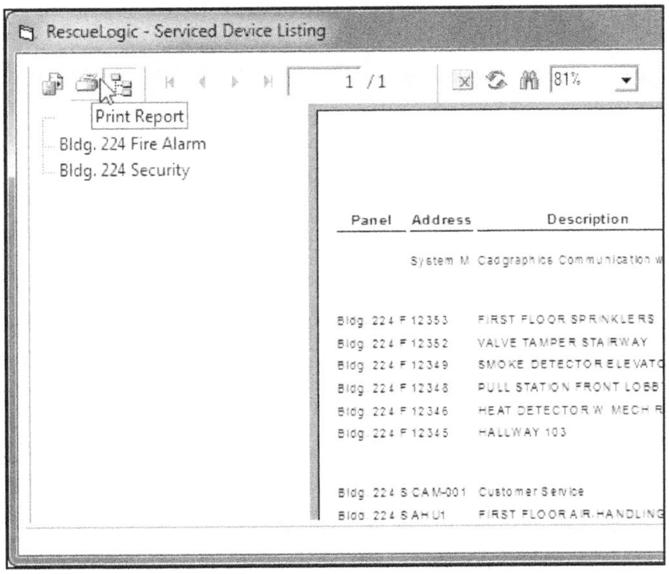

Keep Database Records with Configuration Reports

You can use Configuration Reports to compile and print a list of the devices configured in your database. To create a configuration report, start by opening Configuration Manager. Go to the "Setup" drop-down menu and click on "Configuration Reports."

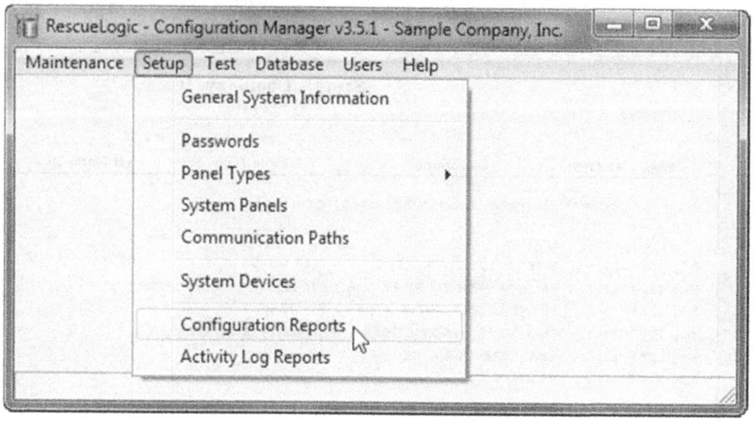

Device Type Filter

When you open Configuration Reports, you will see two tab screens. The first screen, "Device Lists," will compile information about the devices in your system. You can compile and print several types of "Device List" reports. "Device Type" reports will include information about every type of device in your system, such as panels, heat detectors, and waterflow switches.

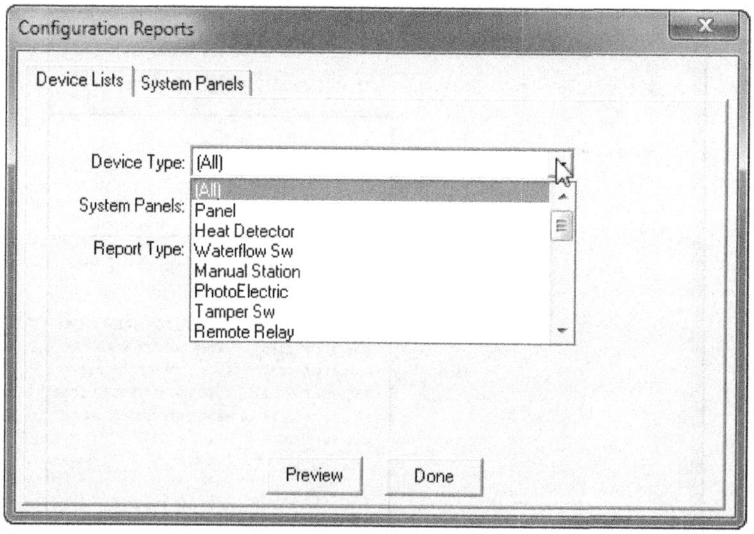

System Panel Reports

"System Panels" reports will include information about all of the panels in your system.

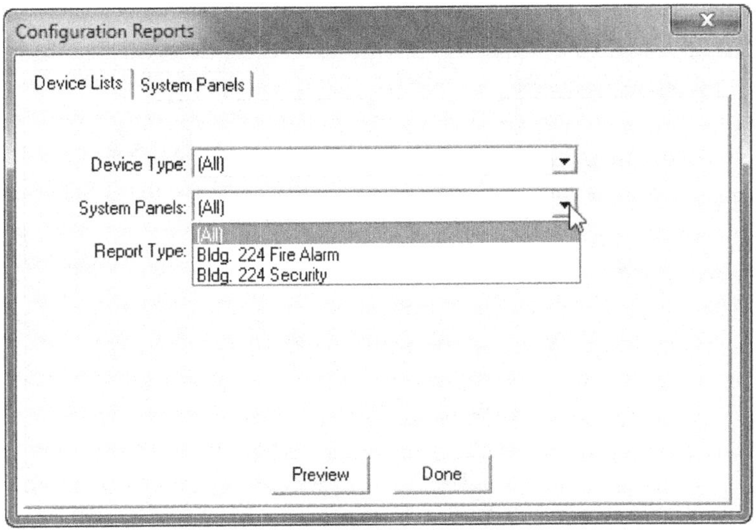

Report Types

You can use the "Report Type" drop-down menu to determine how extensive your report will be. You can choose to compile a report about all of the devices in your system, any devices in your "QuickRestore" list, and any devices that RescueLogic is programmed to ignore.

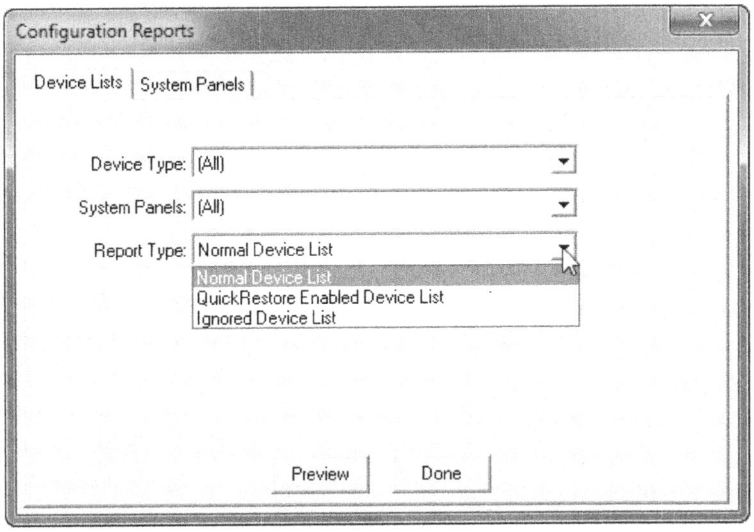

Helpful Hint: If you want to customize your reports even further — if, for example, you want to chart data as bar graphs — RescueLogic report files are compatible with Crystal Reports software.

System Panels

To print a list of all the panels in your RescueLogic system, go to the “System Panels” tab screen and click “Print.”

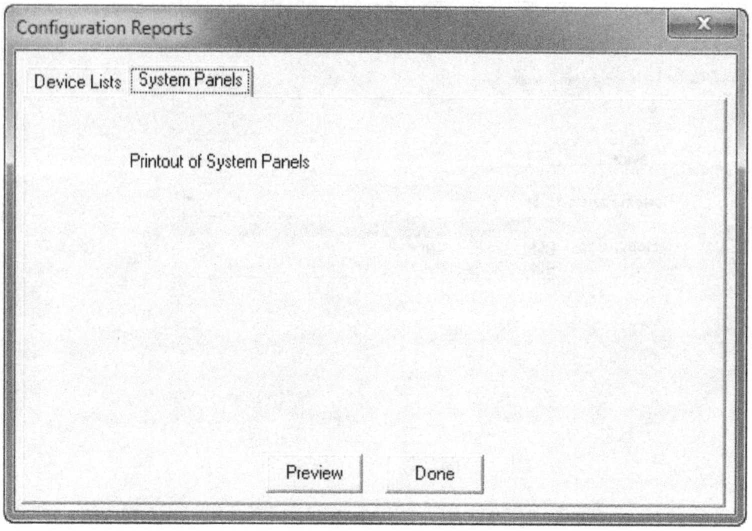

Appendix A: Licensing RescueLogic

In order to add more than ten devices to your RescueLogic system, you will need to activate your copy of the software. Activation is a simple process that you can complete by email.

License Your RescueLogic Software

To begin the RescueLogic licensing process, go to your "Start" menu and open the System Monitor program.

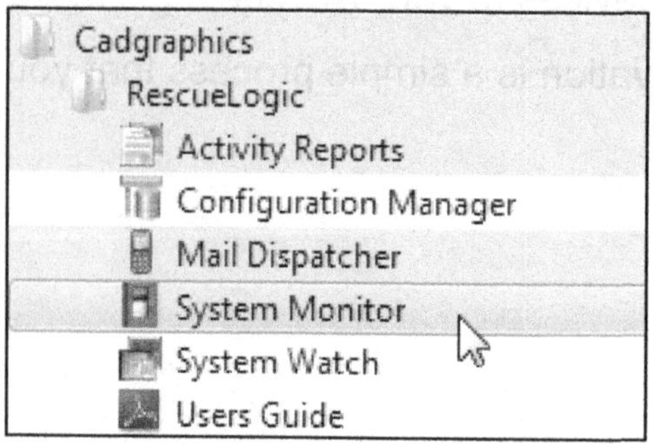

You will be reminded that you are working in demonstration mode. Click "OK" to continue.

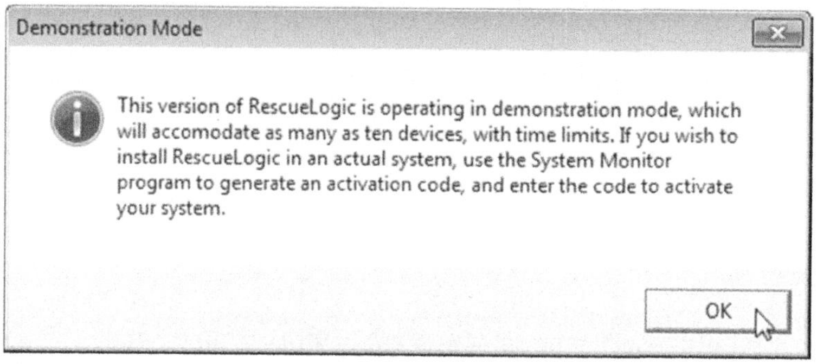

Go to the "Setup" drop-down menu and click on "Product Activation."

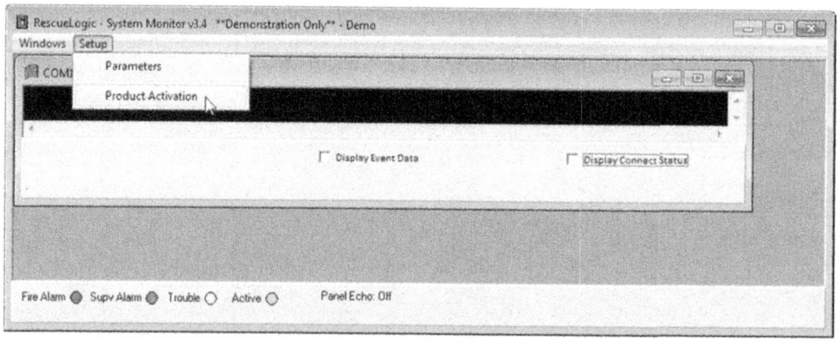

You will see a notice to restart System Monitor after the activation is complete. Click "Yes" to proceed.

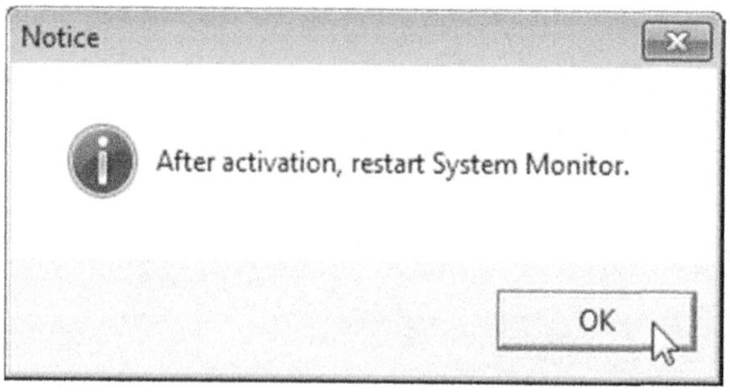

You'll see a product activation screen. Your company name may already be in the box, if it was already entered from Configuration Manager. If the "Company Name" field says "Demo," enter your company name exactly as you would like it to appear throughout the RescueLogic system.

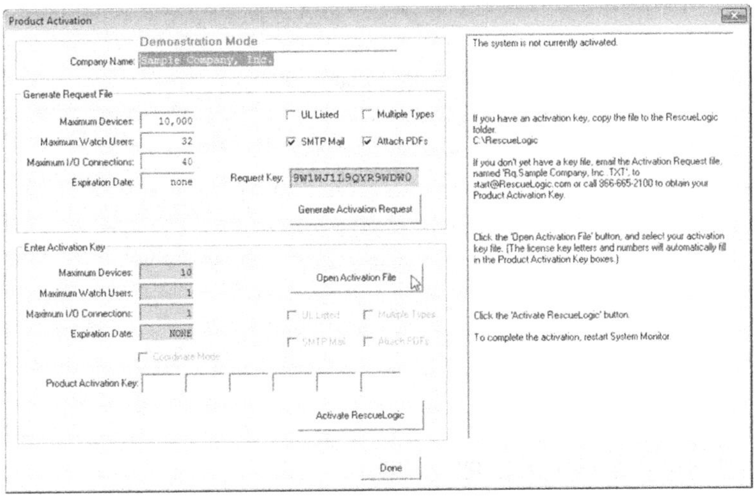

You may be asked to confirm the name change from "Demo" to your company name.

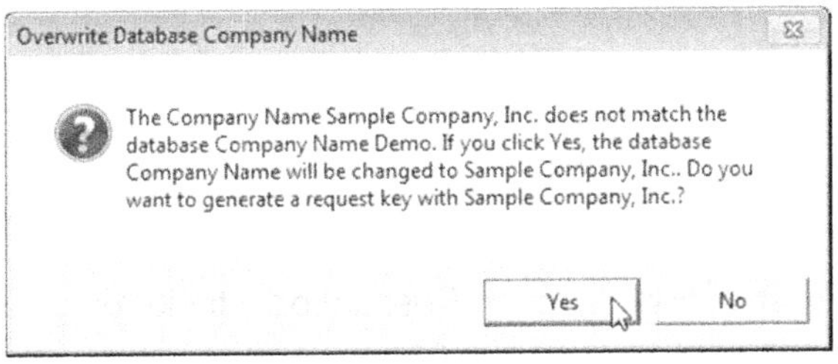

Click the "Generate Activation Request" button.

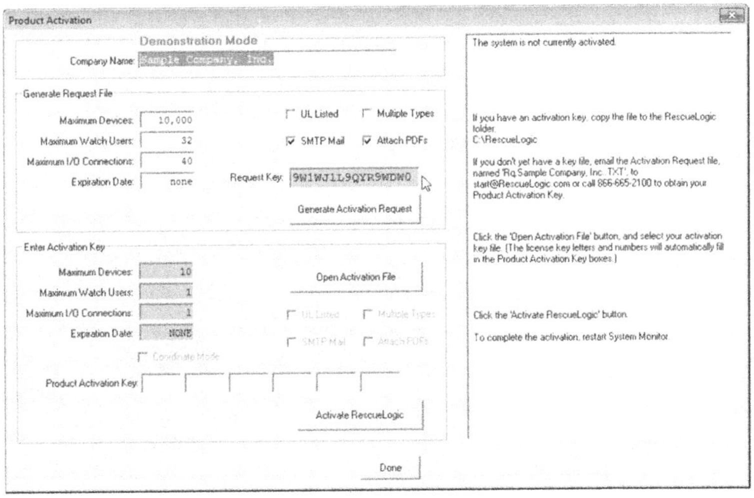

The screen will show an Activation Request number.

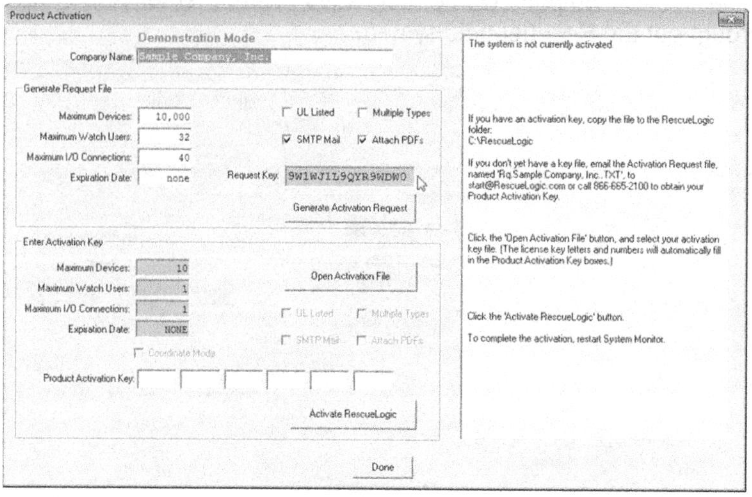

You will be prompted to get your Activation Key by e-mail.

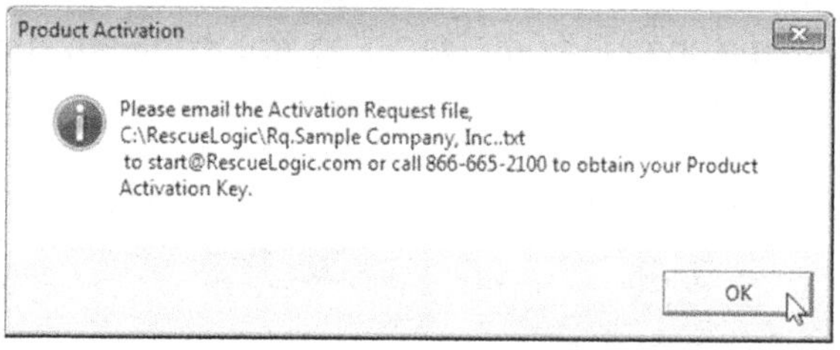

Click “OK,” and then find your activation text file in the RescueLogic folder on your computer.

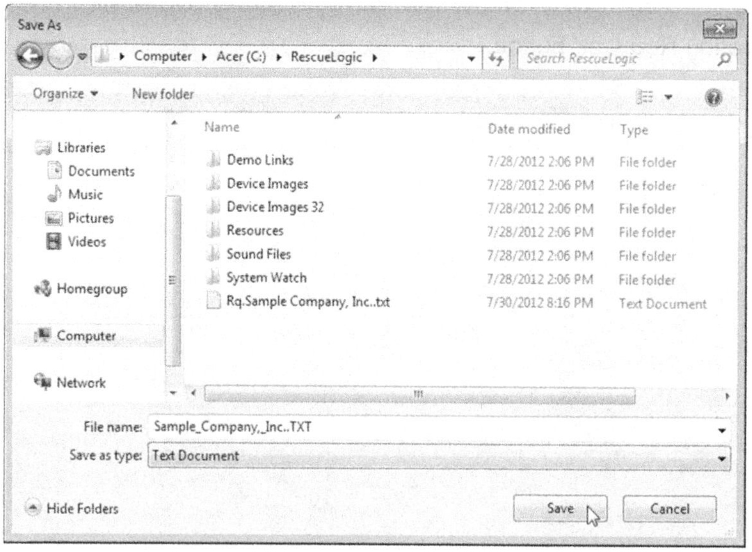

The software will generate an activation request file — a text file called **Rq.*Company Name*.txt**. The text file will be in the RescueLogic folder on your hard drive. At this point, you will not need to look at it. If you choose to open it, however, the text file will look something like this:

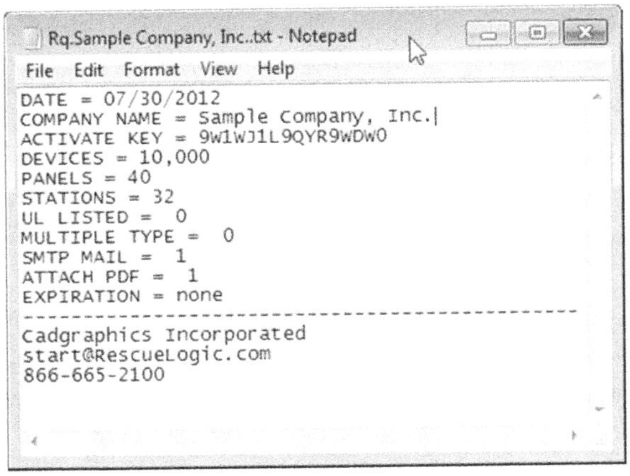
Rq.Sample Company, Inc..txt - Notepad
File Edit Format View Help

```
DATE = 07/30/2012
COMPANY NAME = Sample Company, Inc.
ACTIVATE KEY = 9W1WJ1L9QYR9WDW0
DEVICES = 10,000
PANELS = 40
STATIONS = 32
UL LISTED =  0
MULTIPLE TYPE =  0
SMTP MAIL =  1
ATTACH PDF =  1
EXPIRATION = none
---------------------------------------------
Cadgraphics Incorporated
start@RescueLogic.com
866-665-2100
```

Next, compose an e-mail to *license@rescuelogic.com*, and attach the activation text file. Include your phone number, too.

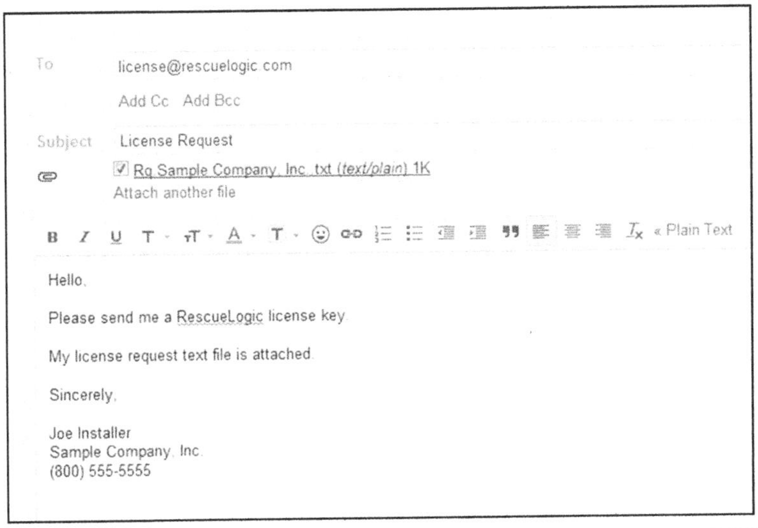

Helpful Hint: RescueLogic software is configured to suit the size of each facility, the type of alarm panels on each site, and the number of people who will use the RescueLogic system. If you would like help to determine which RescueLogic package is right for you, call us at (612) 722-3233 or e-mail info@RescueLogic.com.

By return e-mail, you will get a text file customized with the name of your company. In the case of our example, the file would be named "Sample Company, Inc..TXT."

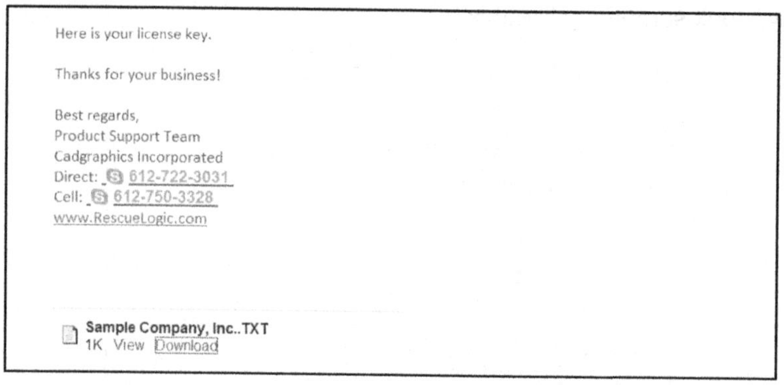

Save the new text file to your RescueLogic folder. First, double-click on the attachment. You will probably get the following "Open Attachment Warning." Select "Save it to disk" and click "OK."

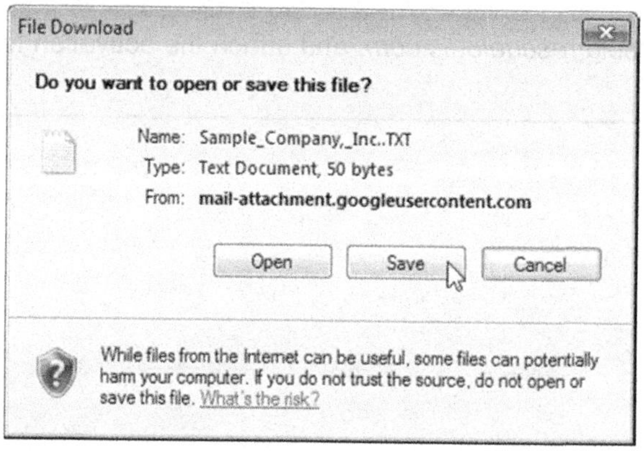

Save the attachment in the RescueLogic folder on your hard drive.

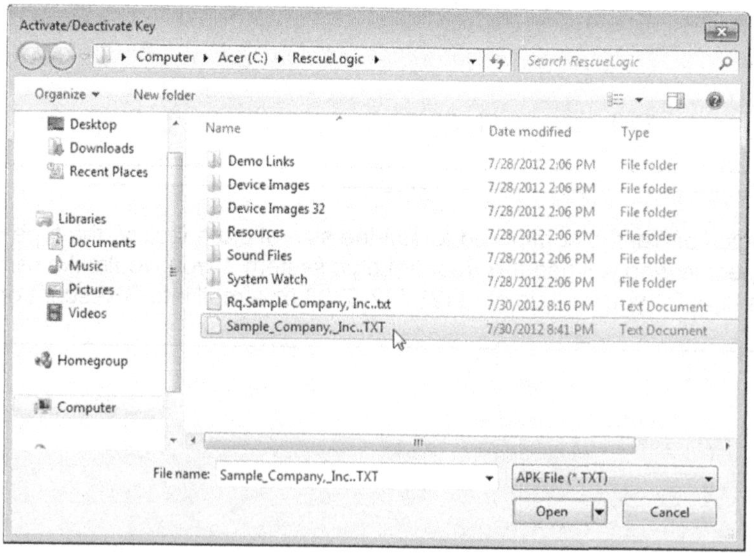

Return to the "Product Activation" window in System Monitor. Click on "Open Activation File."

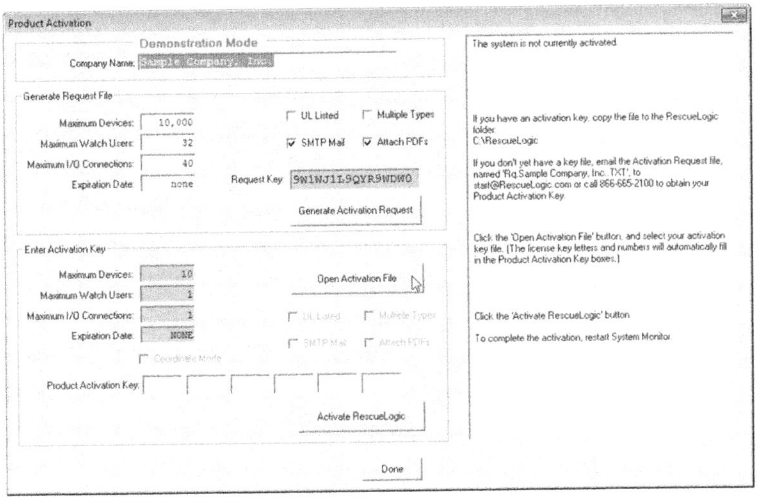

The "Product Activation" window will open. Select the file with your Company Name. (In the image below, note that the file name for the request you send begins with "Rq." The activation file you receive by return email won't have that "Rq." Prefix.)

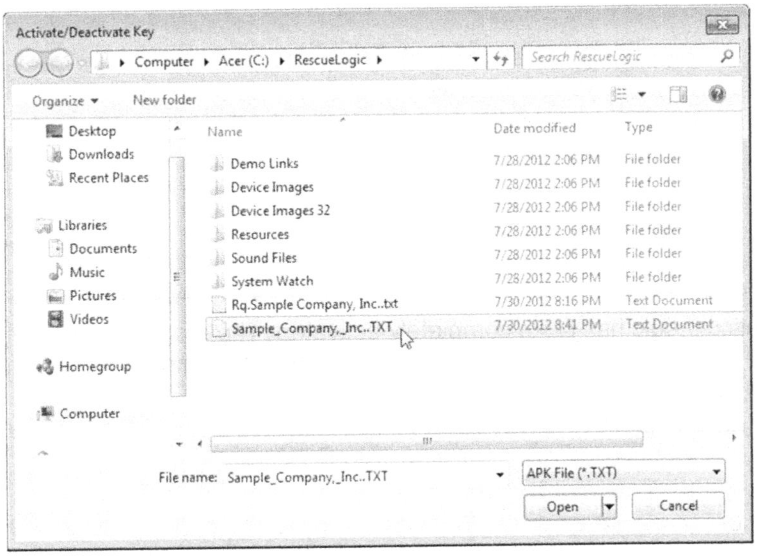

Click the “Activate RescueLogic” button. The license key will be automatically installed.

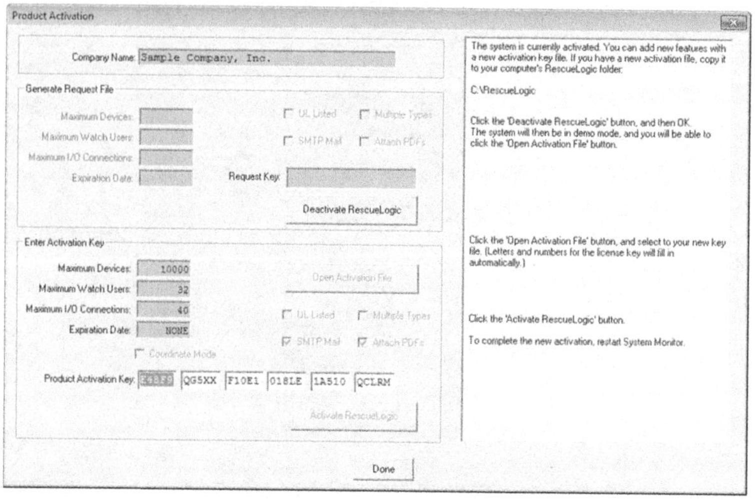

You will see the following message. Read it and click “OK.”

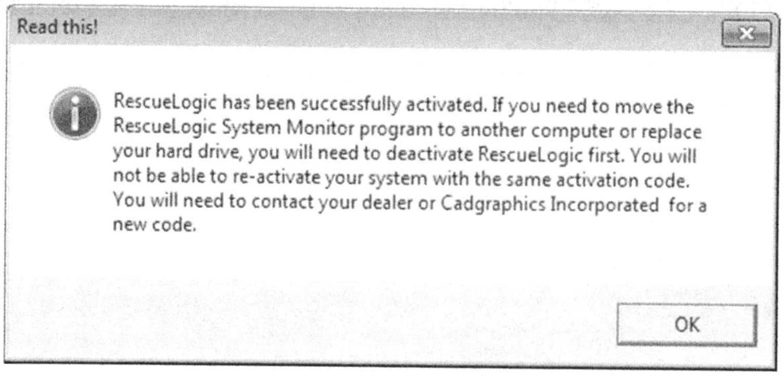

Now you will see that RescueLogic has been completely activated. The program is not running in demo mode anymore. Your company name is filled in, your key codes are complete, and your software is programmed for a maximum number of devices, users, and panels.

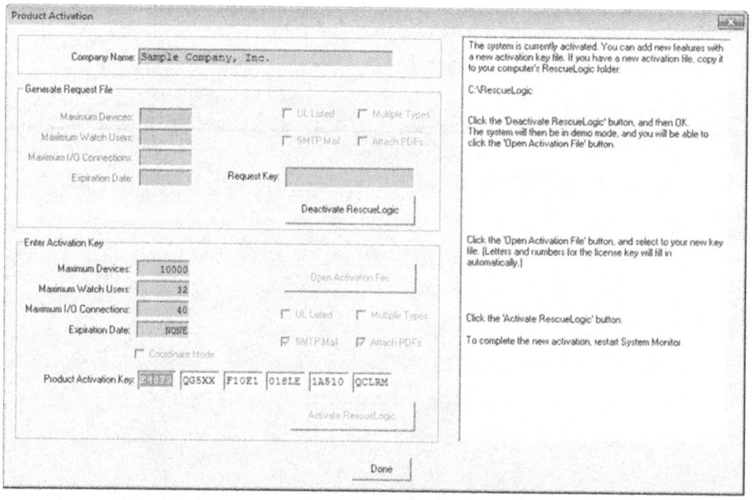

Helpful Hint: Each activation key will work only on one computer. The activation request code that you generate is based on your computer’s serial number and the company name you enter in the database.

Appendix B: Say It in Spanish

In an emergency, you need to communicate clearly with your security team. If your security guards usually read and speak Spanish, your RescueLogic system should include information in Spanish, too. Happily, that's easy to do. As you set up your RescueLogic system, you can include Spanish labels and "Take Action" messages right alongside their English counterparts. Here is a handy guide to a wide range of Spanish words and phrases you can use when you set up your RescueLogic system for Spanish-speaking users. Even if you don't plan to incorporate Spanish in your RescueLogic system, the terms listed here could give you a head start in developing your "Take Action" messages.

Map and Floor Plan Labels

Consult this list as you label your background maps and floor plans.

Access: Acceso
Air Conditioner: Aire Acondicionado
Area: Patio
Atrium: Atrio
Attic: Ático
Audio-Visual Room: Salón de Audio-Visuales
Auditorium: Auditorio
Baggage Claim: Reclamo de Equipaje
Balcony: Balcón
Basement: Sótano
Bathroom: Baño
Battery Room: Cuarto de Baterías
Bedroom: Alcoba
Break Room: Sala de Descanso
Building: Edificio
Business Office: Oficina de Negocios
Bypass: Bipás
Cafeteria: Cafetería
Campus: Ciudad Universitaria
Ceiling: Cielo Raso
Center: Centro
Changing Room: Salón de Cambio
Checkpoint : Punto de Inspección
Chiller: Enfriador
Classroom: Aula de Clases
Closet: Armario
Coat Room: Guardarropa
Command Center: Centro de Mando
Common Area: Área Común
Communications Room: Sala de Comunicaciones
Computer Area: Área de Computadores
Computer Room: Sala de Computadores
Concourse: Vestíbulo
Conference Area: Area de Conferencias
Conference Room: Salón de Conferencias
Control Room: Sala de Control
Copy/Fax Room: Sala de Copia/Fax
Corridor: Corredor
Courtyard: Patio
Critical: Crítico
Customer Service: Servicio al Cliente
Darkroom: Cuarto Oscuro
Data Center: Centro de Datos
Dining Room: Comedor
Directions/ North, South, East, West: Direcciones/ Norte, Sur, Este, Oeste
Directions/ Northeast, Northwest, Southeast, Southwest: Direcciones/ Noreste, Noroeste, Sureste, Suroeste
Display Area: Área de Exhibición
Dock: Muelle
Doctor's Office: Oficina del Doctor
Door: Puerta
Dressing Room: Cuarto de Vestir
Duct: Conducto
East: Este
Electrical Room: Cuatro Eléctrico
Elevator: Ascensor
Emergency Exit: Salida de Emergencia
Emergency Room: Cuarto de Emergencia
Employee Lounge: Sala de Empleados
Enclosure: Recinto
Entrance: Entrada
Entry: Entrada
Equipment Room: Cuarto de Equipos y Materiales
Escalator: Escalera Móvil
Exam Room: Salón de Exámenes
Executive: Ejecutivo
Executive Restroom: Baño de Ejecutivos
Exercise Room: Salón de Ejercicios
Exit: Salida
Eye Wash Station: Estación de Lavado de Ojos
Facility: Facilidad
Fence: Cerca
Fiber Optic: Fibra Óptica
Firefighter's Phone: Teléfono de Bomberos
Floor: Piso
Floors/ First, Second, Third, Fourth, Fifth, Sixth, Seventh, Eighth, Ninth, Tenth: Pisos/ Primero, Segundo, Tercero, Cuarto, Quinto, Sexto, Séptimo, Octavo, Noveno, Décimo
Freezer: Congelador
Furnace: Horno
Gallery: Galería
Garage: Garaje
Gate: Puerta
Generator: Generador
Greenhouse: Invernadero
Guard Station: Estación de Guardia
Gymnasium: Gimnasio
Hall (Large room): Sala
Hall (Corridor): Pasillo
Handicap Access: Acceso para Minusválidos
Headquarters: Sede Central
High-Security Area: Área de Alta Seguridad
Hot Tub: Baño Caliente
Information Desk: Recepción
Janitor's Closet: Armario del Conserje
Kiosk: Quiosco
Kitchen: Cocina
Laboratory: Laboratorio
Landing: Aterrizaje
Laundry Room: Cuarto de Lavandería
Level: Nivel
Library: Biblioteca
Light: Luz
Lobby: Lobby
Locker Room: Vestuario
Loft: Desván
Lounge: Sala (de estar)
Lower Level: Nivel Inferior
Luggage Area: Área de Equipaje
Machine Shop: Taller de Maquinaria
Mail Room: Salón de Correo

Mechanical Room: Salón de Mecánica
Men's Restroom: Baño para Hombres
North: Norte
Northeast: Noreste
Northwest: Noroeste
Nursery: Guardería Infantil
Nurses Station: Estación de Enfermería
Off Limits: Fuera de Límites
Office: Oficina
Open Area: Área Abierta
Parking: Estacionamiento
Pay Phone: Teléfono Público
Pool: Estanque
Press Room: Sala de Prensa
Private: Privado
Public: Público
Public Address System: Sistema Amplificador para Discursos Públicos
Pump: Bomba
Pump Room: Cuarto de Bombas
Quadrant: Cuadrante
Receiving: Recibir
Reception Area: Área de Recepción
Reception Desk: Recepción
Reception Room: Sala de Recepción
Recreation Room: Salón de Recreación
Recycling Station: Estación de Reciclaje
Refrigerator: Nevera
Restricted: Restringido
Restroom: Baño
Revolving Door: Puerta Giratoria
Roof: Techo
Room: Habitación
Sauna: Sauna
Security Room: Cuarto de Seguridad
Shipping: Embarque
Shipping and Receiving: Embarque y Recepción
Shop: Tienda
Shower: Ducha
Shutoff Valve: Válvula de Cierre
Solarium: Solana
South: Sur
Southeast: Sureste
Southwest: Suroeste
Sprinkler Room: Extintor de Incendios
Staff Lounge: Salón del Personal
Stairwell: Hueco de Escalera
Station: Estación
Storage: Almacenaje
Store: Tienda
Studio: Estudio
Sub-Basement: Subsótano
Subfloor: Subpiso
Sunroom: Solana
Supply Closet: Armario de Suministros
Swimming Pool: Piscina
Switch: Interruptor
Switchboard: Conmutador
System: Sistema
Tech: Técnico
Telephone: Teléfono
Telephone Room: Cabina Telefónica
Termination Closet: Armario de Terminación
Tower: Torre
Trash: Basura
Upper Level: Nivel Superior
UPS (Uninterruptable Power Supply) Room: Cuarto de UPS (Suministro de Energía Ininterrumpible)
Vending Machines: Máquinas de Comida Rápida
Vent: Rejilla (de Ventilación)
Vestibule: Vestíbulo
Waiting Room: Sala de Espera
Wall: Pared
Warehouse: Depósito
Water Heater: Calentador de Agua
West: Oeste
Window: Ventana
Wing: Ala
Women's Restroom: Baño de Mujeres
Work Area: Área de Trabajo
Workstation: Estación de Trabajo
X-ray: Rayos X
Yard: Patio

Fire and Security Keywords

Try these keywords when you are setting up your fire and security stations.

Access Card: Tarjeta de Acceso
Air Conditioner: Aire Acondicionado
Alarm: Alarma
Alert: Alerta
Ambulance: Ambulancia
Armed/Disarmed: Armado/Desarmado
Backup Power: Energía de Reserva
Battery: Batería
Biohazard: Bioriesgo
Carbon Dioxide (CO2): Dióxido de Carbono
Chemicals: Químicos
Climate Control: Control del Clima
Control: Control
Control Room: Sala de Control
Coolant: Líquido Refrigerador
Danger: Peligro
Dangerous Chemicals: Químicos Peligrosos
Dangerous Gas: Gas Peligroso
Dehumidifier: Deshumedecedor
Detector: Detector
Device: Mecanismo
Disabled: Inhabilitado
Emergency: Emergencia
Enabled: Habilitado
Evacuate: Evacuar
Explosive: Explosivo
Explosive Gas: Gas Explosivo
Extinguisher: Extintor
Extremely Flammable: Altamente Inflamable
Eye Wash Station: Estación de Lavado de Ojos
Fault: Avería

Fire: Fuego
Fire Alarm: Alarma de Fuego
Firefighter: Bombero
Flammable: Inflamable
Floor Plan: Planta
Furnace: Horno
Gas: Gas
Hazardous Materials: Materiales Peligrosos
Heat: Calor
Heat Detector: Detector de Calor
Heat Sensor: Sensor de Calor
High Temperature: Temperatura Alta
Humidifier: Hemedecedor
Hydrogen Gas: Gas de Hidrógeno
Immediately: Inmediatamente
Intruder Alarm: Alarma contra Intrusos
Ion Detector: Detector de Iones
Loss of Power: Pérdida de Energía
Low Battery: Batería Baja
Low Temperature: Temperatura Baja
Man Trap: Trampa de Hombres
Manual Station: Estación Manual
Map: Mapa
Motion Alarm: Alarma de Movimiento
Motion Sensor: Sensor de Movimiento
Natural Gas: Gas Natural
Needs Service: Servicio de Necesidades
On/Off: Prendido/Apagado
Photo Detector: Fotodetector
Police: Policía
Power Off: Apagado
Power On: Prendido
Propane: Propano
Protected Area/Unprotected Area: Crea Protegida/Área Desprotegida
Pull Station: Estación de Arranque
Pump: Bomba
Radiation: Radiación
Radioactive: Radiactivo
Security: Seguridad
Shut-Off Valve: Válvula de Cierre
Smoke: Humo
Smoke Detector: Detector de Humo
Sprinkler: Extintor
Sprinkler Shut-Off Valve: Válvula de Cierre de Extintores
Sprinkler System: Instalación de Rociadura Automática (para Extinción de Incendios)
Sprinkler Water Flow: Flujo de Agua para Extinción de Incendios
Strobe Light: Luz Estroboscópica
Supervisor: Supervisor
System: Sistema
Tamper Switch: Interruptor de Apretar
Tank: Tanque
Temperature Control: Control de Temperatura
Temperature-Controlled: Temperatura Controlada
Trouble: Problema
Unprotected Area: Área Desprotegida
Vent: Rejilla (de ventilación)
Water Leak: Escape de Agua
Water-Flow Switch: Interruptor de Flujo de Agua
Wire: Cable
Zoom In: Acercarse
Zoom Out: Alejarse

"Take Action" Suggestions

Use these words and phrases as you compose your "Take Action" emergency instructions.

A burglary may be in progress.
Puede estar llevándose a cabo un robo.

A chemical spill may be in progress.
Puede haber un derrame de químico.

A toxic leak may be in progress.
Puede haber una fuga de material tóxico.

Be prepared to use the fire extinguisher.
Esté preparado para usar el extintor de fuego.

Bring a flashlight.
Traiga una linterna.

Call [name] at [555-1212].
Llame a [Nombre] al [555-1212].

Call 911 for a hazardous materials team.
Llame al 911 y pida un equipo contra materiales peligrosos.

Call 911 for an ambulance.
Llame al 911 y pida una ambulancia.

Call 911 for the fire department.
Llame al 911 solicitando los bomberos.

Call 911 for the police.
Llame al 911 solicitando la policía.

Call 911 immediately.
Llame al 911 inmediatamente.

Call a supervisor.
Llame a un supervisor.

Call the building manager.
Llame al administrador del edificio.

Call the electric company.
Llame a la empresa de energía.

Call the gas company.
Llame a la compañía de gas.

Call the head of security.
Llame al jefe de seguridad.

Call the maintenance department.
Llame al departamento de mantenimiento.

Call the service company.
Llame a la compañía de servicios.

Call the telephone company.

Llame a la compañía de teléfonos.

Clear the area.
Despeje el área.

Close all doors and windows.
Cierre todas las puertas y ventanas.

Close all doors.
Cierre todas las puertas.

Close all windows.
Cierre todas las ventanas.

CO2 is deadly.
El CO2 es mortal.

Danger!
¡Peligro!

Do not attempt to handle this emergency alone.
No intente manejar solo esta emergencia.

Do not enter the area.
No entre al área.

Do not forget …
No olvide...

Do not reset this alarm.
No engaste de nuevo esta alarma.

Follow the procedures for this condition.
Siga los procedimientos para esta condición.

Go to …
Vaya a...

Go with a partner.
Vaya con un compañero.

Hydrogen gas is explosive.
El gas de hidrógeno es explosivo.

If you have determined that this is a false alarm that needs service, call _____.
Si ha determinado que ésta es una falsa alarma que necesita servicio, llame a _____.

Investigate.
Investigue.

Make sure all doors are locked.
Asegúrese que todas las puertas estén cerradas con llave.

Make sure everyone has left the area.
Asegúrese que todos han salido del área.

Make sure everyone has left the building.
Asegúrese que todos han salido del edificio.

[Name] has been called automatically.
[Nombre] ha sido llamado automáticamente.

[Name] is disabled and needs help to leave the area.
[Nombre] es minusválido y necesita ayuda para salir del área.

Re-arm the system.
Arme de nuevo el sistema.

Remember …
Recuerde ...

Re-set the system.
Reconfigure el sistema.

Respond immediately.
Responda inmediatamente.

Secure the building.
Asegure el edificio.

Shut off the gas.
Cierre el gas.

Shut off the water.
Cierre el agua.

Someone has activated an alarm.
Alguien ha activado una alarma.

Steps: First, Second, Third …
Pasos: Primero, segundo, tercero...

System malfunction.
Mal funcionamiento del sistema.

Take action.
Haga algo.

The _____ needs immediate attention.
El (la) _____ necesita atención inmediata.

The area is not protected.

El área no está protegida.

The area is protected.
El área está protegida.

The battery needs to be replaced.
La batería necesita ser reemplazada.

The door is closed.
La puerta está cerrada.

The door is locked.
La puerta está asegurada con llave.

The door is open.
La puerta está abierta.

The door is unlocked.
La puerta no está cerrada con llave.

The equipment may be malfunctioning.
El equipo puede estar funcionando mal.

The heat detector has sensed fire.
El detector de calor ha detectado fuego.

The motion detector has sensed activity in the area.
El detector de movimiento ha descubierto actividad en el área.

The power has been cut off.

La fuente de energía ha sido cortada.

The situation may be extremely dangerous.
La situación puede ser muy peligrosa.

The smoke alarm has sensed smoke.
La alarma de humo ha detectado humo.

The smoke detector has sensed smoke.
El detector de humo ha detectado humo.

The system is armed.
El sistema está armado.

The system is not armed.
El sistema no está armado.

The temperature is not within normal range.
La temperatura no está dentro del rango normal.

The temperature is within normal range.
La temperatura está dentro del rango normal.

There is a high risk of explosion.
Hay un alto riesgo de explosión.

There may be a fire.
Puede haber fuego.

There may be a leak.
Puede haber una fuga.

There may have been an explosion.
Puede haber ocurrido una explosión.

This is a drill/This is not a drill.
Este es un ejercicio/Este no es un ejercicio.

This is a test/This is not a test.
Esta es una prueba/Esta no es una prueba.

This is a true emergency.
Esta es una emergencia real.

Tune your radio to channel "x".
Sintonice su radio en el canal "x".

Use caution.
Sea cauteloso.
Wait for _____ to re-set this alarm.
Espere a _____ para reajustar esta alarma.

Wait for the hazardous materials team to arrive.
Espere a que llegue el equipo contra materiales peligrosos.

Wear a gas mask.
Use una máscara antigás.

Wear gloves.
Use guantes.

Wear protective gear: gloves, glasses, gas mask.
Use equipo protector: Guantes, gafas, máscara antigás.

Wear safety glasses.
Use gafas de seguridad

Appendix C: Fire Alarm Codes

In the past, some facility managers worried that computerized monitoring stations would jeopardize the UL-listed status of their fire alarm systems. They don't need to worry any more. The 2010 edition of NFPA 72 makes it clear that supplementary computer systems are a permitted method of monitoring alarm systems.

23.14 Off-Premises Signals.

23.14...

23.14.4* It shall be permitted to provide supplementary transmission of real-time data from the fire system to off-premises equipment.

23.14.4.1 Transmission of real-time data off-premises shall not affect the operation or response of the fire alarm control unit.

23.14.4.2 Any data transmitted shall be consistent with the data generated by the system.

A.23.14.4 Off-site logging of fire alarm data can be useful to preserve information in the face of fire or building failure to facilitate accurate reconstruction of the event. It can also be beneficial to send data off-premises to incident command personnel to enhance situational awareness and response decisions and to maintain safe and efficient operations.

RescueLogic Glossary

ACL-7125 Relay Card: 8-relay circuit board to be installed in computer

Access Point: A device that connects wired and wireless networks.

Active Devices: Smoke detectors and monitoring devices in "alarm" or "trouble" state

Address: The identification code of a device used in communication with a control panel

All Devices: Every smoke detector and monitoring point in the system

Background Map: Picture used to locate devices - usually a floor plan

Binary Log: A RescueLogic Port Capture setting used to create a record file of all characters and codes exactly the way a panel sends them

Button: A graphic on the screen that looks like a 3-D raised button for control

Bytes Read: The number of characters received by the Port Capture program

CD: High-capacity removable disk

COM Ports: RS232 communication port with a connector at the back of the computer, named COM1: through COM128:

Command Post: Location of the RescueLogic monitoring computer

Configuration: The act of customizing RescueLogic for your site

Configuration Manager: The program used to customize RescueLogic for your site

Data Bits: One of the communication parameters between the RescueLogic computer and a control panel that must match

Data Rate: The speed setting of communication between RescueLogic and a control panel

Default: A RescueLogic setting assigned before customization for your site

Device Image: A Windows metafile or icon picture that looks like a device

Device State: The reported status of a system device: Alarm, Trouble, or Normal

Device Type: A specific category of device, such as smoke detector or heat detector, for input of alarms or control of the fire system

Dialogue Box: A small pop-up window with a message or a question for you to answer

Directory: A folder that holds files on a disk drive

Disk Drive: A device in the computer that can store large amounts of data. A floppy disk drive (usually a:) can be used to transfer data to or from the computer

DNS Server Address: The Domain Name System allows Internet host computers to have a domain name (like www.RescueLogic.net) and one or more eight-digit IP addresses.

Done Button: The button on a RescueLogic input screen that will save the information you've entered and take you back to a main menu

DOS: Operating system; Windows can allow DOS commands

Double Click: Click the mouse pointer button twice, quickly

Drag and Drop: Point to an item on the screen, hold the mouse button down, and the item will follow your movement. You may drag it to any location, then release when you are finished moving it

Error: A reported problem that the computer cannot process

Ethernet: A local area data communications network that uses unshielded twisted pair wire.

Ethernet Adapter: A circuit board in the computer that allows another computer or an entire network to share programs

EULA: End User License Agreement

Exit: Quit the current program

Fire Alarm: A message that one of the devices has reported a fire

Floor Plan: An image that represents a building floor, much like a blueprint

Graphic: An individual image on the computer screen

Group: An association of devices that can be named and identified with a unique graphic

Hard Drive: See "disk drive"

Hardlock: A copy-protection device with software drivers

Icon: A coarse graphic image 16, 32, or 48 pixels square

Incoming Data: Information about the status of a fire system as received by RescueLogic' System Monitor program

Incoming Event: A status change identified in the fire or security system

Infrastructure: An integrated wireless and wired Local Area Network

Interface: A method of connecting dissimilar entities, such as a control panel, a computer, and an operator

ISP: Internet Service Provider

LAN: Local Area Network

License: An agreement between the owner of software and the user who has purchased the right to use it

Locate Button: The System Watch button that will automatically select a floor plan and locate a device

Maintenance Menu: The Configuration Manager menu used to keep site records current and accurate

Malfunction: RescueLogic constantly monitors system components to ensure that alarms will be reported. A malfunction is usually reported as "Trouble" or "Fault."

MB: Megabyte, or 1 million bytes: A unit of measure used to determine the size of computer information

Menu: A list of program selections

Message Box: A small window with information about your computer

Message Mapping: The RescueLogic process of mapping information from fire and security panels to points and categories that can be displayed

Monitor: The process of reading information from field panels; also, the computer component with a screen, to make viewing that information possible

Mouse: The common device used to select or point to items on computer screens

Next Device Button: The System Watch button used to select the next device in the list, allowing you to view a graphic or read "Take Action" instructions

Next Page Button: The System Watch button used when lists fill more than one screen

Panel: A computer device mounted on a wall to monitor and control devices throughout a facility

Panel Data: Messages communicated from a panel to another computer device to report events and system status

Parity: A communication parameter setting between a panel and a RescueLogic computer that must match

Port: See "COM Ports"

Port Capture: A RescueLogic software program that records data exactly as a panel reports it

Port ID: The name of a communications port, COM1: through COM128:

Previous Device Button: The System Watch button used to select the previous device in the list, allowing you to view graphics or read "Take Action" instructions

Previous Page Button: The System Watch button used when lists fill more than one screen

Print: Sends current window data to the system printer

Processor: The central part of a computer's control system; Pentium processors are the most common

RAM: Random Access Memory; stores and transfers information quickly, but holds data only while the computer is on

Remove Cleared Button: The System Watch button used to remove normal (properly running) devices from the "Active" warning list

Rocketport Card: A circuit board installed in the computer to provide more COM: ports for multiple control panels

RS232/EIA282: RS232 cable is commonly used to connect computers and peripherals. It transmits data according to RS232 data transfer standards. The RS232 standard was renamed the EIA232 standard in the early 1990s.

Run: Activate a software program

Security Alarm: A system device has reported a security breach

Setup Menu: The Configuration Manager menu that will be used for initial installation

Software: Computer information and programs that run inside computer hardware

Start: The Windows menu used to select and start programs

Stop Bits: One of the communication parameters between the RescueLogic computer and a control panel that must match

Supervisory Alarm: Something in the system has been turned off or is not running correctly

SVGA Video Card: The circuit board in the computer that connects to a display screen

System: Equipment and software designed for a particular purpose

System Architecture: The structure and design of a system

System Monitor: The RescueLogic program that reads information from panels and updates the RescueLogic.mdb database

System Watch: The RescueLogic program that displays a color-coded device list and graphics

Take Action Button: A System Watch program button that displays instructions for action in response to reports of "Alarm" or "Trouble"

TCP/IP: Transmission Control Protocol/Internet Protocol, the standard for data transmission over the Internet

Timed Log: A RescueLogic Port Capture setting that creates a file with each line timed to the millisecond it was transmitted

Touchscreen: A computer display screen with a touch-sensitive map that allows users to select items with a touch of a finger instead of a mouse

Trouble: See "Malfunction"

Video Card: See "SGVA Video Card"

WAN: Wide Area Network

Zone: An association of devices that can be named and identified with a unique graphic

Index

About the Author

Dan Horon is the President of Cadgraphics Incorporated, makers of RescueLogic software for fire alarm and security systems. Dan was the chair of the NFPA Task Group on Circuits and Pathways when the chapter was added to NFPA 72. He still serves on the NFPA Protected Premises Technical Committee, as well as the Technical Correlating Committee Task Group on Networks. You can email him at *dan@rescuelogic.com*.

Made in the USA
Monee, IL
08 November 2026

67972905R00131